VICTORY IN WORLD WAR II

VICTORY IN WORLD WAR II

THE ALLIES' DEFEAT OF THE AXIS FORCES

NIGEL CAWTHORNE

Picture credits

AKG Images: 136, 180

Corbis Ltd: 321; /Bettmann: 72, 100, 280; /Dmitri Baltermants Collection: 241; Hulton-Deutsche: 41; /Michael St Maur Sheil: 452; Yevgeny Khaldei: 314

Getty: 14, 17, 20, 24, 77, 91, 108, 126, 176, 185, 224, 227, 255, 263, 298, 343 and 355, 382, 421; /Time-Life: 367

Imperial War Museum: 319 and 333

Mary Evans Picture Library: 273

Popperfoto: 97 and 114, 153

Topfoto Ltd: 36

This edition published in 2017 by Arcturus Publishing Limited
26/27 Bickels Yard, 151–153 Bermondsey Street,
London SE1 3HA

AD005866UK

Printed in the UK

CONTENTS

INTRODUCTION

On 1 September 1939, under the flimsiest
of pretexts, the German army launched an
assault on Poland. By 6 October, all Polish
resistance had ceased, and Hitler was
busying himself sharing out his new territory
with his newfound ally, Josef Stalin.

The early years of the Second World War had gone well for Germany. After Hitler had occupied the Rhineland, Austria, and most of Czechoslovakia, the major European powers, Britain and France, locked together in a policy of appeasing Hitler, hoped that this would be the end of his territorial demands in Europe. This hope was doomed to failure from the start. On 1 September 1939, under the flimsiest of pretexts, the German army launched an assault on Poland. By 6 October, all Polish resistance had ceased, and Hitler was busying himself sharing out his new territory with his newfound ally, Josef Stalin. A little over two years later, German troops had swept through Scandinavia, Holland, Belgium, France, the Balkan countries, Greece and Crete, and German Panzer troops were entrenched outside the very gates of Moscow itself. Hitler had succeeded in his aim of creating a new German Empire, a Third Reich. At its height, this German empire stretched from Stalingrad in the east to the English Channel in the west, and from the northernmost tip of Europe to the North African desert.

In the Far East, Japan had also been building an empire. Japanese leaders had long felt that they had been denied the benefits they regarded as their due as a victor in the First World War, and the tension in the region had increased steadily throughout the 1930s. By 1941, the new Japanese military government felt strong enough to launch an all-out assault on the possessions of the Western powers in the Far East. The Japanese strategy also involved a swift defeat of the USA, before that vast country could mobilize to its full potential. Admiral Yamamoto, the Japanese commander at Pearl Harbor, believed that if Japan could defeat the US within a year, all would be well;

if they could not, the outlook would be bleak.

The Japanese attack on Pearl Harbor was followed up by a series of lightning victories; in Malaya, Singapore, the Dutch East Indies, the Philippines, Burma, and a host of strategic Pacific islands. These victories would see the Japanese forces over-extended, and vulnerable, however. Just six months after entering the war, the US Navy smashed the Japanese carrier fleet at the Battle of Midway. As the Japanese gains in the Pacific fell one by one to the US Marines over the next three years, Yamamoto's gloomy prognosis would be borne out.

For Hitler, November 1942 would see him at the apogee of his power, as his elite Sixth Army stood poised to capture Stalingrad. Three months later, the commander of Sixth Army, Field Marshal Paulus, would surrender to the Red Army amidst the devastated shell of the city, and 90,000 German soldiers would begin the long, weary march into Soviet captivity. After Stalingrad, the German army would begin a long retreat which would only end in Berlin. At the same time, the German army in North Africa was in retreat after the Battle of El Alamein towards Tunisia, where the US would make its presence felt outside the Pacific. The defeat of the German forces in North Africa would open the door to the Allied invasion of Italy in early 1943. In retrospect, Midway, Stalingrad and El Alamein were the turning points of the Second World War. That is not to say, however, that they came close to ending the war – far from it. How the Allies built on their successes, and emerged victorious from the war, is told in the following page, beginning with the moment Hitler's worst nightmare came true and he found himself fighting a war on two fronts: D-Day, 6 June, 1944.

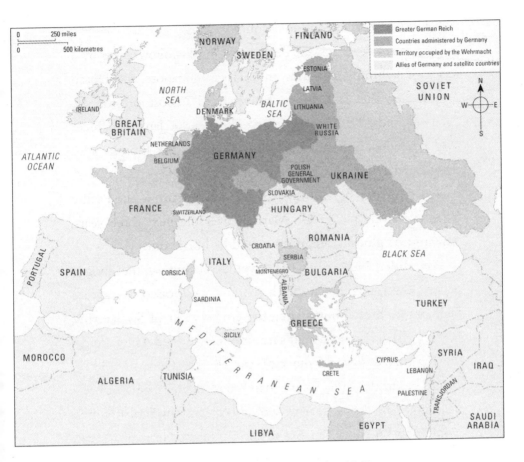

Hitler's Empire The Third Reich at its peak, November 1942.

SECTION ONE
D-DAY

Operation Overlord – the D-Day invasion of Normandy on 6 June 1944 – was the largest seaborne invasion in history. By nightfall on 6 June, the Allies had put over 150,000 men ashore on five beaches, and had secured a springboard from which to mount the liberation of France.

CHAPTER 1

Planning Operation Overlord

The war in the west, the German Field Marshal Rundstedt once remarked, would be won or lost on the beaches of Normandy. Unfortunately for Rundstedt and the German army, this was not a view shared by the German Führer, Adolf Hitler.

Ever since the Soviet Union came into the war in 1941, following Hitler's invasion of its territory, it had been urging Britain to begin a second front in western Europe. And when the US entered the war, they wanted to make an attack on the Germans in France as soon as possible. The British were more circumspect. Having been in the war longer than their new allies, the British felt that it would be foolish to risk everything in one reckless operation. Many of the British commanders had experienced the carnage of the First World War and were afraid of throwing men against enemy lines in a frontal assault – inevitable when making an amphibious assault against a fortified coastline. As First Lord of the Admiralty in the First World War, Churchill himself had been responsible for the ill-fated amphibious assault at Gallipoli in the Dardanelles where 250,000 men, largely

Australians and New Zealanders, were lost before the 83,000 survivors could be evacuated. Britain's worst fears were realized when 5,000 Canadians, 1,000 British and 50 US Rangers staged a disastrous raid on the Channel port of Dieppe in August 1942, in which 2,600 men were killed or captured. The US Army was still untested, so President Roosevelt was persuaded to join the war in North Africa.

When this was brought to a successful conclusion, Churchill proposed an attack on the 'soft underbelly of Europe'. On 10 July 1943 an Anglo-American force landed on Sicily. Italian resistance collapsed and on 25 July Mussolini fell from power and was arrested. The German forces, under Field Marshal Kesselring, were then evacuated from Sicily and prepared to defend the Italian mainland.

On 2 September, a small Allied force landed on the 'heel' of Italy and quickly captured the ports of Taranto and Brindisi. On 3 September Montgomery's Eighth Army crossed the Strait of Messina and landed on the 'toe' of Italy, meeting little resistance. That day, the new Italian government agreed to change sides and its capitulation was announced on 8 September. The following day, the combined US–British Fifth Army under General Mark Clark landed at Salerno on the 'shin'. This was where Kesselring had expected the attack to come. The situation was precarious for six days, but the Fifth Army eventually broke out, taking Naples on 1 October.

On 13 October 1943, Italy declared war on Germany. This was not unexpected and Kesselring had already consolidated his hold on central and northern Italy. He held the Allies at the Gustav Line, a defensive line that ran right across the narrow peninsula of

Italy some sixty miles south of Rome. To get round this, the Allies landed 50,000 men north of the Gustav Line at Anzio. At first they met with little resistance, but instead of driving directly on Rome, the landing force stopped to consolidate the beachhead. Kesselring quickly counterattacked, nearly pushing the Allies back into the sea.

The main Allied force was held up by the German defenders at Monte Cassino, a mountain-top monastery pivotal in the Gustav Line. The Eighth Army was then switched from the Adriatic side of the peninsula to the western flank. On the night of 11 May 1944, the Allies managed to breach the Gustav Line to the west of Monte Cassino, which was outflanked and fell to the Polish Corps of the Eighth Army on 18 May. On 26 May, the main Allied force joined up with the beachhead at Anzio and on 5 June 1944 the Allies drove into Rome.

However, progress on such a narrow front up the Italian peninsula was bound to be slow, and did little to divert German strength from the Russian front. By this time the Red Army was making good progress against the Wehrmacht. By sheer weight of numbers it would eventually overwhelm the German army and overrun Germany. Even if the Allies pushed Kesselring all the way to the Alps, it would have been impossible to cross them before the Red Army swept right across Germany and, perhaps, took the rest of western Europe, as many people feared. By the spring of 1944, a landing in France was politically vital.

THE ATLANTIC WALL

The delay in staging an amphibious assault across the English Channel gave the Germans time to fortify the coastline. They

The Atlantic Wall *The Atlantic Wall took four years to complete, and slowed the Allies up by less than twenty-four hours on D-Day: as D-Day historian Stephen Ambrose has pointed out, this probably qualifies it as a great military blunder.*

built what they called the 'Atlantic Wall' down the west coast of Europe from the Arctic Circle to the Pyrenees. By the time of the invasion, 12,247 of the planned 15,000 fortifications had been completed, along with 943 along the Mediterranean coast. Half a million beach obstacles had been deployed and around 6.5 million mines had been laid.

The huge extent of the wall was partly due to a campaign of misinformation called Operation *Fortitude*, designed to give the Germans the idea that a landing might come anywhere at any time. To defend his empire against attack from the west, Hitler would have to spread his forces thinly.

At the beginning of the war, the British had arrested every German spy in Britain and turned many of them, so that they could be used to feed false information back to their spymasters in Hamburg and Berlin. False information was also conveyed by radio traffic that the Germans intercepted. The British had also broken the German Enigma code, so they could see whether their deception was working. On occasions, the British even fed the Germans information that the invasion would come in the south of France or Norway, through the Balkans or in the Black Sea. This forced Hitler to disperse his troops to the four corners of his empire.

However the major purpose of *Fortitude* was to convince Hitler that the Western Allies would take the most direct route. They would take the shortest Channel crossing at the Straits of Dover to the Pas de Calais, where it would be easy for them to support the landings with air and artillery cover from England. It would also give them the shortest route to Paris and Germany itself. This deception was reinforced by the invention of the First US Army Group, or FUSAG. This was a non-existent army, apparently mustered in Kent, ready for embarkation at Dover. Radio traffic poured out of Kent, and set-builders from theatres and film studios were employed to mock up tanks and landing craft that would look like the real thing in German aerial reconnaissance photographs. One badly-wounded prisoner of war, a Panzer officer who was being returned to Germany, actually saw FUSAG with his own eyes – though the tanks and trucks he saw were not in Kent at all but in Hampshire, ready for embarkation at the southern ports. He was also introduced to General Patton, who German intelligence had been led to believe was commanding officer of FUSAG. Hitler became so convinced that FUSAG existed and that this was where the attack would come that he kept his mighty Fifteenth Army in the Pas de Calais and his Panzers east of the Seine for seven weeks after the Allies had landed on the beaches in Normandy.

The Calvados coast in Normandy was chosen as the site of the landings because it had a number of wide, flat beaches close enough together that the forces landing on them could quickly join up and form a single bridgehead. It was poorly defended. The fortifications there, and in other places, had been built by slave labourers who had weakened them with deliberate sabotage. Many of the defenders were Russians, Poles or other eastern Europeans who had little motivation to fight against the Americans or the British. What Germans there were, were mostly either to old to fight on the Russian front, too young, or had been wounded there.

The other advantage of the Calvados coast was that it did not have a major port. The conventional wisdom was that, for an invasion to succeed, the landing force would have to seize a port to get men and materiel ashore quickly enough to defend against a counter-attack that would aim to push them back into the sea. This was another reason why Hitler and his High Command were so convinced that the attack would come in the Pas de Calais, where there were three ports – Calais, Boulogne and Dunkirk. But the raid on Dieppe had taught the British that an attack on a heavily defended port was not a good idea. Even if a landing force managed to take it, the Germans placed demolition charges in the harbour facilities of all the ports they occupied. Once these had been set off they could render the port useless and the invasion would inevitably fail. Instead British planners came up with an ingenious solution – the Allies would bring their own. Two prefabricated 'Mulberry' harbours would be built in sections which would then be towed across the Channel and assembled at the landing beaches. The Americans laughed when they first heard the idea, but began to take it very seriously when they realized that landing in an area that had no existing port would give the invasion force the element of surprise.

The Allies' plans were well advanced when, in November 1943, Hitler sent his most trusted and most able commander, Field Marshal Erwin Rommel, to take charge of the Atlantic Wall. He found it wanting, especially in Normandy, and began strengthening it, for example, supervising the laying of over four million mines in little more than four months. Then, with just a

Tour of Inspection *Field Marshal Erwin Rommel inspects defences in the Caen area with his senior staff officers, May 1944, one month before D-Day.*

week to go before the Allied landings, the battle hardened 352nd Infantry Division was switched direct from the Russian Front to man the defences along what was to become Omaha Beach.

BUILDING UP TO INVASION

During the late spring of 1944, southern England had become one huge parking lot for tanks, trucks and aeroplanes. There were weapons and ammunition dumps in country lanes, and village pubs were full of soldiers from every part of the English-speaking world, along with Poles, Czechs, Hungarians, Free French and Jews from Germany, Austria and all parts of Nazi-occupied Europe. In all, more than six million people were involved in the D–Day landings. Twenty US divisions, fourteen British, three Canadian, one French and one Polish division were billeted in southern England, along with hundreds of thousands of other men who belonged to special forces, headquarters' units, communications staff and corps personnel. Then, as this huge force made its way silently at night to the embarkation ports, these men simply disappeared.

In the ports and waiting out to sea were 138 battleships, cruisers and destroyers which would bombard the French coast. They were accompanied by 279 escorts, 287 minesweepers, four line-layers, two submarines, 495 motor boats, 310 landing ships and 3,817 landing craft and barges for the initial assault. Another 410 landing craft would join them as part of the ferry service to get more personnel and equipment ashore after the beachhead had been secured. A further 423 ships, including tugs, would be involved in the construction of the Mulberry harbours and the laying of the PLUTO (Petroleum Line Under The Ocean) pipeline, that would pump petrol under the Channel, and the telephone cables that would connect the commanders on the ground to SHAEF (Supreme Headquarters, Allied Expeditionary Force) in London. Another 1,260 merchant ships would also be involved in supplying the landing force, making a total of over 7,000 vessels.

Some 10,000 aircraft were also deployed in Operation *Overlord*, as the D-Day plan was known. They would bomb key fortifications, drop paratroopers, tow gliders carrying airborne troops, attack enemy formations and protect the airspace above the beaches.

For political reasons the head of the invasion force had to be an American, and Churchill worked well with General Eisenhower, who had demonstrated his competence as a commander in Operation *Torch* and the landings on Sicily and Italy. Under him, actually running the landings, would be four British officers – Eisenhower's deputy, Air Chief Marshal Sir Arthur Tedder; Admiral Sir Bertram Ramsay, commanding the operation at sea; Air Chief Marshal Sir Trafford Leigh-Mallory in the air; and on the ground, General (later Field Marshal) Bernard Montgomery. This caused some resentment among American officers, who felt that they should have been represented at the high levels of command. However, one of the reasons Eisenhower had been picked as overall commander was the skill he had already shown in handling the rivalries between the British and the Americans.

When Montgomery was appointed on New Year's Day 1944, the first thing he did was to throw away the invasion plans American planners had been working on since 1942. He considered that the front in the American plan was too narrow and that the assault force was not big enough to do the job. He upped the number of divisions landing on the beaches from three to five and the number of airborne divisions from one to three. Montgomery presented his plan to the military commanders and senior politicians at St Paul's School in West Kensington on 15 May 1944. It was accepted. A key part of the plan was that on D-Day itself, equal numbers of British and American troops would be landed. But as losses mounted, the battle ravaged British proved unable to sustain this commitment, while the US had an almost bottomless well of recruits. Eventually, the war in western Europe would become a predominantly American affair.

Commanders Air Chief Marshal Arthur Tedder, General Dwight Eisenhower and General Bernard Montgomery look on as the preparations for D-Day continue.

To reflect this, Eisenhower himself would take over command of the land forces once the beachhead was well established.

D-Day was to be 5 June 1944. By that time, the Allies had complete air superiority over France and the bombing campaign had softened up the enemy. Much of it was directed against the railways to prevent men, weapons and ammunition being brought to the front. Bombing and sabotage by the French Resistance had knocked out 1,500 of the 2,000 locomotives available. Eighteen of the twenty-four bridges over the Seine between Paris and the sea had been destroyed, along with most of those over the Loire. Marshalling yards, crossings and other vital parts of the railway system had been attacked, and bombs and rockets had knocked out nearly all the radar stations along the northern coast of France.

As 5 June approached, the fine, sunny days that had lasted throughout May came to an end. The defenders along the Atlantic Wall, who had been kept on constant alert by false alarms for months, began to believe that the Allies had missed their chance. Rommel himself took the opportunity to go back to Germany to see his wife on her birthday. On the following day, 6 June, he was to have a meeting with Hitler.

The Allied first-wave troops had already embarked on 4 June when the weather worsened and a storm blew up. Eisenhower had no option but to postpone the invasion. However, that night the meteorologists thought that there might be a break in the weather the next day and Eisenhower gave the order for the invasion fleet to sail. Broad lanes across the channel had been swept by navy minesweepers and, as the invasion fleet headed out to sea, huge waves of RAF heavy bombers flew overhead to blast the coastal defences with 5,200 tonnes of bombs. As dawn broke on 6 June, the USAAF's medium bombers and fighters took over and continued the pounding of the emplacements behind the invasion beaches.

Under Montgomery's plan, the US had two landing beaches – Utah, at the base of the Cotentin peninsula and Omaha, further to the east along the Calvados coast. The three British beaches – Gold, Juno and Sword – lay to the east of that. The two fronts were each about twenty miles long.

CHAPTER 2

The Airborne Assaults

Impressed by the German airborne invasion of Crete, the Allies decided that the infantry on D-Day would benefit from the support of airborne troops. Had they known the extent of German losses on Crete, however, it is possible they would have decided otherwise.

The use of airborne troops was a rather late addition to the D-Day plan. General Omar N. Bradley, commander of the American landing forces, was the only senior commander who favoured their use. He proposed dropping the 82nd 'All American' and the 101st 'Screaming Eagles' behind the Atlantic Wall to seize the causeways that ran inland from the American beaches, and cut off the Cotentin Peninsula to prevent the Germans reinforcing Cherbourg. Air Marshal Leigh-Mallory was against it, and Montgomery would only consent if Bradley took full responsibility for the operation. Bradley agreed to do so.

A DIFFERENCE OF OPINION

The British caution was natural. The use of airborne troops was relatively new and did not have a good track record, although it had started out well enough. On 10 May 1940, a German paratroop regiment had seized Holland in a single day, and in

April and May 1941, the German airborne assault on the island of Crete took the island in just eight days. During that operation, forty-six RAF planes were lost and 12,000 British prisoners of war were taken. However, the Germans lost between 4,500 and 6,000 men and between 271 and 400 aircraft. The loss of so many of his elite paratroopers so appalled Hitler that he forbade future large-scale paratroop operations and, for the Germans at least, the day of the paratrooper was over.

However, the Allies did not know the extent of the German losses on Crete and continued planning paratroop operations of their own. These had begun on 22 June 1940, when Churchill had ordered the formation of a corps of airborne troops within forty-eight hours. He envisaged an initial force of 5,000. They were to be trained that summer. Their first action was on 10 February 1941, when thirty-five of them were dropped in Southern Italy to destroy the Monte Vulture aqueduct which supplied the towns of Brindisi, Bari and Foggia where there were dockyards and military installations. Then, on 12 November 1942, the 3rd Battalion of Britain's 1st Parachute Brigade captured the Bône airfield in North Africa after being dropped by USAAF C-47s.

On 16 August 1942, the US 82nd and 101st Airborne Divisions were officially activated. They comprised 17,650 'lean and mean' volunteers, some of whom did not survive their rigorous and dangerous training. The first mass airborne drop of Allied troops occurred over Sicily on 10 July 1943. Four hours after the jump, Colonel James M. Gavin, commander of

Opposite: Death from above German paratroopers landing on Crete, the largest airborne operation of the war.

the 82nd Airborne, could only muster twenty men out of the 3,400 that had boarded planes in North Africa. Some of the troops landed sixty miles east of the drop zone. The British fared little better. Only fifty-seven out of their 156 planes dropped their troops anywhere near the target. In all, 605 officers and men were lost, including 326 who landed in the sea and were drowned. Eisenhower wrote to Marshall in Washington, telling him that he had no faith in airborne troops as, once the force had been scattered, he doubted that it could ever be melded back into an effective fighting unit.

Marshall disagreed, at one point even suggesting that the invasion of Normandy should be primarily an airborne assault, with the landings on the beaches a subsidiary action. Eisenhower rejected this out of hand, but slowly became convinced that an airborne operation might make a decisive difference on the Cotentin Peninsula and in the battle for Cherbourg. Later, a British airborne landing to the east of the beaches was planned to protect the flank and continue the deception that the invasion would take place at the Pas de Calais.

THE US AIRBORNE ASSAULTS

The Americans were unlucky in their choice of drop zones. Utah Beach was at the base of the Cotentin Peninsula. Behind it run the Merderet and Douve rivers. Napoleon's engineers had devised a series of canals and ditches there which the Germans used to flood the area. The 101st Airborne, under Major-General Maxwell D. Taylor, had to seize the roadways and causeways that ran through these flooded fields so that the landing force could escape from the beach. The 82nd Airborne, under Major-General

Matthew B. Ridgeway, were to land at the Merderet River, west of the village of St Mère-Église and seize the village and the crossroads there to prevent the Germans counter-attacking from the north-west. Fortunately, the Germans were not expecting the Allies to land there. They had laid out their defensive formations and their *Rommelspargel*, or 'Rommel's asparagus' – sharpened poles that were deadly both to paratroopers and gliders trying to land – further to the rear.

At 0100 hours on 6 June 1944, the Pathfinders went in. These were an advance force who were to mark the drop zones with radio direction finder beacons and lights in large 'T' shapes on the ground. But there were problems. A cloud bank over the coast forced the Dakotas carrying them to climb above it or drop below it. This meant that the Pathfinders jumped from too high or too low an altitude. Anti-aircraft fire also forced the pilots to take evasive action, throwing them off course. One Pathfinder team landed in the Channel and only one, out of eighteen, landed where it was supposed to.

Half an hour later, and five hours before men hit the beaches, the Germans saw the 925 C-47s of the United States IX Air Force Troop Carrier Command fly over, and six regiments – some 13,400 men in all – descend from the skies. Again there were problems. For most of the pilots, it was their first combat mission and they had not been trained for night flying, bad weather flying, or flak avoidance. They flew in groups of nine, separated from the planes on each side by just 100 feet – a C-47 measured 95 feet from wing-tip to wing-tip. Each group was separated by just 1,000 yards from the groups before and aft. They flew without navigation lights and all they could see of the

plane ahead was a tiny blue dot on the tail.

They crossed the Channel at 500 feet to avoid detection by German radar, following a course sent up a radio beacon carried by a British patrol boat and a light carried by a British submarine. Over the Channel Islands, they climbed to 1,500 feet to avoid anti-aircraft fire. The batteries on the Channel Islands opened up, but their only effect was to wake the American paratroopers who had been knocked out by the anti-airsickness pills they had been issued. Over the coast they were to descend again to 600 feet: the jump height was set low so that the paratroopers would spend less time in their vulnerable descent. But as they crossed the coastline, they too ran into the cloud bank. The planes automatically dispersed to avoid the danger of mid-air collision. When they emerged, some found they were alone.

It was then that all hell broke loose. Search lights and tracers raked the skies. The Dakotas were hit by 88mm shells, 20mm shells and machine-gun fire. Some planes exploded, others plunged towards the ground. The pilots had been instructed to slow down to 90 mph for the drop, to minimize the shock to the jumpers. But a plane flying at 600 feet and 90 mph is a sitting duck, so the pilots threw the throttle forward until they were doing 150 mph. They had no real idea where they were, except that they were somewhere over the Cotentin Peninsula. The pilots wanted to get out of it, and flicked on the red light, telling the paratroopers to stand up and hook up, as they passed over the Channel Islands. At the first possible opportunity, the pilots then flicked the light to green, hoping to get rid of their charges and return to England as fast as possible. The men then made the $10,000 jump – so called as GIs were required to take out a

$10,000 life assurance policy to provide for their families in the event of their death. As they jumped, many saw planes below them. Some planes got hit by equipment dropped from above them. One paratrooper got caught on the wing of a plane below.

Some men had already been wounded by shrapnel inside the plane. Others refused to jump when they saw the fireworks outside. Those who did jump found themselves either too low or too high. And they were sitting ducks as flares lit up the night sky. The Germans even set fire to a hay barn, so they could pick off the US paratroopers as they came down. Those who made it to the ground found the situation confused, to say the least. Men from the 82nd Airborne found themselves in the 101st's drop zone and vice versa. In the dark, they were supposed to identify each other by the metallic toys that made the click of a cricket. Unfortunately, this was hard to distinguish from the sound of a safety catch being taken off.

General Taylor of the 101st found himself completely alone. After twenty minutes, he hooked up with a private and a lieutenant, his aide. They tried to find out where they were with a map and a flashlight, but between the three of them they came to three different conclusions. More men turned up. Soon Taylor had gathered a group consisting of two generals, four colonels, four lieutenants, a handful of NCOs and a dozen privates. 'Never have so few been commanded by so many,' Taylor commented sardonically.

But Taylor and his men were lucky. Some landed in areas that the main force would not reach until twenty-five days later. Lieutenant-Colonel Louis Mendez walked for five days, covering ninety miles, without encountering another American, though he managed to managed to kill six Germans on the way. Some of the paratroopers fell in the Channel, while others were captured as soon as they landed.

Rommel had ordered the lock gates on the Merderet River opened at high tide and closed at low tide, so the area where the 82nd Airborne were to land was flooded. This had not shown up on aerial reconnaissance. Although the water was only a metre deep, it was enough to drown a fully-laden paratrooper, or one who could not detach his chute fast enough. The British had a quick-release device on their harnesses, but the Americans had fiddly buckles on theirs. Thirty-six troops of the 82nd drowned that night. A complete stick – that is, the squad of men who jump from one plane – went missing. One hundred and seventy-three men broke an arm or leg, and sixty-three were taken prisoner.

Only four per cent of the 82nd landed in their target zone to the west of the Merderet river. Three days later, the 82nd was still at one-third strength, and 4,000 men were missing. This meant they could not secure all the causeways across the Merderet and Douve rivers. The 101st were even worse off. They could only muster 1,000 out of their 6,000 men.

LIBERATING ST MÈRE-ÉGLISE

General James Gavin was in command of the men who were supposed to take St Mère-Église. While over the Channel he had kept a watchful eye on the twenty planes in his formation. But by the time his plane had emerged from the clouds and the green light came on, he could only see two others. It took him almost an hour to find the twenty men who jumped with him. He only discovered where he was when a patrol he had sent out found a railway line. More patrols managed to muster 150 men, but none of them was armed with anything heavier than a rifle or carbine. Heavy equipment had apparently landed in the flooded fields and disappeared under the water. Stragglers informed him that there were Americans on the other side of a bridge at the village of La Fière which was one of the division's objectives. Gavin headed there, but he found his way barred by German armour that held the bridge. There was a stand-off. Without anti-tank weapons they could not dislodge the Germans and join up with the rest of the division, while the Germans were heavily outnumbered and could make no headway. The stalemate was only broken four days later when American armour arrived from the beachhead.

The 506th Regiment landed near the target of St Mère-Église, but had scattered, while the 505th had the misfortune of landing on the village itself. They were shot as they fell from the sky – the Germans had a machine-gun in the bell tower of the church. One shot hit a man's grenades and an empty chute was left floating to the ground. Another man was sucked into a house that was on fire. Men were shot down when they landed in the village square or left hanging from trees or telegraph poles. But some made it to the ground safely and managed to take revenge on the Germans. In the one success of the night, 1,000 troops mustered outside St Mère-Église, out of the 2,200 that were supposed to be there. By dawn it was the first town in France to be liberated and the Stars and Stripes hung outside the town hall where the Nazi swastika had hung for four years. Unfortunately that was only the beginning of the town's troubles. The Germans shelled St Mère Église for the next two days, flattening many of the buildings and killing dozens of the inhabitants. The first US casualty report came from St Mère-Église. It listed 756 missing, 347 wounded and 156 dead.

While the Americans on the ground found themselves disorientated and confused, the Germans were no clearer on what was happening. Lost Americans did the one thing they could do – cut the enemy's communications. Telegraph poles were blown up and wires cut, and German units found themselves isolated. Even reports that did reach the German command posts were garbled and incomplete. The German commanders could make little sense of the wide dispersal of the American landings and the High Command decided that the attack on the Cotentin Peninsula was an Allied diversion.

On the ground, the American paratroopers outnumbered the German defenders two to one and, with the dawn, they began to make headway. The 506th Regiment, whose target was to capture the dry land to the rear of Utah Beach, managed to assemble two battalions. They seized and held the nearby roadways. Then one battalion routed the German defenders at Pouppeville, while the other fought its way against fierce resistance to the southern end of the beach.

Lieutenant-Colonel Steve Chappius found that the rest of his 502nd Regiment had landed three miles south of the drop zone. Nevertheless, he rounded up a dozen men and struck out for his objective, the powerful artillery battery at St Martin. When he arrived, he found that the guns had been removed. He reported this to General Taylor, who had set up divisional headquarters in an old monastery about a mile away.

THE GLIDER FORCES

One of the paratroopers' main aims was to clear the way for the second wave of the invasion – the glider force. The idea of using gliders also came from the German actions on 10 May 1940, when ten DFS 230 gliders, carrying nine paratroopers each and towed behind Junkers 52 transport planes, landed in a grassy compound on top of Belgium's allegedly impregnable Fort Eben Emael. This cleared the way for the German Panzers to outflank the Maginot Line. The British began training their own glider force after Dunkirk and the US Army Air Force began training glider pilots in May 1942.

The British used the Horsa, a high-winged 67-foot monoplane with an 88-foot wingspan. This could carry thirty men, or a jeep and ten men, and weighed eight tons when loaded. They also deployed the massive Hamilcar glider with a take-off weight of eighteen tons. This could carry forty men and even a light tank, and its 110-foot wingspan dwarfed the Halifax that towed it.

The Americans plumped for the smaller Waco, which carried fifteen men. Prefabricated in Ohio, they were shipped to England where they were to be assembled. Initially, untrained British civilians were employed, but of the first sixty-two they put together, fifty-one were not airworthy. The semi-skilled airmen from the US 1st Air Force then stepped in and assembled another two hundred, a hundred of which were destroyed by a thunderstorm. With just five weeks to go before D-Day, glider mechanics were flown in from the US. Working around the clock, they managed to assemble a total of 910 Wacos.

More than a hundred were to land in the Cotentin drop

zones, just two hours after the paratroopers. They would carry the essential 57mm anti-tank guns that would be needed if the Germans counter-attacked. But the scattered paratroopers had had no chance to prepare the gliders' landing sites. Many disintegrated on landing. Many fields in the drop zone were too small to land in, causing gliders to crash into buildings or hedgerows. The latter were a lot thicker than expected. Although they could be seen by aerial reconnaissance, they were assumed to be like the hedges in England that could be cleared by foxhunters. In fact, they were six feet high or more and impenetrable. The trees were also taller than expected, making it almost impossible to clear them and land without hitting the hedge at the other end of the field. It was one of the major failures of intelligence. Of the 957 men of the 82nd Airborne's glider force who landed in Normandy that night, twenty-five were killed, 118 wounded and fourteen were missing – giving an overall casualty rate of sixteen per cent before they even got into action. Four of the seventeen antitank guns they carried with them were unserviceable, as were nineteen of the 111 jeeps. A second wave of gliders that landed on the evening of 6 June suffered even greater losses, and not one of the Wacos that landed in Normandy survived intact.

THE BRITISH AIRBORNE ASSAULTS

The British airborne operation away to the east aimed to take control of the five-mile area between the Rivers Orne and Dives, to protect the flank of the seaborne landings from the German armoured reserves, massed east of Caen. It was to be undertaken by the 6th Airborne Division, who were to destroy most of the bridges over the Dives to prevent a German counter-attack, and capture intact the bridges over the Orne and the Caen Canal so that reinforcements could reach them from the beaches. Again one of the major hazards they would face was a flooded area.

The paratroopers were to go in and mark out the landing zones with flares. An hour and forty minutes later the gliders were to arrive. As it turned out, the gliders arrived only about five minutes after the paratroopers had gone in and they had had no time to find the landing zones. When the gliders were cast free by their Halifax tow planes, they descended rapidly; visibility was poor and there were no flares in position on the ground to tell them where to aim for. One Horsa landed so close to the Caen Canal Bridge – known to posterity by its codename Pegasus Bridge, after the 6th Airborne's winged insignia – that it came to rest with its nose inside the wire defences of the bridge. The force that held this bridge controlled the movement of forces between the Normandy beaches and the east, specifically the Pas de Calais. Had it been in German hands it would surely have been freely used to switch divisions from the more northerly coast to the Normandy beaches once it became clear that they were the site of the invasion.

PEGASUS BRIDGE

It was on Pegasus Bridge that the first German victim of Allied land-based troops was claimed. It was a young sentry, cut down as he fired a flare to alert fellow soldiers to the presence of enemy paratroopers. Moments later, the first British casualty was felled by German machine gunners. It took barely eight seconds for Lieutenant Herbert Denham Brotheridge to enter history as the

first Allied soldier to die on D-Day. He had been hand-picked by Major John Howard to lead one of six 30-man companies into action that night. Brotheridge's glider crash-landed into the barbed wire defences at about 2am on 6 June and his men were first on to the bridge.

The story of Lieutenant Brotheridge and the audacious assault by six gliderborne platoons of the 2nd Battalion the Oxfordshire and Bucks Light Infantry ranks among the Second World War's greatest adventures, and was later dramatized in the film The Longest Day, starring Richard Burton, Sean Connery and Robert Mitchum.

Brotheridge's daughter Margaret discovered the truth about her heroic father years later: 'The bullets hit him in the neck, literally within seconds. They eventually managed to get him to Madame Gondrée's cafe at the far end and she was with him when he died a short time later.'

Before the 50th anniversary of D-Day, Margaret made a low-key visit to the cafe – the first house in Nazi-occupied Europe to be liberated. With only limited French, she could offer no explanation other than hand her passport to Madame Gondrée.

'She stared at me for a few seconds,' Margaret recalled. 'Then she shoved all her customers out, closed the door and sat holding my hand in silence.'

Members of Madame Gondrée's family had risked their lives prior to D-Day to provide intelligence about the bridge and its defences. The captors of the bridge had lost their radio

*Opposite: **Pegasus Bridge** Paratroopers and glider soldiers of 6th Airborne Division at Pegasus Bridge. The Horsa which landed them can be seen in the background.*

equipment in the drop and were unable to contact their brigade HQ, although they did make contact with another glider company which had taken the Orne Bridge.

THE CAPTURE OF MERVILLE

The 9th Parachute Battalion under Lieutenant-Colonel Terence Otway was charged with taking the coastal battery at Merville. The battery's two artillery pieces and ten heavy machine guns threatened both the invasion fleet and the British invasion beaches. It was defended by machine-gun pits, ringed by barbed wire and minefields and garrisoned by two hundred men. On the night of 5 June, its reinforced concrete fortifications were attacked by a force of one hundred Lancaster bombers, but they caused scarcely any damage. Otway was to be dropped a mile-and-a-half away at 0050 and take the battery by 0515. He was then to send up a Very light, otherwise British warships would start a naval bombardment – though no one thought it likely that naval guns would succeed when a hundred Lancasters had failed.

Things began to go wrong when Otway's planes came under heavy antiaircraft fire over the coast. A direct hit on the tail of Otway's own plane made it impossible to steer. Although they were nowhere near the drop zone, Otway and his men jumped. They landed in an old Norman farmhouse that the Germans were using as a headquarters. One even crashed through the roof of the conservatory, much to the surprise of the Germans. But some Canadian paratroopers who had landed nearby opened fire and the Germans fled. Running well behind schedule, Otway finally reached the assembly point at 0200. But by 0230 he had only mustered 150 men; 650 were missing. They had lost all their heavy equipment, including their radios; they still had a Very pistol, however. They quickly advanced on the battery at Merville, arriving there with an hour to spare. Fortunately for them, their reconnaissance party had dropped on target and had already cut the barbed wire and marked a path through the minefield. But as soon as the demolition squad blew up the last of the barbed wire, the German machine guns opened up. Otway's men were caught out in the open, but some of them made it into the defensive trenches inside the wire, leading up to the walls of the fortifications. They began pouring machine-gun fire through the embrasures, causing a blizzard of ricochets inside, and the Germans quickly surrendered. The Very light went up fifteen minutes before the naval bombardment was to start. Seventy-five British troops — half of Otway's party — had been killed or wounded, while only twenty-two of the two hundred German defenders survived.

But this was the one success of the 9th Parachute Battalion. Mistaking the Orne for the Dives, the pilots dropped the rest of the battalion in the wrong place. Some landed in the American sector. Others were captured or killed in skirmishes, while nearly two hundred men were never found. Otway and his men ran into more trouble later. When they left the Merville area, they were mistaken for a German detachment and were bombed by the USAAF.

THE BRIDGE AT TROARN

One of the Dives bridges was taken out by a single British sergeant who, having borrowed some explosives from some

Canadians who were not supposed to be there, walked up to the bridge unchallenged, planted his borrowed explosives and blew it up.

The most important bridge over the Dives was at Troarn. This carried the main road from Caen to Le Havre and Rouen. Although the bridge was within striking distance of the British beaches, it was outside the perimeter secured by the paratroopers. A party under Major J.D.A. Rosveare was to land in gliders, with jeeps and trailers carrying the demolition charges, and

Generals Two of Germany's most successful military commanders, Field Marshals Gerd von Rundstedt (l), and Erwin Rommel.

make a dash for the bridge before the Germans knew what was happening. The landing, was, as usual, confused. Major Rosveare mustered just seventy-three of his men, with no jeeps and trailers. They collected all the explosives they could find, loaded them onto handcarts that they found in local farmyards and set off. The first road sign they passed told them they were eleven kilometres from Troarn and they realized that they could not make it there by dawn on foot. At this moment, a Royal Army Medical Corps jeep with a trailer happened by. Rosveare commandeered it, unloaded the medical supplies, loaded what explosives it could carry and sent the rest off with a detachment to blow another bridge nearby. When Rosveare and his party reached the village of Troarn they crashed into a roadblock made of wire. The German sentry loosed off one shot, then ran. But it took valuable minutes to extricate the jeep. The party then careered on though the village, shooting wildly at any German who showed himself. Rosveare lost two men, either to enemy fire from a machine-gun post, or they might simply have fallen off the speeding jeep. When they reached the bridge they found it unguarded. It took two minutes for Rosveare and his men to blow it. They abandoned the jeep and disappeared into the undergrowth. By evening they had found their way to British lines, by which time the remaining bridges had been dynamited and the British forces landing on the beach were safe from any armoured counter-attack from the east.

THE GERMAN REACTION

Although the British airborne troops had achieved their objectives more successfully than the Americans, both had managed to spread confusion among the enemy. This did not mean, however, that there was not serious opposition waiting for them in the area. At 0130 Colonel Hans von Luck of the 125th Regiment of the 21st Panzer Division received his first reports of the airborne landings. Immediately, he gave orders for his regiment to assemble and within the hour his officers and men were lined up beside their tanks, which had their engines running. Von Luck's plan was to go and seize Pegasus Bridge from the British, but the only person who could give the order for the Panzers to go into action was Hitler, and Hitler was asleep. So was von Rundstedt, and Rommel was at home with his wife. In St Lô, a birthday party for General Marcks had ended around 0100. Marcks was just about to retire for the night when his operations room informed him that there was a great deal of aerial activity over the Cotentin Peninsula. He telephoned General Max Pemsel at the Seventh Army headquarters in Le Mans and told him that he believed the airborne landings were not isolated raids. Pemsel woke the Seventh Army's commander, General Friedrich Dollmann, in Rennes and told him that the invasion had begun.

He also woke General Hans Speidel, Rommel's Chief of Staff, with the news. Speidel called von Rundstedt. Admiral Kranke and Luftwaffe commander Field Marshal Hugo Sperrle also called von Rundstedt with news of enemy activity. However, between them, they decided that this was not the long-awaited invasion. Just before 0300, Pemsel phoned Speidel again, saying that the air drops were continuing and enemy ships had been seen off the east coast of the Cotentin Peninsula. Speidel was still not convinced and told Pemsel that the parachutists were probably secret agents being dropped to aid the Resistance, or Allied airmen who had bailed out of damaged planes. However, both the German Seventh Army and LXXXII Corps were now on the alert. Their switchboards tried to make contact with forward units, but failed. The phone lines had been cut. The Luftwaffe were scrambled, only to find themselves chasing radar decoys – strips of aluminium foil miles away from the aircraft that were dropping paratroopers and gliders over Normandy. Further confusion was generated when British radio operators cut in on the Luftwaffe frequency and started issuing misleading orders. Throughout the night, German headquarters received sporadic reports of paratroopers landing. But the troops and the French Resistance set about cutting the telephone wires so it was impossible for anyone in command to get a clear picture of what was going on. At 0245, General von Rundstedt's headquarters received a report saying, 'Engine noise audible from the sea on east coast of Cotentin'. This was dismissed, and the Germans only became aware of the impending invasion when the landing craft were twelve miles off shore. Even then, it was thought to be a diversionary attack to draw the German defenders away from the Pas de Calais where the real invasion would come. As H-Hour, the start time of the operation approached, the Allied airborne troops were enjoying some measure of success, while the German military, despite having some alert junior commanders, was effectively leaderless. The initiative, then, was with the Allies. It remained to be seen whether they could force their advantage home.

CHAPTER 3

Sword Beach

Sword Beach was the key to Montgomery's plan for the invasion. It would put British troops within striking distance of the town of Caen, whose capture would prevent any German reinforcements arriving from the Pas de Calais area.

Sword was the most easterly of the invasion beaches. It ran the two miles from Lion-Sur-Mer to Ouistreham and the mouth of the Orne Canal. It was the key beach in Montgomery's invasion plan, putting the Allies within striking distance of Caen, whose capture – on the first day, Montgomery hoped – would prevent any reinforcements coming in from the Pas de Calais.

The first on station at Sword was the seven-metre-long midget submarine X23, under the command of Lieutenant George Honour. Shortly before dawn the X23 surfaced, and raised an 18-foot mast, topped with a sonar beacon, to act as guidance for naval artillery. Soon after, as dawn broke, all hell broke loose with it. The Eastern Naval Task Force opened up and five-inch shells from its destroyers and fourteen-inch shells from its battleships came screaming overhead. Bombers and fighters attacked the beaches simultaneously, and Honour had his cap blown off by the blast of the rockets fired from an LCT (landing craft, tank).

By 0530 British soldiers were mustered on the boat decks of the landing ships, infantry (LSIs) which were hove to ready to launch the assault. Men from the South Lancashire and East Yorkshire Regiments clambered onto their LCAs (landing craft, assault), and were lowered into the swell. They were to be followed by battalion headquarters and reserve companies. As they headed for the beaches past HMS *Largs*, a bugler of the East Yorkshire sounded a general salute. This was acknowledged by Admiral Talbot and the Divisional Commander, General Tom Rennie.

ONTO THE BEACH

With the lead infantrymen huddled in their LCAs, the artillery in the landing craft behind them opened up as the craft ran in. At around 0630, 15,000 yards from shore, the LCAs adopted an arrowhead formation, attended by a motor launch equipped with radar to calculate the opening range. At 0644 – one minute late – the first ranging rounds of white tracer were fired by A Troop of the 7th Field Regiment. They were joined by gunfire from the battleships, cruisers and destroyers at 0650. The self-propelled guns of the 3rd Division Artillery opened up at 10,000 yards, joined by field guns aboard the LCIs.

The enemy returned fire with 88mm gun batteries a couple of miles inland, and mortars and machine-gun fire from pillboxes and positions set up in the remains of the seaside villas along the top of the dunes, and the water round the leading landing craft was soon foaming.

As they approached the beaches, Major C.K. 'Banger' King of the 2nd Battalion, East Yorkshire Regiment, read inspiring extracts from Shakespeare's *Henry V* over the Tannoy, while Brigadier Lord Lovat, commanding officer of the Commando brigade, had his piper play a highland reel. The lead LCAs hit the beaches along with an LCT carrying 'Hobart's Funnies', armoured vehicles specially adapted to deal with beach hazards such as mines and ditches, at 0726. As the infantry ran down the ramp into the surf, Royal Marine frogmen went over the sides of the landing craft to destroy submerged beach obstacles.

Next, the amphibious tanks arrived after a run-in of almost an hour. As soon as their tracks hit the shelving sand of the beach, they began to rise out of the water. Once the bottom of the flotation skirts were clear of the water, the air was released, the struts holding them in place were broken and the tank was ready for action. Within a minute they were pounding the enemy positions in front of them with shells and machine-gun fire. The enemy replied with 88mm mortars and machine-guns, mainly aimed at the infantry who were still struggling ashore. Smoke gave the infantry some cover, but machine-gun fire running along the length of the beach took its toll.

STRONGPOINT COD

Among the infantry, casualties were heavy, but most of the men made it across the beach into the dunes. This left them temporarily helpless as they had outrun their tanks, some of which found themselves stranded, having dropped their flotation skirts, by the incoming tide. Others were hit, immobilized but still firing. The infantry who had made it into the dunes soon took over the task of putting down suppressing fire.

One of the major threats was Strongpoint 0880, codenamed

Cod. This was a pillbox surrounded by a zigzag of trenches, which stood almost directly across the beach from where B Company of the East Yorkshires had landed. The company commander, Major Harrison, was killed almost immediately. Lieutenant Bell-Walker took command and decided that, if he was going to get his men off the beach, he had to do something about Strongpoint Cod. Acting with suicidal bravery, he managed to creep around behind it, toss a grenade through the gun slit and follow up with a burst of Sten gun fire. He was cut down by machinegun fire from the rear positions, but his company got off the beach more or less intact.

When the first wave of LCTs discharged their Hobart's Funnies, the Crabs – Sherman tanks with flail chains attached – drove up the beach with their chain-drums flailing to explode mines. At Lion-sur-Mer, a German anti-tank gun was in action, but a bridge-carrying Sherman dropped its bridge directly onto the emplacement, putting the gun out of action. Other Hobart's Funnies set various ingenious explosives to blow gaps in the barbed wire and dunes. Bundles of logs were dropped into antitank ditches and bridges were laid over the sea walls. These allowed the Crabs, which had made several passes down the waterline and back, to deploy inland to clear the way for the troops.

The immediate area of the beach had been cleared of the enemy as early as 0830. But a strongpoint 500 metres inland, that boasted five multi-gunned machine-gun posts, three 81mm mortars, a 75mm and a 37mm gun, and two 50mm anti-tank guns, took three hours to clear and cost the invaders dearly. The German resistance there was only overcome by a joint effort of the East Yorkshires and South Lancashires, along with support tanks and infantry from the 5th Battalion Kings Regiment and elements of No. 4 Commando. The arrival of a machine-gun platoon from the 2nd Battalion Middlesex Regiment with universal carriers finally cleared the German trenches and fifteen survivors surrendered at 1000 hours.

By 0900, elements of the South Lancs had pushed south and taken the village of Hermanville, which was held by two hundred Germans. A Company, which had turned west, found itself held up by snipers and machine-gun fire from the German stronghold codenamed Trout, in Lion-sur-Mer itself. In a nearby wood, the Germans had a battery, protected by trenches and sandbags, that continued to lay down fire across the beach as the Suffolks were coming ashore. A naval forward observer with the commandos only got within range at 1441. He called in a bombardment from the Polish destroyer Slazak. After an hour and almost a thousand rounds, the Slazak had to break off, but the battery remained in operation for another two days. Despite this German battery, the odd mortar and occasional sniper fire, the fighting on the beach itself was over and men moved at a leisurely pace off the beaches, towards the fighting which was now taking place inland.

MOVING INLAND

As the initial wave of infantry had been engaging the enemy, the Royal Engineers had been working on the beach obstacles. They had suffered badly under enemy fire and some had drowned. On D-Day, the sappers would suffer 117 casualties, and twenty-six Crab flail tanks were knocked out with forty-two casualties among their crew. By 1030, the tide – aided by a strong wind

– was covering the sand rapidly and the sappers turned their attention to clearing the exits from the beach. Clearance teams went in to remove mines, stakes and other obstacles at the top of the beach that would slow the landing of further troops. This operation was slowed by the need to remove knocked-out tanks that were scattered along the beach and were blocking the exits. The only way for armour to get clear of the beaches was to move westwards, then down the road to Hermanville, which ran along a narrow causeway over the flooded marshland behind the dunes. The delay in clearing the exits caused a back-up. Vehicles choked the narrow strip of sand, which was all that was left of the beach. Fifty self-propelled guns stood in the surf, firing inland. And by 1200 it was decided that landings would have to be suspended for thirty minutes to allow the traffic jam to clear.

THE COMMANDOS

The Commandos, including a large French contingent, spearheaded the fighting inland. Moving with a little more dash and determination than other infantrymen, they overcame the German defenders in Ouistreham, and in the casino at Riva-Bella in heavy fighting.

Major R. 'Pat' Porteous lost nearly a quarter of his men by the time they had got over the seawall, and casualties would have been worse if their smoke grenades had not impeded the aim of the German machine guns in the pillbox to their left. Their objective was a coastal battery, but when they reached it, they found that it housed only telegraph poles. The guns had been moved three kilometres inland a few days before, and the Germans began shelling the old battery position as soon as the British reached it. The bombardment was directed from a fire-control tower in a medieval fortress. Snipers there also harassed them. They tried to storm the tower, but the Germans rolled grenades down on them. A PIAT (Personal Infantry Anti-Tank) hollow-charge missile fired at the tower had no effect and their flame-thrower did not have enough pressure to reach the defenders. So Porteous and his men gave up, and headed for Pegasus Bridge, where, together with 4 Commando under Lord Lovat, they joined up with the airborne troops on the eastern side of the Orne at 1300, achieving their first and most vital objective.

ON TO COLLEVILLE

The 3rd Division took less than an hour to secure their beach, and begin their thrust inland, spearheaded by the 1st Battalion of the Suffolk Regiment. The aim was to meet up with elements of 6th Airborne on the strategically vital Orne River.

Their first objective was the village of Colleville, which was cleared without serious resistance. There were, however, still two German strongpoints in the immediate vicinity, codenamed Morris and Hillman. Although Morris put up relatively light resistance, its occupants having been heavily shelled by HMS Dragon and HMS Kelvin, Hillman would prove of sterner stuff, and it was not until tanks from the Staffordshire Yeomanry arrived that progress was made. The tanks were ordered through the gap. When the lead tank stopped, refusing to run over the body of a dead British soldier, the driver was told to 'f***ing well get on with it'. Troops followed the tanks through the gap and fanned out, taking cover in shell holes. After grenades were

Take cover *A group of Allied troops shelters from enemy shelling in a battlefield crater outside Caen. The town was finally captured by British and Canadian troops after five weeks of intensive fighting, during which it was all but destroyed.*

tossed down the ventilation shafts, the occupants came out with their hands up. Other concrete emplacements were blown up. By 2000 hours, there was no further resistance, only some fifty German soldiers waiting to be taken prisoner.

The only serious counter-attack mounted by the Germans on D-Day came at the western end of Sword Beach, where the aim was to link up with the Canadians landing on Juno Beach about two miles away. The 22nd Regiment of the 21st Panzer Division under Colonel Oppeln attacked into this gap, and actually reached the beach at 2000. The British and Canadians, however, succeeded in bringing up tanks and anti-tank weapons, so when the 22nd Panzers went in they had to run a gauntlet of fire. The lead tank suffered a direct hit and exploded. Inside a couple of minutes, five Panzers had been destroyed. The Royal Canadian Air Force then joined the attack. Oppeln had to call off the advance. The best he could hope for was to hold his position and he dug in. The 192nd Panzergrenadiers were left in the gap, stranded, as, by late afternoon, the rest of the 716th Division was in full retreat.

NIGHTFALL

By the end of the first day, the British had put 29,000 men ashore at Sword. They had suffered 630 casualties, but inflicted many more and taken large numbers of prisoners. Even as dusk fell, landing craft were queuing up to land more men on the beaches and an enormous force was waiting in the transport area in the Channel, ready to be landed the next day. Sections of the Mulberry Harbours were already on their way from England. However, the British invasion force had not secured its vital, though over-optimistic, objective – taking Caen itself. By the end of the first day they were still five kilometres short of the outskirts. But the Germans showed no signs of exploiting this failure. The 21st Panzer Division had failed to push the British back into the sea, and the bulk of German armour was still in the Pas de Calais, awaiting an invasion there.

That night a new wave of 6th Airborne gliders came in. This time the weather conditions allowed less troublesome landings. These were followed by a massive airdrop of equipment. As the sky filled with coloured parachutes, the tired and blooded British troops took great heart from this overwhelming display of air power.

Although the Germans had lost their one opportunity to push the British back into the sea, the British were now dug in, holding a defensive line instead of going after the enemy, giving German units the chance to do the same. To the north of Caen, 21st Panzer Division took up position, flanked by 192nd Panzergrenadiers to the east. These units were reinforced by elements of 12th SS Panzer Division *Hitlerjugend*, a young and elite formation of a very different class to the majority of the German defenders on D-Day.

In the air, however, the Allies were in supreme control. Fighter-bomber attacks and concentrated artillery fire halted German advances, and 25th SS Panzergrenadiers, who with the support of tanks from 12th SS Panzers had retaken the village of Cambes, were forced to abandon the village and dig in along the road to Caen in defensive positions.

To the rear, the Lincolns had cleared Lion-sur-Mer, then moved up to St Aubin d'Arquenay and the Benouville bridges, which were being defended by Fox Troop of 92nd Light Anti-Aircraft Regiment of the Royal Artillery. These bridges were vital for the British getting off the beaches, and over the five days following D-Day, the Luftwaffe mounted eight attacks on them, losing seventeen planes to the British defenders.

Ouistreham was cleared. The South Lancashires also cleared the villages of Cresserons and Plumetot, and moved on to Douvres. This allowed the British from Sword Beach to join up with the Canadians who had landed on Juno, though Douvres radar station remained in German hands until 17 June – D+11. The radar facility itself had been bombed out of action three weeks before D-Day itself, but the station had a secure telephone line to Caen and the Germans hung onto it as a forward observation point.

Although the British failed to take Caen again on D+1, their actions on land, along with the continuing bombardment from the guns of the Royal Navy, seriously disrupted any attempt by the Germans to counter-attack.

BEYOND D-DAY

Both sides now dug in, and for the next two weeks the situation would freeze in these positions. Although Montgomery's initial plan called for the occupation of Caen, he now used the static position at the eastern end of the invasion beaches as a pivot for the invasion as a whole. It pinned down the German forces in Normandy, allowing the Americans on the westerly beaches to push west, then south, then east without meeting any serious opposition.

CHAPTER 4

Juno Beach

*The 1942 Allied raid on the port of Dieppe had
cost many Canadian troops their lives. For many of
their countrymen, the landing on Juno Beach would be
their opportunity to even the score a little.*

The Canadians landed on Juno Beach, which lay between
the two British beaches, Sword and Gold. It centred
on Courseulles-sur-Mer, the most heavily defended point
in the British sector. At the extreme left of the beach were
the strongpoints of Langrune and St Aubin, but these were a
kilometre apart, and the 716th Infantry Division, under General
Wilhelm Richter, had only horse-drawn transport to haul their
guns and supplies. The men manning the strongpoints were
mainly under eighteen or over thirty-five. There were some
veterans of the Eastern Front in their mid-twenties, but most
of them were badly injured or disabled, and the numbers were
made up by Ost battalion troops from Poland, Russia and Soviet
Georgia. Certainly, the German troops were no match for the
young, tough, fit and well-trained Canadians, who were highly
motivated. Canadians had suffered the bulk of the casualties at
Dieppe in 1942. The raid was a national disaster and Juno Beach
was the place where the Canadians, specifically the 3rd Infantry

Division, were going to pay the Germans back. The odds were in their favour, as they outnumbered the defenders six to one. The first wave would put 2,400 Canadians on the beach to face just 400 German troops.

TO THE BEACHES

On the morning of 6 June, some 366 ships assembled in an area just five miles wide by ten miles deep off Juno Beach. At 0530, the slowest LCTs, carrying the amphibious tank squadrons, began their run in. An hour later, the heavier support craft, with a destroyer escort, set off. Next came the engineering groups who would knock out the beach obstacles. They were followed by the assault tanks, the flail tanks and other specialized vehicles designed to cope with the beach defences. Behind them were the first wave of the infantry, with two companies of each battalions. The other two companies followed up in a second wave fifteen minutes later. Behind the infantry spearhead were the LCTs carrying rocket launchers. Following them were the self-propelled artillery regiments, who would fire three shells every two hundred yards as they sped towards the beaches.

Some of the LCAs found it hard going. Towed craft broke their lines. It was considered too dangerous to launch the amphibious tanks, and the decision was made to beach their LCTs so they could drive straight onto dry land. But after they passed the 7,000 yard mark, the commanding officer of the 7th Brigade, decided his tanks would swim ashore after all, though the sea conditions meant they landed only just ahead of the infantry.

Although the German emplacements on Juno had been heavily bombed by both the RAF and the USAAF, they were

Spearhead *Men of 48 Royal Marine Commando come ashore at Juno Beach.*

virtually all still intact as the first wave of Canadian landing craft began their approach to the beach around 0730.

The demolition teams went in first, setting off the small Teller mines that marked the outer reaches of the obstacles. Nearly a quarter of the landing craft were damaged by explosions, but the troops still managed to struggle ashore. Fortunately for the Canadians, many of the obstacles were quickly submerged because of the strong north-westerly wind that piled up water over them. By 0800, the first wave of LCAs were dropping their ramps and the assault teams were wading ashore. As they made their way through the obstacles and up on to the beach, the Germans opened fire.

There was a high sea wall at the back of Juno Beach, but specialized tanks carried bridges to help the infantry over it.

Crab flail tanks dealt with the minefield on the other side. Tanks carrying fascines breached the anti-tank ditches, while bulldozers shifted the barbed wire. Once they were through the coastal defences, the Canadians found themselves in flat, open country with few fortifications and very little opposition. However the men on the beaches had to suffer intense flanking fire from fortified pillboxes, until tanks with flame-throwers took them out. At Juno Beach, one in eighteen was killed or wounded: there were 1,200 casualties among the 21,400 men landed. However, this figure is misleading as most of the men were landed in the late morning or afternoon, while most of the casualties occurred during the first hour when the casualty rate was more like one in two.

The Regina Rifle Regiment landed at Courseulles where the German defences were strongest, and took heavy casualties: forty-five men of the Regina Rifles were killed on D-Day, mostly in this action.

The Royal Winnipeg Rifles also ran into difficulties. They were fired on while still at sea. They arrived six minutes ahead of their tanks and many were shot while they were still chest-high in water. When the tanks did turn up, there were only six of them, due to an accident at sea. The infantry's only chance was to charge directly at the enemy. By the time they got into Courseulles itself, only twenty-six men were left standing.

B Company of the Queen's Own Rifles also found themselves in trouble to the east in Bernière. The wind and tide had carried them two hundred yards east of their planned landing position, dropping them directly under the village's two 50mm guns and seven machine guns. The amphibious tanks of the Fort Garry

Horse had not been launched out to sea and were not there to support them. B Company took sixty-five casualties and huddled under the beach obstacles. Then Rifleman William Chicoski, Lance-Corporal René Tessier and Lieutenant W.G. Herbert made a dash for the sea wall. It was ten feet high at Bernière and it afforded them enough shelter to work their way along to the strongpoint. There they used Sten guns and grenades to overcome the defenders.

MOVING INLAND

The eastern flank of Juno Beach was taken by the North Shore Regiment. They arrived at 0740, at the same time as their tanks, to find that the concrete gun shelter that towered above the beach at St Aubin was still intact. Two tanks were knocked out in the surf by the emplacement's 50mm anti-tank gun. It loosed off seventy-five rounds until it was finally silenced by two high-velocity shells from the Fort Garry's Sherman tanks, a sustained bombardment by a 95mm howitzer of a Royal Marine Centaur and a concrete-smashing charge laid by the Royal Engineers.

Along the entire five-mile stretch of Juno Beach, fighting continued for two hours after the Canadians had first hit the beaches. The Reginas found that the tunnels and trenches that they thought they had cleared when they first landed had been re-occupied by the Germans, and the Canadians had to perform the hazardous job of trench-clearing all over again. On the other side of the harbour, the Royal Winnipegs were fighting the Germans through the ruins of houses there. In Bernières, the Queen's Own Rifles found themselves under attack when they emerged from the landward side of the village, and the North

Shore Regiment suffered casualties in the booby-trapped house at the rear of St Aubin.

The situation was little better on the beaches. As the landing craft pulled back from the shore, they set off more mines and a quarter of the LCAs were put out of action. The leading company of Le Régiment de la Chaudière, reserve battalion to the Queen's Own Rifles and the North Shores, lost all but five of its landing craft. The men swam ashore, but those who made it to the beach had to shelter under the sea wall at Bernières until the Queen's Own Rifles returned to relieve them. And the Canadian Scottish, the reserve battalion of the Reginas and the Winnipegs, found itself held up on the beach by a minefield – 14,000 mines had been laid between Bernières and Courseulles – and suffered heavy mortar fire.

Nevertheless, by H+2, the two leading brigades were ashore and the reserve brigade, the 1st, and its armoured regiment, the Sherbrooke Fusiliers, were landing against little resistance. The beach was jammed with men and vehicles, while Crabs made gaps through the minefields so they could leave the beach. At Bernières there was an additional difficulty as the area behind the dunes was flooded. An ingenious solution was found. At 1200 hours, a tank was sunk in the mire and used as a pier for a bridge. This bridge remained in place until 1976. When it was replaced, the tank was removed: it is now a local war memorial.

Fighting continued in St Aubin until 1800 hours, and the North Shore Regiment was still engaging the coastal command post of the 2nd Battalion of the 736th Grenadier Regiment at 2000 hours. But otherwise the Canadians pushed on into the countryside with negligible resistance, as the area behind the beaches was practically deserted, both by the French inhabitants and the defending forces. Richter was so short of men that he had had no choice but to put them all on the coast itself, and once they were overcome, resistance was at an end. There were a few snipers at Banville and Colombiers-sur-Selles, and a little resistance in the village of Anguerny, but even this was overcome by the late afternoon. By the end of D-Day the North Nova Scotia Highlanders, who had landed on the beaches at noon, were at Villon-les-Buissons, just three miles from the outskirts of Caen.

Montgomery and Eisenhower were delighted. The Canadians drove deeper into France than any other troops that first day. Better yet, they had not suffered a tragedy comparable with Dieppe, which had been the great fear. Heavy casualties had been expected. Losses of 2,000, including 600 drowned, had been anticipated. In fact, the Canadians suffered just 1,000 casualties, including 335 dead, and the enemy had been completely overcome. Of the four German and two Russian battalions stationed in the area, only one battalion at eighty per cent strength could be mustered by the end of the day. To all intents and purposes, the German 716th Division was no more. The Canadians were still a few kilometres short of their D-Day objective: N13, the main road that joined Cherbourg and Caen to Paris. However, it is generally agreed that all D-Day objectives were wildly over-optimistic.

CHAPTER 5

Gold Beach

Although resistance on Gold Beach was less than on neighbouring Omaha, casualties were nevertheless initially high. Once ashore, however, the 50th Division moved further inland than anyone bar the Canadians on Juno Beach.

To Gold Beach, the most easterly of the British–Canadian sector, were assigned the 50th (Northumbrian) Infantry Division, with support from 47 Royal Marine Commando, and units of the Royal Engineers. Casting off at 0615, six miles from shore, the Royal Engineers and the Underwater Demolition Teams hit Gold Beach at 0753. H-Hour on Gold was one hour later than on the American beaches, as the tide swept from west to east and low tide came later on the British beaches. However, the strong wind was piling up the water so that some of the beach obstacles were underwater before the Underwater Demolition Teams could destroy them.

There were two German concentrations along Gold Beach, one at La Rivière on the left flank where Gold met Juno Beach, and one at Le Hamel in the centre, and there was also a series of well-concealed gun emplacements on the steep cliffs near Longues-sur-Mer to the west of Gold Beach which were left unscathed by air strikes and the initial bombardment. Soon after dawn, the guns began firing on the battleship USS *Arkansas* off Omaha Beach and forced HMS *Bulolo*, the headquarters ship for Gold Beach, to change position. The light cruiser HMS *Ajax*, which had famously seen action off Montevideo against the Graf Spee in the Battle of the River Plate, moved in to take on the fortification. Fortunately for the Allies, the exact co-ordinates of the emplacements had been paced off by the farmer who owned the land, and his blind son. They had got the figures to André Heintz, professor of history at Caen University, who transmitted them to England on a homemade radio. The first twenty minutes of the Ajax's bombardment forced the Germans to abandon two of the emplacements because of the concussion caused by the shock of the Ajax's 6-inch shells hitting the concrete. Then a shell entered the embrasure of a third emplacement while a shell was being loaded into the 155mm gun's breech. The shell exploded, setting off the magazine. No-one survived.

TO THE BEACHES

Sherman tanks on the LCTs had 25-pounder guns, and more 25-pounder field pieces towed behind them fired three rounds a minute, starting when they were twelve kilometres out and ending when they were three kilometres from the beaches. The noise on board the LCAs caused by this bombardment and the rockets being fired at the beaches was deafening.

The lead LCAs each fired twenty-four Spigot bombs, each containing thirty pounds of high explosive each, from a range of about 400 yards. These were aimed to land among the beach obstacles and clear a path twelve yards wide and eight yards long.

The idea was that the amphibious tanks and Hobart's Funnies on their LCTs to the rear would have a clear lane to the top of the beach, so they could deal with the defenders there before the first infantrymen arrived. The lead LCAs were conscious of the strange silence that engulfed the shore once the naval bombardment was over. They had also been issued with 'sticky bombs', explosive charges that they were supposed to attach to remaining beach obstacles. These were new items of equipment and no one had been trained to use them. Few of them would stick, and men trying to attach them came under sniper fire.

The infantry had major trouble avoiding being run down on the high seas by the LCTs behind who passed them on the run-in. German snipers also prevented the Underwater Demolition Teams clearing lanes of mines. This being the case, the pilots of the landing craft behind them had been told that the best tactic was to approach the shore at full tilt. Twenty of the LCTs hit mines, losing both men and tanks. But two companies of Hobart's Funnies were landed near Asnelles.

When the LCAs bringing the infantry assault teams hit, the men rushed ashore. One commando said that their eagerness to get ashore was because they would rather have fought the whole German army than go back onto the landing ships. Everyone had been seasick after a breakfast of fried eggs washed down with a tot of rum, which was mandatory for all those going ashore. Fortunately, there was little resistance, other than from a strongpoint at Le Hamel, which kept the beach under a constant fire until taken out in the afternoon by the 1st Hampshires, with the support of an AVRE and a Sexton tank of the Essex Yeomanry. Elsewhere, opposition was easily overcome. Even the strongpoint at La Rivière only held out until 1000 hours, though it cost the lives of ninety-four men of 69th Brigade, including six officers, to take it. The 47 Royal Marine Commandos, landing to the far right near St Côme de Fresne, came under heavy machine-gun fire from the crack German 352nd Division as they tried to negotiate the beach obstacles. This damaged fifteen out of their sixteen landing craft and caused the loss of forty-three men and their signalling equipment. They headed west towards the small harbour town of Port-en-Bessin where they were supposed to meet up with the Americans from Omaha Beach. The Royal Marines took the town from the rear on D+2 at the cost of two hundred lives.

THE VICTORIA CROSS

As the lead assault companies of 6th Battalion of the Green Howards landed on the King section of Gold Beach, they saw what looked like a pillbox. Company Sergeant-Major Stan Hollis of D Company, a hardened veteran, grabbed a machine gun, balanced it on the ramp of the LCA, and gave the pillbox a burst. There was no response – probably because it was not a pillbox at all but a shelter for the tramline that ran along the sea front. As Lieutenant-Colonel Robin Hastings, the commanding officer of the 6th Green Howards, hit the beach, he saw that A Company was pinned down by a German 105mm gun emplacement and a pillbox. But a tank from B Squadron of the 4th/7th Royal Dragoon Guards, supporting 6th Green Howards, managed to 'post' a shell through the emplacement's embrasure, silencing the 105mm. Then Lance-Corporal Joyce, who Hastings had got out of a Glasgow cell after a drunken spree on embarkation leave in Scotland, jumped up on to the sea wall, threw a grenade into the pillbox, then rounded up the survivors. This earned him the Military Medal. Once Hollis and D Company were through the minefield they headed for their next objective, the gun battery at Mont Fleury. A short way up the road, they came under fire in the area of a house, but they continued towards the battery. Following with company headquarters, Major Ronnie Lofthouse spotted that the small-arms fire was coming from a concealed pillbox and pointed it out to CSM Hollis. Single-handedly Hollis charged the pillbox, Sten gun blazing. The Germans returned fire but miraculously missed. When he reached the pillbox, Hollis shoved the muzzle of his Sten gun through the firing slit and gave it a burst. Lying on the roof of the pillbox, he dropped a grenade through the slit. Once it went off, he jumped down the back and opened the door. He found two dead Germans inside, along with a number of wounded. The rest surrendered. Quickly changing the magazine on his Sten gun, he followed a trench leading to another pillbox, whose occupants surrendered. In all, he had thirty or so prisoners on his hands. He directed them towards the beach, from where they would be shipped back to prisoner of war camps in England.

For this action, and for later extracting a Bren gun team under fire, CSM Hollis was awarded the Victoria Cross, the only one to be won on D-Day. That night 6th Green Howards were a mile short of their D-Day objective, St Léger on the Bayeux-Caen road. They had suffered ninety casualties.

Six miles inland from the coast, to the right of the beach, a German battle group was stationed at Bayeux. The Germans were depending on this unit for their response to an invasion in that area. However, the battle group had set off at 0400 to Isigny, where enemy paratroop landings had been reported. This was something of a wild-goose chase and they were ordered back to their base at 0800. They were to counter-attack towards Crépon, but the order took an hour to reach them; it then took them five hours to get back, as many of the French trucks they commandeered had broken down. By that time, one battalion had been hived off to face the Americans landing on Omaha Beach. When they reached their assembly point at Brazenville they found it was already in British hands.

THE BATTLE FOR CREULLY

At about midday, British troops reached the small village of Creully, about five miles inland. The eight men in German uniforms who were to have defended the beach there – five Russians and three Lithuanians – surrendered immediately. The British then pushed on to the N13 main highway, which they reached at the village of St Léger, halfway between Bayeux and Caen, at 1500. The squad that arrived there climbed a tree to spy out the land, only to see a German halftrack rumble into the village and park at the bottom of the tree while the six-man German crew got out to relieve themselves. Two more German half-tracks arrived. Two of the half-tracks headed off – one to the east, one to the west – leaving the third parked in the village square. As soon as they were sure the Germans had gone, the Tommies shinned down the tree, hot-wired the half-track and made off back to Creully where the British had just met up with the Canadians from Juno Beach.

In the afternoon of D-Day, Creully had been the site of a

crucial tank action between the 4th/7th Dragoon Guards and German Panzers. Part of 8th Armoured Brigade, 4th/7th Dragoon Guards had been put under the command of 69th Infantry for the invasion, with one tank squadron assigned to each infantry battalion. B Squadron would support 6th Green Howards; C Squadron would support 5th East Yorkshires to their left. The plan had been for the tanks to swim ashore, landing five minutes ahead of the assault battalion. A Squadron would support 7th Green Howards, the reserve infantry battalion, and land at H+45, forty-five minutes after H-Hour. Their tanks had been fitted with flotation screens and a Duplex-Drive that operated a small propeller from the tank's main engine. However, some of A Squadron's Shermans had had their 75mm guns replaced by 17-pounders, which were more effective at knocking out Panzers. As the barrel of the 17-pounder was too long to fit inside the flotation screen, A Squadron's landing craft would deliver them directly to the beaches. At the last minute, they were supplied with a roll of beach matting. When the ramp dropped, two men were supposed to run forward, unrolling this. Then the tank would drive up it. A Squadron were not impressed, having already practised the landing without this new-fangled device. During the Channel crossing, the matting went overboard.

As it was, the sea was too rough off Gold Beach to launch the amphibious tanks, so B and C Squadrons were unloaded in shallow water a few hundred yards off shore. They made it to the beach with few casualties. A Squadron, who followed up at 0830, lost two tanks, which sank in underwater shell holes. After breaching a minefield, they headed down the road past Crépon to Creully with the 7th Green Howards. The 1st and 3rd Troops led, with the 2nd and 4th following with the infantry riding on them. By this time there was little opposition and the few Germans they encountered were eager to surrender.

Their aim was to reach the bridge at Creully as quickly as possible. It was a key crossing point of the River Seulles that otherwise might prove a significant tank obstacle. There were reports that a German Panther tank was holding the bridge, but it had withdrawn before A Squadron arrived. The British tanks quickly crossed the bridge and drove nervously into the village itself. Tanks are more vulnerable in a built-up area where men with anti-tank weapons can get up close in the narrow streets, and snipers can pick off the tanks' commanders, who have their heads out of the tank turrets. But A Squadron made it through the village without incident and out into the cornfields on the other side. This was perfect tank country and the experienced tank commander Major Jackie d'Avigdor-Goldsmied deployed his squadron for a rapid push south. Suddenly two of his tanks exploded and he ordered the rest of the squadron to make a dash for a line of trees four hundred yards ahead. They made it, but another tank was hit there. Like the others, it burst into flames. The Germans called Shermans 'Tommy cookers' because of their tendency to catch fire when hit. Even though he saw this inferno, Lieutenant Alastair Morrison, leader of the 4th Troop in the rear, made a dash for the trees. When he reached them, he saw another tank go up but, by chance, he spotted a distance gun flash near the bottom of a telegraph pole. He did not dare roll his tank forward to the edge of the trees to engage the enemy directly. Instead, he called in indirect fire, which hit the target with the second shell. Suddenly shells were bursting all around them. Both A Squadron and 7th Green Howards suffered heavy casualties. It was discovered later that the fire came from HMS Orion after someone ashore called in artillery support. When they withdrew to a more secure position to tend to their casualties, they were attacked by an American Thunderbolt fighter. It was only on his third pass that he spotted the orange smoke from a smoke grenade Morrison flung into the cornfield to warn the pilot he was attacking friendly forces.

By the end of the day, A Squadron had lost seven killed, four injured and four tanks. By the evening of 6 June the Caen–Bayeux highway had not been cut, and there were still hostile forces between Gold and the Americans on Omaha. The British had, however, put 25,000 men on Gold Beach, at the cost of 413 casualties, penetrated six miles inland, captured the heights of Port-en-Bessin, and linked up with the Canadians on Juno. It was, by any standards, an impressive start to the campaign.

CHAPTER 6

Omaha Beach

'Two kinds of people are staying on this beach; the dead, and those who are going to die. Now let's get the hell out of here.'

COLONEL GEORGE TAYLOR, US 16TH INFANTRY REGT

While the British and Canadian assaults on Sword, Juno and Gold, and the American assault on Utah, had progressed as well as the planners had hoped, and far better than many had feared, the same could not be said of Omaha. The US 1st Infantry Division was tasked with taking the beach and, ambitiously, the villages of Colleville-sur-Mer, Saint-Laurent-sur-Mer and Vierville, cutting the Bayeux-Isigny road and linking up with the British on Gold. Omaha would prove to be their Calvary.

As the site for an amphibious landing, Omaha Beach was about as far from ideal as it is possible to imagine. Its 7,000 yards of sand and shingle were overlooked by a hundred-foot escarpment which provided the enemy with a natural fortress. But it was vital that Omaha Beach was taken so that the American forces landing on Utah Beach to the west could join up with the British forces landing to the east to form one continuous beachhead.

Omaha Beach had other disadvantages. It was crescent-shaped,

Beach obstacles on Omaha, designed to prevent landing craft coming in near to the shore. They would provide some cover for the men of the US 1st Division, however.

allowing guns along the top of the bluff to concentrate their fire on the troops landing below. The bluff itself was cut up by five wooded ravines or draws which provided the only exits from the beach and the Germans concentrated their firepower down these draws. Strong offshore currents created sand bars and gullies that were exposed at low tide and created difficulties for the landing craft and vehicles coming ashore. To these natural hazards the Germans had added three bands of obstacles their own. Near the low-water mark there were iron structures about ten feet high with Teller anti-tank mines on their uprights. Above those were two rows of wooden poles driving into the sand at a shallow angle, carrying a mine or shell on the tip. Then about halfway up between the low-water mark and the high-water mark were rows of 'hedgehogs': two or three pieces of angled steel joined in the middle, which could puncture the hull of a landing craft.

Mines had been laid on the shingled embankment under the bluff along with improvised booby traps hidden in great coils of barbed wire. Along the top of the bluff were a series of strongpoints which overlooked the draws. Although some of the concrete emplacements had yet to be finished, these strongpoints were well protected. In them there would be one artillery piece, a 50mm cannon and ten machine-guns manned by a thirty-strong platoon. Overlooking Omaha Beach there were eight concrete bunkers containing heavy 88mm or 75mm guns, sixty light artillery guns, thirty-five small artillery pieces in pill boxes and eighteen anti-tank guns. One central strongpoint also had automatic flame throwers. Between the strongpoints there were infantry trenches with at least eighty-five machine-guns. To the rear there were forty pits housing rocket launchers and mortar positions. Communications between these defences were good and all this fire power could be directed by one man in the central strongpoint overlooking the beach. However, there was one weakness to this defence: shells had to be brought up to the gun emplacements by truck and these had been targeted in air attacks and naval bombardments. While the invasion was being planned, the defences on Omaha Beach were manned by 716th Coastal Defence Division. This division was made up mainly of Slavs and Poles. It was undermanned and its morale was low. But the week before D-Day, elements of the 352nd Infantry Division, veterans of the Eastern Front, had been moved up.

ASSAULT ON POINTE DU HOC

At the western end of Omaha was a formidable German battery, codenamed Maisey, on top of the 100-foot cliff at Pointe du Hoc. Both Omaha and Utah beaches were in range of the six 155mm guns there. It was manned by 210 men: eighty-five artillery men and 125 infantry. Its destruction was crucial if the landings on Omaha and Utah were to have any chance of success. Of the 300 enemy installations in the American sector, the destruction of Maisey was given top priority. The job was given to the US Army Rangers. The Rangers had been trained by the British Royal Marine Commandos in Scotland, where they practised coastal assaults against cliffs.

Delays at sea meant the Rangers arrived at Pointe du Hoc late, and found themselves pinned down at the foot of the cliff by German machine-guns, mortars and grenades.

The USS *Satterlee* moved close in to the shore, and engaged the pillbox on the top of the Pointe. After savage gun battles, at 0728 the naval fire control party hauled themselves up to the top of the cliff and established communications with the fleet. *Satterlee* and USS *McCook* began picking off enemy positions. One gun was blown up and another was knocked off the cliff. The accuracy of the naval artillery support saved many Rangers' lives.

Those who made it to the top of the cliff found shelter in shell and bomb craters. By 0745 all the Rangers were up the cliff and their commander, Colonel James Rudder, established his command post near a destroyed anti-aircraft emplacement. By 0830, a party of Rangers had fought their way through to the road from Vierville to Grandcamp, where they established a defensive perimeter and a roadblock. Although the Rangers had achieved their objectives, German counter-attacks were not long in coming, and the only reinforcements that could get through were three paratroopers from the 101st Airborne who had somehow made it through the German lines.

The Rangers held the position throughout D-Day and the following day, despite repeated German counterattacks, until they were finally relieved, and at 1130 on 8 June Old Glory was raised on Pointe du Hoc. Rudder's men had overrun a fortified garrison, held off five counter-attacks and suffered both enemy artillery and friendly fire. Rudder himself had been injured a second time by shards of concrete blown off a bunker by US naval gunfire. In all, his assault force suffered 70 per cent casualties.

ON OMAHA BEACH

While the Rangers had been fighting on Pointe du Hoc, Omaha Beach itself had seen some ferocious fighting. The beach lay three miles to the east of the Pointe. Things had begun badly there too. At 0540, H-50, thirty-two amphibious tanks from two companies of the 741st Tank Battalion were launched over ten miles out to sea. There was a heavy swell with three to four foot waves. Given the conditions, the tanks were launched too far out. Their flotation screens were simply swamped or pounded by the waves until they gave way. Twenty-seven of the tanks sank. Of their 135 crewmen, few survived. The five tanks that did get ashore fared little better. Three fell victim to German anti-tank guns almost immediately. The amphibious trucks carrying 105mm field guns also sank, so the assault troops were left with practically no artillery support.

The naval bombardment on Omaha started at 0550. Soon after the German batteries began their reply, though Maisey on the Pointe du Hoc was notably silent. At 0600, 480 B-24 Liberator bombers dropped 1,285 tons of bombs. These were aimed at thirteen specific targets. But the cloud ceiling was low, visibility was poor and the bombs were dropped late. Some landed as much as three miles inland, leaving the beach defences unscathed. When the naval bombardment finished at 0625, 3,000 rounds had been fired, again to little effect. British LCTs had also launched a fusillade of 5-inch rockets, but most of them fell short.

Having seen the fate of the 741st's tanks, the Navy Lieutenant in charge of the 743rd's decided to take them into shore. B Company, which landed opposite the Vierville draw, were soon lost to the fire from the German defences there. But A and C Companies landed successfully. They were soon followed by the assault troops in their LCAs.

Each landing craft carried thirty-one men and one officer. Each had six riflemen in the bow carrying an M-1 rifle and ninety-six rounds of ammunition, a four-man wire-cutting team carrying M-1s, a demolition team with TNT charges and Bangalore torpedoes at the ready, two two-man machine-gun teams carrying Browning automatic rifles, two bazooka teams, a four-man mortar team carrying a 60mm mortar and fifteen to twenty mortar rounds, a flame-thrower team, a medic and a section commander in the rear, along with the coxswain. A sergeant or senior NCO was the last to leave the landing craft to make sure that everyone else had left. Soldiers wore clothing impregnated with chemicals to guard against gas attacks and an assault jacket with built-in packs. Each man carried his weapon, five grenades, half a pound of TNT, a gas mask, a life preserver, six packs of rations, a canteen, a first aid kit, a knife, an entrenching tool and any other specialist equipment his job required. When fully equipped, an infantry man carried between sixty and ninety pounds, depending on the type of weapon he carried. Many also carried cigarettes, extra socks and other nonessential items. However, every extra pound made it harder to cross the beach

Reinforcements *for the 1st Infantry Division disembark from their landing craft at Omaha Beach.*

under fire. The boats were arranged in sections of six with each section carrying a company, whose headquarters group would come in with the second wave at 0700.

Of the first wave, only the 16th Infantry Regiment of the 1st Division had combat experience, both in the Western Desert and Sicily. As they jumped down as much as twelve feet into the pitching landing craft sometime before dawn, most men who had no experience of amphibious assaults comforted themselves with the thought that everything would be all right. Those who had assaulted a beach before were less sanguine. The ride from ship to shore took two to three hours. In the heavy seas the men were soaked and cold before they reached the beaches, leaving trigger fingers numb. Almost everyone suffered from seasickness. Most regretted the heavy breakfast of eggs and bacon they had eaten before leaving the transport ship. They had been issued with anti-seasickness pills, but few took them, fearing they would make them drowsy. At least ten landing craft sank. Once in the water, few men survived. The weight of the equipment strapped to them quickly dragged them to the bottom. The men on other boats could do nothing to save them as they were forbidden to stop on their run-in.

Once the naval bombardment stopped, the 800 German defenders returned to their positions and prepared to engage the enemy. They were not stunned and disorganized as the D-Day planners had hoped. The fortifications were undamaged and, in the sector of the beach assaulted by the 16th Regimental Combat Team at least, there was little tank support.

The Germans waited until the first wave of forty-eight landing craft reached the shoreline, where they were confronted by a solid wall of obstacles. Then the Germans unleashed heavy artillery, mortar and machine-gun fire. Survivors recalled the firing being so heavy that running out onto the beaches was akin to committing suicide. But they had no choice.

The German defences had been left unscathed by the air and artillery attacks and the battle-hardened veterans of the 352nd gave courage to the green troops of the 716th. From the eighty-five machine-gun posts and numerous strongpoints along the bluff, the Germans rained down intense fire on the invaders. It was easy for the German machine-gunners to concentrate their fire on the landing ramp of an LCA as it hit the shore. It was bound to drop at any moment, exposing thirty men huddled together – the perfect target. Soon the water was choked with the dead and wounded, and new landing craft coming had no choice but to run over them. Inside the LCAs, the assault troops would hear the bullets bouncing off the metal ramp, knowing that the moment they hit the beach that protection would be snatched away from them.

The heavy fire caused some of the coxswains to drop their ramps too early, dropping the troops into water that covered their heads. Others hit unexpected sandbars and left men stranded too far from the beach to wade ashore. This meant that valuable equipment had to be discarded and men arrived at the beach without weapons and too exhausted to advance. Those who kept hold of their guns found them jammed with wet sand. Some of those too tired to move drowned when the tide came in.

Thirty-two 'Stonewallers' from the 116th RCT of the 29th Division were wiped out to a man as they left their LCA. To avoid the machine-gun fire coming in through the ramp opening, some men jumped over the sides of the landing craft, only to drown. Three LCAs of A Company of the 116th RCT were hit by concentrated fire and suffered appalling casualties. Other LCAs were blown up when they ran into mines or were hit by shells. The other two LCAs of A Company had not even made it to the beaches. Within twenty minutes, the Company lost sixty per cent of its men and was left 'inert, leaderless and almost incapable of action', according to one surviving private.

The strong wind and tide had pushed the landing craft well to the east. Some hit the beach a thousand yards from where they were supposed to be and could find no familiar landmarks to orientate themselves. Following the infantry were the engineers. Their larger landing craft were targeted and many destroyed. They were particularly vulnerable as they were full of TNT to clear the mines and beach obstacles. Some sixty per cent of the engineers' equipment was destroyed on Omaha Beach on D-Day.

Ten bulldozers were lost on the run-in. Another three were shot up on the beach, leaving just three working vehicles. One landing craft, mechanized (LCM) received a direct hit as it approached the beach, detonating the explosives and killing the entire navy team. Only one of an eight-man navy demolition team survived when their heavily laden rubber dingy was hit by shrapnel. Once on the beaches the engineers were confronted with worse problems. There were few tanks to give them covering fire and their task was to blow up the beach obstacles that many of the infantry were using as cover. Several engineers were killed when bullets hit the explosives they were planting. One team preparing a thirty-metre gap was wiped out when a mortar set off their primer.

Those infantrymen who made it across the beach found shelter behind a small bank of shale, but to get there they had to run the gauntlet of murderous crossfire from the German machine-gunners. To make that sprint, most men abandoned their heavy packs, so they arrived at the shale without the equipment they needed to move on. The men who huddled there were badly disorientated and disorganized. Few had any idea where the rest of their unit was and they received no orders as all their radio equipment had been lost. Some tended to the wounded. Others searched for their unit leader, cleaned their weapons or simply stared out into space. They were trapped. Ahead of them lay a minefield; beyond that the bluff. Behind them more and more men were being landed. The men sheltering behind the shale had to watch as those that followed them were butchered: blown up and cut to pieces by machine-gun fire. Anyone who attempted to make it down to the water and drag a wounded buddy to safety was cut down.

Even though what remained of the forward fire controllers had no way of communicating with their ships, the navy saw what was happening and saved the day. The destroyers moved in so close that they were hit by German rifle fire. They began pounding the beach defences. This boosted the morale of the troops trapped on the beach and gave the infantry the break they needed.

When the second wave hit at 0700, they expected to find the beaches cleared and move directly inland to their objectives. As it was, most of the beach obstacles were still in place. Only six of the proposed sixteen fifty-metre-wide lanes had been cleared, and only one fully marked. Landing craft sailed up and down the shore looking for a clear place to land. If they did not find one, they nudged their way gingerly through the obstacles, some of which were rigged with mines.

Many were hit by artillery fire in the water and the survival rate was little better than the men in the first-wave boats. Those who made it to the beaches faced a suicidal dash to the sea wall. Finding themselves in the wrong position, some tried to move laterally to the place where they should be, taking heavy casualties on the way. But some units got lucky. Grass on the bluffs to the west of the draw that led up to St Laurent caught fire and smoke obscured the right end of the beach. K Company of the 3rd Battalion of the 116th Infantry made it to their beach exit with only one casualty, a lieutenant who had been stabbed accidentally with a bayonet while still on the landing craft.

But it was soon clear to anyone on the beach that the situation was generally a disaster. A Company from the 116th and C Company from the 2nd Rangers had been cut to pieces and had effectively ceased to exist as fighting units. G and F Companies were scattered and disorganized, having suffered heavy casualties, and E Company was disorientated. With the tide coming in, the weak and the wounded were left to drown. Others hid behind the shale or the sea wall, unsure of what to do.

The second wave brought headquarters units and with them General Norman D. Cota, who landed at H+57. Realising the situation was desperate, he exposed himself to enemy fire leading his men over the sea wall. He personally supervised the siting of a BAR (Browning Automatic Rifle) and brought fire to bear on an enemy position. By 0830, the commanders of both the 16th Infantry, Colonel George Taylor, and the 116th Infantry, Colonel

Charles D.W. Canham, were ashore, along with the assistant division commander, General Willard G. Wyman, but still no one in that sector had advanced off the beach. However, some sort of a command structure was in place and new, makeshift units were formed.

SLOW PROGRESS

Men gave their lives to cross the minefield, their mutilated corpses marking the path for those who followed. One young officer threw himself down on the ground to clear the last few feet of a minefield for his men, detonating a mine which killed him. His men advanced over him. Slowly the soldiers began making their way towards the bluff.

To the east of the beach, things were particularly confused. Currents and navigational errors had delivered the bulk of the force into a German killing zone where there was not so much as a sea wall for cover. The men had to cross 500 yards of open beach before they could find cover in the sand dunes. There they were pinned down by machine-gun fire from the bluff high above. They were trapped in this position until Colonel George Taylor turned up at 0830.

Colonel Taylor told his men, 'Two kinds of people are staying on this beach, the dead and those who are going to die. Now let's get the hell out of here.'

Along the beach, ragged bunches of men began to realize that it was better to try and fight their way off the beaches than stay in the Germans' well-planned killing zone. A sergeant shoved a Bangalore torpedo under the wire at the top of the dune and blew a gap in it. Then Colonel Taylor led his men through it.

They dashed though a flat area towards the base of the bluff. It was heavily mined and there were many casualties.

By 0900 there were five thousand men on the beach. The situation still looked grim, but between 0900 and 1000 hours, elements of the 16th Infantry managed to find their way to the top of the bluff and, in close hand-to-hand fighting, they moved along it, clearing German fortifications. A platoon led by Lieutenant Spaulding attacked a strongpoint that covered the east side of one of the draws. Five machine guns and an anti-aircraft gun housed in two pillboxes and four concrete shelters covered the beach exit. There was a close exchange of hand grenades and small arms fire. Eventually one German officer and twenty men surrendered. By the time reinforcements arrived on the eastern sector of the beach at 1000, the exit was secure. Even so, another twenty-eight landing craft were lost to underwater obstacles.

Thanks to General Cota, the 116th Infantry began to make progress too. He sent a man forward to blow a hole in the wire with a Bangalore torpedo. But the first man through the gap was cut down by German fire and no one seemed eager to follow him. So Cota seized the moment. He ran through the gap and across the road beyond it, then he shouted for his men to follow him. They did and, miraculously, not one of them was hit. They advanced 100 yards through reeds and grass to the base of the bluff. A German trench, which was luckily empty, provided some cover. But at the other end of it they found themselves in a minefield. Nevertheless, they headed onwards and upwards, suffering a number of casualties by the anti-personnel mines. Those who were not wounded were further motivated by a horrendous sight down below: the Germans were machine-gunning their own men who had surrendered to the Americans.

Cota's group reached the top of the bluff at around 0900. The General then split his makeshift unit into fire teams, and sent them to take out a machine gun that stood between them and the draw at Les Moulins. They then moved around to take Vierville from the rear. There they met other elements of the 116th, who were greeted by Cota walking down the main street twirling his pistols like a character in a Western film. Colonel Canham had also fought his way up the bluff and met up with Cota in Vierville too. Together they cooked up a plan to get their men off the beaches. Canham would clear the draw at Les Moulins by attacking the Germans from the rear, while Cota would unplug the draw below Vierville where a paved road ran down to the shore.

Cota took just five men with him down the draw. The German positions below them were now coming under fire from the 14-inch guns of the USS Texas. Between 1223 and 1230, six shells hit the German fortification. The concussed occupants put up only a token resistance. After a brief firefight, they surrendered to Cota's tiny force. Using the Germans as guides to take him through the minefield, Cota made his way back to the beach where a horrifying scene of destruction met him. Quickly he marshalled some explosives to blow an obstruction in the draw that prevented armour leaving the beach. Soon men and machines were marching up the draw and General Cota made his way east along the beach encouraging other men to move forward.

To the commanders viewing the beaches from offshore, the situation was still far from clear. They decided to throw the reserves into the battle and at 1045 the 115th Infantry arrived on the beach. Still the exits had not been secured, but the 115th moved up the bluff and took the village of St Laurent, which dominated the road system directly inland. By 1200 there were four major breaches in the German defences. As the afternoon progressed the breaches were widened and American troops began to move inland. However, this could not be seen by those out on the ships. There was little radio communication as seventy-five per cent of the assault force's radios had been lost. General Omar Bradley, in command of the American First Army, considered evacuating the beach and taking his men to the British sector where the landings seemed to have gone more smoothly. When he reported back to SHAEF that the landings on Omaha Beach were a disaster, Eisenhower ordered the Allied air forces to bomb Omaha Beach. The attack was to begin at 1330. Luckily, this could not be done. It would have turned a disastrous situation into a catastrophe.

Fortunately, the German commander General Kraiss was receiving similarly inaccurate reports. It seemed to him that the defences at Omaha had held. If Kraiss had sent his reserves that morning, they would probably have been able to push the Americans back into the sea. Instead, the reserves were sent out to track down paratroopers, but they found it difficult to move during daylight due to harassment by Allied fighters. Kraiss decided that any spare manpower should be concentrated on the British beaches where the situation seemed more desperate from the German point of view.

At 1600, the 1st Infantry Division commander General Clarence R. Huebner came ashore to direct operations on the beach personally. With him came the artillery that the infantry needed to secure its advance. The 26th Regiment landed at 1930.

It was redirected to clear Colleville, behind the beaches occupied by the 16th, and advanced through St Laurent inland to Formigny.

By dark, after a disastrous start to the day on Omaha Beach, fire support was in place and it became clear that the Germans were in no position to counter-attack. At the end of D-Day, the 1st Infantry Division at Omaha Beach controlled a strip of Normandy 10,000 yards wide and 2–3,000 yards deep. It was not much, but it was a foothold. For this tiny piece of land, they had paid with 2,000 casualties.

By midnight, the Vierville draw was secure and the coast road was cut. The 116th Infantry held positions to the west and south of the village. The 2nd and 5th Rangers tried to swing to the west to meet up with their comrades on Pointe du Hoc, but were stopped by German outposts. The 115th Infantry under Colonel Eugene N. Slappey moved off the beach up the Les Moulins draw but they ran into opposition from Germans occupying the village of St Laurent, which blocked the exit to that draw and another one, a dirt path that led down to the beach. Slappey sent his 1st Battalion around to the south of the village to prevent the German garrison being reinforced, and he sent his other two battalions into the village from the east. They ran into stiff resistance and St Laurent did not fall to the Americans until the next day. To the east, Colleville changed hands several times that day. It ended up being held by the Germans that night, though it was virtually encircled. When the Americans had held it earlier that day, due to a communications mix up, the village had been raked by naval gunfire, killing sixty-four men.

German positions on the bluffs were cut off and retreating German troops found themselves falling into ambushes where the GIs took understandably savage revenge. But most of the defenders stayed in place until their ammunition ran out. They had been ordered to do so. The Führer himself had told them not to give up an inch of his murderous empire and Rommel's plan was to stop the invasion cold on the beaches. This was a mistake. Maintaining their positions on the bluff meant that the Germans could go on killing Americans, but could not win the battle. They could not fall back and form up to stage concentrated counterattacks. Inland was bocage country, but the Germans only managed to stage a piecemeal defensive action there. Although the remaining defenders on the bluff would slow the Allies down and inflict numerous casualties, they were bound to fail in the end as they were receiving no reinforcements while wave after wave of fresh troops were coming in over the beaches.

That is not to say that the Germans were not good soldiers. When an American officer was interrogating a German prisoner about the whereabouts of minefields, the German would only give his name, rank and serial number, as stipulated by the Geneva Convention. So the American fired his carbine between the German's legs. The German pointed to his crotch and said, 'Nicht hier', then pointed to his head and said, 'Hier.' The interrogator gave up.

Even though they had got up the bluff, it was difficult for the Americans to maintain the momentum of their advance. Troops who had survived the hell of the beaches understandably felt that they had done their job for the day. They wanted a rest. Those who made it into villages found wine and took a drink. However, to the west of Vierville, the Rangers determinedly pushed on towards their buddies on Pointe du Hoc.

Once they were off the beaches, the Americans also had to switch to a new style of fighting. Bold leadership worked when soldiers were storming the bluff, but when fighting from hedgerow to hedgerow, those who went boldly ahead got killed. Sheltering behind the ridge of shale or behind a seawall, a soldier could see that he had two choices: advance or die. In bocage country, those who stayed under cover survived.

Vierville itself remained the weakest part of the American line that first night. Its church was taken out by USS Harding after Colonel Canham suspected that its steeple was being used by a German artillery spotter. Many of the churches in Normandy suffered a similar fate.

On Omaha Beach, the American V Corps suffered 2,400 dead, wounded and missing, and put ashore 34,000 troops out of its 55,000 assault force. On D-Day alone, they had a casualty rate of 7.2 per cent, which would normally be considered horrendous, though it was five per cent less than expected. German losses were only half that of the American – 1,200 in all – but that was twenty per cent of their defence force, and they had not succeeded in their objective, snuffing out the invasion on the beaches.

The following day, not only did the Americans hold on to their foothold, they expanded it.

CHAPTER 7

Utah Beach

The most westerly of the invasion beaches, Utah was assigned to the US 4th Infantry Division, whose task was to seize the beach, link up with airborne troops from the 101st Airborne, and attack towards Cherbourg.

H-Hour on Utah Beach was 0630, the earliest of all the beaches. As on Omaha, things went wrong from the start.

At 0455, the first of twenty-four waves of landing craft headed for Utah Beach and at 0550 Allied warships began their bombardment of the German fortifications. Then a fleet of bombers dropped over four thousand 250-pound bombs on the enemy positions, which were simultaneously hit by 1,000 rockets. Unlike on Omaha Beach, this bombardment was successful, leaving many of the defenders disorientated and eager to surrender. But that did not mean that the rest of the assault went smoothly.

The plan was for the thirty-two amphibious tanks to land first at 0630, directly the warships had lifted their bombardment. Twenty LCAs would follow, each carrying thirty men from the 2nd Battalion, 8th Infantry. Ten of them were targeted at the German strongpoint at Les Dunes de Varreville at the north end of the beach. A second wave of thirty-two boats would arrive

D+3 *US troops advance across the seawall on Utah Beach, 9 June 1944.*

five minutes later, carrying the 1st Battalion, 8th Infantry, along with naval demolition teams and combat engineers. Ten minutes after that, landing craft would land regular Sherman tanks on the beach, along with bulldozer tanks. Two minutes later, the fourth wave would hit, carrying detachments of the 237th and 299th Engineer Combat Battalions.

STRUGGLING ASHORE

Nothing in this plan worked out. Everyone landed at least a kilometre south of where they were supposed to be. Most were late. This was partially due to the heavy seas and smoke obscuring the beach, but the main problem was that three of the four boats controlling the assault were lost to mines out to sea before the run–in even began. On the beach, Brigadier-General Theodore

Medic *His face set in a look of quiet determination, a young American soldier with a head wound is treated on Utah Beach.*

Roosevelt, second-in-command of 4th Infantry, and Colonel James van Fleet, commander of the 8th Infantry Regiment, had a decision to make. Should they move the entire landing force a mile northwards up the beach and go back to the original plan, or strike inland from where they were as assault troops were already crossing the sea wall and the engineers were clearing obstacles from the beach? Roosevelt was famed for saying, 'We'll start the war from right here.'

Van Fleet disputes this. He said that he made the decision, saying, 'We've caught the enemy at a weak point, let's take advantage of it.'

Whichever the case, it was Roosevelt who made the decision

stick. As second-in-command of the 4th Infantry Division, he had the authority to order the succeeding waves to remain where they had landed, without anyone countermanding his orders. This flexibility won the day at Utah Beach and General Roosevelt was awarded the Medal of Honor.

The Germans were taken by surprise by the Allies' amphibious tanks. Lieutenant Arthur Jahnke, the twenty-three-year-old veteran of the Eastern Front commanding the strongpoint at St Marie du Mont, thought he must be hallucinating as a result of concussion from the bombardment when he first saw them, until realization dawned. Despite the determination of its defenders, the naval bombardment of St Marie du Mont was too much for them and the strongpoint was overrun. Jahnke himself was captured in a makeshift dugout, shooting at Americans with his rifle. A tank blasted his position with 75mm cannon and a GI dragged him out. Jahnke tried to make a grab for the GI's machine-gun, but the American calmly pushed his hand aside and told him to take it easy. With the other survivors he was marched down to the beach with his hands on his head and waited to be taken out to Allied ships. Although the resistance of coastal defenders soon ceased, the beach came under continued attack by artillery further inland until D+13, Jahnke himself being wounded by shrapnel from an incoming German shell as he waited in the POW enclosure on the beach.

Naval Seabee (combat demolition units) teams began clearing the beach of obstacles, making way for succeeding waves of infantry hitting the beach. Although 88mm guns inland were still firing at the beach, they had little effect as the Germans had no forward observers.

MOVING OFF THE BEACH

Advanced elements of the American infantry quickly made their way inland across the causeways directly behind the beaches and came under mortar fire. They also found that bridges in the causeways had been wired for demolition, but they were not blown. Although there was sporadic resistance by German snipers, most of the defenders, when challenged, gave up without a fight.

At 1110, scouts at the western edge of the flooded area behind the beaches saw a helmet behind a bush. Not knowing whether the owner was an American or a German, they set off an orange flare. Two men stood up. They were wearing the Stars and Stripes on their shoulders. The 4th Division had linked up with the 101st. The 101st had already taken Pouppeville, killing forty Germans. Together they secured St Marie du Mont.

Landing so far to the south was a problem for the 12th Infantry Regiment as their first objective was St Martin de Varreville, which lay to the north. The causeway leading inland from the beach was jammed with tanks, trucks and troops, and the next exit was coming under fire from four 155mm guns at St Marcouf. The commanding officer of the 12th Infantry, Colonel Russell 'Red' Reeder made the decision to have his men wade though the flooded area to St Marie de Varreville. According to aerial reconnaissance, there was just eighteen inches of water in the irrigation ditches. Elsewhere it was only supposed to be ankle-deep. But when the men set out, they soon found that it was waist deep in the flooded fields, while in the irrigation ditches it was over a man's head. Brave souls would swim across and throw a rope back to haul the rest of the unit across. For nearly two kilometres the troops struggled on in constant danger of drowning. One slip and the weight of their equipment would pull them under. Men cursed the navy for trying to drown them on their way to the beaches and cursed the army for trying to drown them on the land. The Germans' sporadic sniper fire was merely an irritant.

By late afternoon, US infantry had hooked up with the 82nd Airborne at St Germain de Varreville, St Martin de Varreville and Chef du Pont.

Much of the credit for the speed of the American advance belonged to the navy. Every time the 4th Division ran into enemy armour, they called back to the warships for artillery support. The USS Nevada fired so many salvos that the paint peeled off the gun barrels, leaving the steel burnished blue underneath. Normally, they kept the empty shell cases for reloading, but these hindered the movement of the gun turrets so they were thrown overboard. The sheer force of the volleys distorted the superstructure of the ship. Doors fell off, bulkheads shifted, light fittings broke, and many men reported hearing loss.

By the middle of the afternoon, Utah Beach had been cleared of obstacles and a small city had taken shape. There was no doubt in anyone's mind that Utah Beach was secure. Next day they would set off to take Montebourg, seal off the Cotentin peninsula and go on to take Cherbourg.

SUCCESSFUL LANDING

American losses on Utah were comparatively light. The 12th Regiment suffered sixty-nine casualties, mainly caused by mines. The 8th and the 22nd Regiments suffered 106 wounded and twelve dead. In all, the 4th Division lost twenty times more men during training following the disaster in Lyme Bay, where German torpedo boats attacked during a practice session, at a cost of 749 American lives.

The landing on Utah Beach was one of the major successes of D-Day. The paratroopers' role was vital, confusing the enemy, holding the western exits to the beaches and preventing any German counter-attack. Even though the plan of attack had to be abandoned within minutes of hitting the beaches, the 4th Division got close to all their D-Day objectives. They got their men ashore at an astonishing speed. In fifteen hours, more than 20,000 American troops landed on Utah Beach, along with 1,700 vehicles. Jodl estimated that it would take the Allies six or seven days to put three divisions into France. The Americans did that on Utah Beach in one day.

CONCLUSION

Although the Americans suffered appalling casualties on Omaha Beach, and few Allied units managed to reach their primary objectives on that first day, they nevertheless managed to secure a broad beachhead. By midnight on 6 June, eighteen hours after the landings had begun, the Allies had 150,000 troops ashore in Normandy, with more arriving all the time. They had also landed artillery, ammunition, armour, and supplies. In conclusion, it can be said that the D-Day landings were a success.

SECTION TWO
THE ITALIAN FRONT

After the Allied victory in North Africa,
the logical place to attack next was Italy.
The capture of Italy would provide a way,
in Churchill's phrase, into the 'soft
underbelly' of Europe.

CHAPTER 8

Mussolini's War

By 6 June 1944, the war in Italy was already well advanced. Following the Allied seizure of Sicily in August 1943, the attack on the Italian mainland was launched on 3 September. The German occupation forces in Italy would not give up lightly, however.

Benito Mussolini, the Fascist dictator of Italy, and Adolf Hitler had announced an 'axis' binding Rome and Berlin on 25 October 1936. This had been strengthened to a full military and political alliance by the Pact of Steel on 22 May 1939. When Britain and France declared war on Germany on 3 September 1939, the Allies were unsure whether Italy would live up to its treaty obligations to Germany. When Winston Churchill became prime minister on 10 May 1940, he still hoped to convince Mussolini to side with Britain and France, as Italy had done in World War I. But once the British Expeditionary Force had been evacuated from Dunkirk and France collapsed, Italy joined the war on the German side on 10 June.

Italy had occupied Libya in 1911, and, in 1940, had an army of 300,000 men under Marshal Rodolfo Graziani stationed there. The British had a mere 36,000 in Egypt. The Italians seized the opportunity to invade with the aim of taking the Suez Canal.

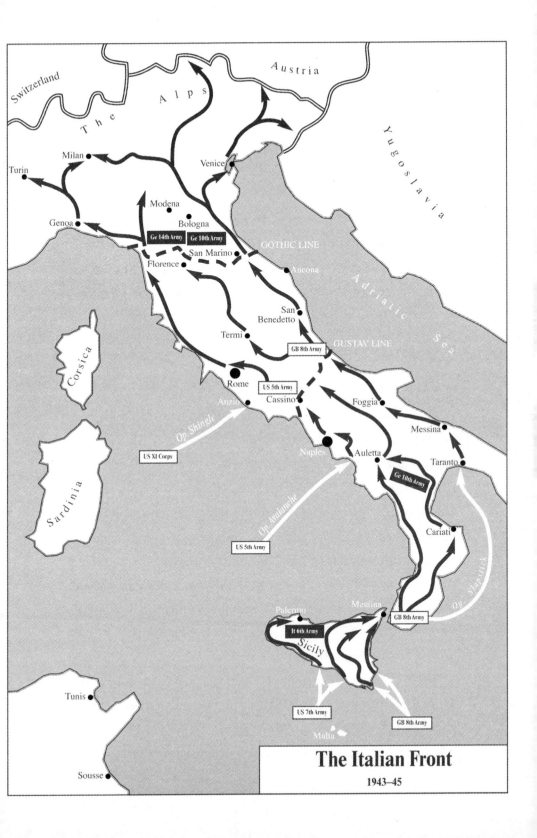

The Italian Front
1943–45

Il Duce Mussolini addresses his troops from on top of an Italian light tank.

The British counter-attacked and crushed the superior Italian force and were only prevented from driving the Italians out of North Africa completely by Churchill's commitment to defend Greece against German invasion. Troops were diverted there. Meanwhile, Hitler sent General Erwin Rommel and his Afrika Korps to North Africa, who forced the British back.

The battle front then ebbed and flowed across the deserts of North Africa until the British won a decisive victory at el-Alamein in October 1942. By this time America had joined the war. Beforehand, Winston Churchill and President Franklin D. Roosevelt had agreed that, once America came into the war

– which seemed inevitable – the Anglo-American Allies' first priority would be to defeat Hitler in Europe. After that, they would turn their attention on Japan.

Still smarting from the unprovoked attack on Pearl Harbor on 7 December 1941, the Americans were eager to make the kind of amphibious assault on France that eventually occurred on D-Day. However, Churchill persuaded them that the Allies were not remotely ready for such a risky venture. Instead, America should join Britain in fighting the Germans and Italians in North Africa. As Britain's Eighth Army under General Bernard Montgomery pushed Rommel's forces back from Egypt in the East, American forces under General Dwight D. Eisenhower landed in Morocco and Algeria to the west of the Axis forces. Together they drove the Axis forces out of North Africa completely in May 1943.

At the conference in Casablanca in January 1943, Churchill persuaded Roosevelt that the Allies' next move should be to attack the 'soft underbelly' of Europe. At this point in the war, Italy was looking particularly weak. When Mussolini had mobilized on 10 June 1940, he had an army of seventy-five divisions. Since then twenty more had been raised, but that did not cover their losses. Two divisions had been lost when the British overran the short-lived Italian East African Empire, which comprised Italian Somaliland and Abyssinia (now Ethiopia). Another twenty-five had been lost in North Africa. Mussolini had also sent an Italian Expeditionary Force – later renamed the Italian Eighth Army – to join Hitler's 'crusade against Bolshevism' in the Soviet Union. Of a force of 229,000 men, 84,830 had been killed and over 30,000 wounded. In three years of fighting more than a third of Mussolini's army had been lost. Less than half the rest were available to defend the homeland. Thirty-six Italian divisions were fighting guerrillas in the Balkans, or occupying France.

Italy had invaded Albania in 1939. Then, on 28 October, without informing Hitler, Mussolini sent seven divisions – 155,000 men – across the border into Greece. The Greeks not only halted the Italian Army, they pushed it back into Albania and joined the war on the Allied side. The British already had air bases in Greece and landed troops on Crete. Hitler then drew Hungary, Bulgaria and Romania into the Axis and was forced to send troops into Yugoslavia and Greece to bolster his Italian ally. However, even by 1943, the Axis forces had not pacified the Balkans. For the first five months of the year, the government in Rome posted casualties of 10,570 in Yugoslavia and Greece. More were being killed by the *Maquis*, supplied with guns through Corsica, in the Savoie and Dauphiné regions which Italy occupied in southeast France. In 1944, only thirty divisions were available to defend the Italian peninsula, Sardinia and Sicily – and some of those were not combat-ready. The Blackshirt M Armoured Division had not completed its training on its German-built tanks. And the *Centauro* and *Ariete* divisions, which had been badly mauled in Russia, were then being hastily reconstituted. So there were only twenty divisions, no better equipped than they had been in 1940, available to face an Allied invasion. Along with the regular army there were 'coastal defence' units, which were the Italian equivalent of Britain's home guard. Although they comprised an impressive twenty-one divisions and five brigades, their members were largely old men. In Sicily, for example, the unit was commanded by two second lieutenants who had been retired in 1918 and had only recently been called back into active service. The units were also poorly equipped. Much of their weaponry came from the Vichy French army, which had been disbanded in 1942 after Allied forces had landed in French North Africa and the French fleet had been scuttled in Toulon. These weapons often came with parts missing or without ammunition. In some cases, they had been deliberately sabotaged. The coastal defence units were also strung out along Italy's long coastline. In Sicily, there were just forty-one men per mile. This was not a force that could repel a determined Allied invasion.

The Italians had little in the way of air defences. Their air force was small and antiquated, and Italian airfields were already being bombed regularly by the Allies. The German Luftwaffe promised help, but it had already suffered grievously in the Battle of Britain and on the Eastern Front.

Allied bombers flying from North Africa had also forced the Italian navy to withdraw from its base in Tarranto. On 12 April, the cruiser *Trieste* had been sunk by air attack off La Maddalena, northern Sardinia, and on 5 June, flying fortresses had damaged the battleships *Vitorio Veneto*, *Littorio* and *Roma* at La Spezia. Shortages of fuel and supplies had also forced the Italians to lay up the cruisers *Cesare*, *Dora* and *Duilio*.

On 14 June 1943, Mussolini wrote a note to his chiefs of staff, saying: 'In the present state of the war the Italian forces no longer hold any possibility of initiative. They are forced onto the defensive. The army ... lacks among other things room to manoeuvre. It can only counter-attack the enemy who lands at one point on our territory and drive him back into the sea.'

Even this assessment was wildly overoptimistic, as Mussolini would go on to admit.

Like Rommel in Normandy, chief of the Italian general staff, General Vittorio Ambrosio, knew that there would be no stopping a well-equipped army once it had established a beachhead and was making its way inland. The Italians, particularly, did not have the armour for that. The only way to defend Italy was to smash the invasion force on the beaches. However, it was clear that the Italians did not have the artillery to do that either. As Mussolini gloomily concluded in his memo of 14 June: 'He who defends himself dies.'

The Allies had another meeting in Washington from 12 to 25 May 1943. There it was decided that, while the invasion of France set for late spring 1944 was to be the principal Allied operation against Germany, they should also mount 'such operations as are best calculated to eliminate Italy from the war and to contain the maximum number of German divisions'.

'THE MAN WHO NEVER WAS'

Hitler and the Italian *Comando Supremo* expected the Allied attack to come in Sardinia. From there the Allies could take Corsica, laying the entire west coast of Italy open to attack. However, reserving their strength for the Normandy landings, the Allies took the easier option of invading Sicily in Operation *Husky*. From there they could take southern Italy and, once the huge airfields at Foggia and Naples were in their hands, they could begin bombing the oil fields in Romania which supplied the petrol that kept the Germany Panzers on the move. And by taking the airbase on Sicily itself, the Allies could stop the

Luftwaffe pounding the beleaguered island of Malta and allow convoys to pass through the Mediterranean.

The problem to the Allies was that it seemed blindingly obvious to anyone who could read a map that their next move would be the invasion of Sicily.

'Everyone but a bloody fool would know it's Sicily,' said Winston Churchill.

Even though the invasion of Sicily was the easy option, it would be no push over. The island's mountainous terrain favoured the defender. An attack against a well-entrenched force would be costly, or might even fail. What was more, the build-up to Operation *Husky* would be impossible to conceal, so the Germans would know that the attack was coming. It was vital, therefore, to keep Hitler and the Italians focused on Sardinia.

Two members of the XX – 'double cross' – Committee, Squadron Leader Sir Archibald Cholmondley and Lieutenant Commander Ewen Montagu, came up with a cunning plan. They would deliver forged documents, showing the Allies were going to attack Sardinia, into German hands. However, if such information reached the Germans by conventional means they would immediately suspect it was a ruse and redouble their defences on Sicily. No live spy could be used to hand over the documents as there was always the possibility that such a person might be a double agent, or break under torture. Instead, they decided that their courier would be dead. In fact, he would be a fiction and he became known as 'the man who never was'.

Initially Cholmondley considered dropping the documents with a corpse and a partially opened parachute. They quickly abandoned that scheme for a number of reasons. An Allied agent or air crewman would not be carrying the sort of high-level documents necessary to make the whole thing in any way credible. Allied couriers who did carry high-level documents were not allowed to fly over enemy-held territory. And a post mortem would show that the body had been dead long before it hit the ground.

Instead, Montagu suggested that they should deliver the document using a body floating in the sea. It would be dropped by submarine off the coast of Spain, where the Fascist government worked closely with the Abwehr, German military intelligence. The body could then credibly be that of a courier as he would not have been lost flying over enemy territory. And as a body could have been in the sea for several days before it washed ashore, this would also overcome the problem of the time of death established in the post mortem.

There was, of course, no shortage of dead bodies in wartime London. But they would have to find one of the right age and appearance to be a courier. If possible, he should be a victim of drowning. The search for a suitable corpse was necessarily low-key to avoid provoking gossip. Then there was the ticklish problem of getting permission from the next of kin.

Initially they had little luck, and Montagu was about to give up when he heard about a man in his early thirties who had just died of pneumonia. The disease filled the lungs with fluid which would convince a Spanish pathologist that the man had died from drowning at sea. The dead man's family were contacted and told the body was needed for a worthy cause. Montagu assured them that it would eventually receive a proper burial, although under another name. The family agreed on the condition that the corpse's true identity never be divulged.

Montagu then started Operation *Mincemeat* to build the corpse a convincing identity. First there was the tricky problem of giving him a name. This would have to be printed in the newspapers as the Abwehr were sure to check the casualty list. He could not have been in the army as the army's system made it impossible to file a fake casualty report. He could not be a sailor, as the Royal Navy at that time did not wear a standard battle dress and they did not want to call in a tailor to make him a uniform. So the corpse became Royal Marine Captain (acting Major) William Martin, as that was one of the most common names on the navy list. The name would not arouse the suspicion of his brother officers, as the dead man could be any one of several William Martins.

Montagu filled the corpse's pockets with keys, coins and other bits and pieces. There was a love letter from his fiancée Pam, and a picture of a girl in a swimsuit provided by one of the secretaries in Montagu's office. He also decided to make Major Martin appear careless, the sort of person who might end up in the sea off the coast of Spain. Montagu's team produced some overdue bills, an irate letter from Martin's bank manager and a stern letter from his father. There were theatre ticket stubs and a book of matches. Everything was all carefully co-ordinated to build a seamless picture of the major's life in the last few days before he left England. Montagu's team found a living person who resembled the dead man to pose for the photograph on his ID card. To reinforce the careless side of Martin's nature, Montagu gave him a replacement ID card, issued 'in lieu of No. 09650 lost'. The serial number of the supposed missing original was that of Montagu's own navy ID card.

Zero Hour *The start of the Allied invasion of Sicily – zero hour has arrived and the men of the Allied forces receive the word 'Go'.*

While Major Martin lay in cold storage, Montagu's team filled his briefcase with documents indicating that not only were the preparations for Operation *Husky* actually a build-up to the invasion of Sardinia, but that the Allies were also planning an attack on Greece and the Balkans. It was felt that to feed the Germans bogus operational plans was too obvious. Instead the briefcase would contain, among other things, a letter between two officers that merely alluded to Sardinia and Greece. Montagu got the vice-chief of the Imperial General Staff, General Sir Archibald Nye, to write a letter to General

Sir Harold Alexander, the British commander in North Africa under the American General Dwight D. Eisenhower. It explained why Eisenhower's request for a cover operation centred on the Greek islands had been denied. That cover was already assigned to the operation to be launched from Egypt by Field Marshal Sir Henry Wilson, the commander in chief in the Middle East. Consequently Eisenhower would have to make do with an attack on Sicily as a cover for his own operation. This suggested that two different operations would be launched in the Mediterranean, one in the east and one in the west. As Sicily was the cover for the true target in the west it could not be the target itself. That left Sardinia.

Major Martin also carried a letter establishing the purpose of his trip. It was from Lord Louis Mountbatten, chief of Combined Operations, to Admiral Andrew Cunningham, British naval commander in the Mediterranean, introducing Martin as an expert on landing craft on loan from Mountbatten's staff for the planning of the Mediterranean operations. As an aside, Mountbatten noted Martin had been right about the Dieppe raid when most of the Combined Operations staff had been wrong. This was the first admission by the British that the raid on Dieppe had not been a success and lent the stratagem extra credibility.

On 19 April 1943, the corpse was packed in a special canister packed with dry ice aboard the submarine HMS *Seraph*. Just before dawn on the 30th, *Seraph* surfaced about a mile off the Spanish coast near Huelva and launched the body, which floated off in a Mae West with the briefcase securely attached to its wrist by a chain. The currents were sure to carry the body inshore and a few hours later a fishing boat picked it up. To make the story all the more convincing, the British government asked the Spanish for the briefcase back. They obliged. When it was returned, after a short delay, the contents were given a minute examination, which revealed that the envelopes had been opened, presumably to copy the contents. The Spanish post mortem confirmed that Major Martin had drowned and, a few days later, he was buried in Huelva with full military honours. Flowers were sent by his fiancée and family while, back in London, the 4 June edition of *The Times* included Martin's name on the casualty lists.

The letters in the briefcase were equally convincing. The Abwehr reported back to Berlin: 'The authenticity of the captured documents is beyond doubt.' Hitler ordered the strengthening of fortifications on Sardinia and Corsica, and he sent an additional Waffen SS brigade to Sardinia. One panzer division was sent from France to Greece. Another two panzer divisions were sent from Russia, immediately before history's greatest tank battle at Kursk. And Rommel was posted to Athens to form an army group.

THE INVASION OF SICILY

Indications of the Allies' true intentions came as early as 6 June when Allied planes began bombing the island fortress of Pantellia that lies in the channel between Tunisia and Sicily. Over six days, 6,550 tons of bombs were dropped, and on 12 June, Vice Admiral Gino Pavesi surrendered the garrison of 12,000 men, though only fifty-six had been killed and 116 wounded. Even so Hitler continued to insist that the Allies, 'by neglecting to attack Sicily immediately after their landings in North Africa, had virtually thrown away the war in the Mediterranean,' according to General Frido von Senger und Etterlin, who saw the Führer on 22 June.

On 10 July 1943, Montgomery's Eighth Army and General George Patton's Seventh Army landed on the southern shores of Sicily. The success of Operation *Mincemeat* meant its defenders were drawn up along the north shore, facing Sardinia. However, they knew an attack was coming. For much of the previous month, the island's defences had been pounded by four thousand Allied planes under Air Chief Marshal Sir Arthur Tedder. Five thousand tons of bombs fell on Messina alone. In response, the defenders could put up just 200 Italian and 320 German planes, and much of the island's defences and infrastructure, including the airfields, had been wiped out.

Even so, Operation *Husky* nearly turned into a disaster. The previous evening, Axis aircraft had spotted the Allied fleet leaving Malta. That night the armada was hit by a storm which almost forced it to turn back. However, because of the heavy weather, the defenders dropped their guard. High winds took their toll on the airborne troops, blowing gliders and parachutists out to sea to their deaths. Those who landed on the island, at around five o'clock in the morning, were widely dispersed. Nevertheless, they succeeded in hampering the enemy's movements, and around a hundred British airborne troops took a vital bridge at Primsole, south of Catania, and held it for five days until the Eighth Army arrived to relieve them.

At dawn on the 10th, the coastal defences were attacked by tactical aircraft and pounded by naval gunfire. Then a fleet of 2,590 ships, including 237 troop transports and 1,742 landing craft began putting ashore 115,000 British and Canadian troops and 66,000 Americans. Facing them were the 230,000 men and 150 guns of the Italian 6th Army, who had few motorized units, supported by the 15th Panzergrenadier Division, which was only partially motorized, and the 1st Paratroop Panzer Divison *Hermann Göring*, which had only two battalions of infantry and less than a hundred tanks – though these did include a company of the feared Tiger tanks. There was also a division and a brigade of the coastal defence force holding 120 miles of the south coast against six British and American divisions, while to the west of Licata the American 3rd Division were opposed by just two battalions.

The Italian coastal defence force put up a heroic defence. But facing superior numbers supported by tanks they were virtually wiped out. By the evening, the commander of the Italian Sixth Army, General Alfredo Guzzoni ordered the 15th Panzergrenadier Division to hold the central town of Enna, while the *Hermann Göring* Division and the Italian *Livorno* Division attacked the American bridgehead at Gela. The following morning the Panzers ran into the forward posts of the 1st American Division, but when they got with 2,000 yards of the beach they came under fire from six destroyers and the cruisers Savannah and Boise, which loosed off 3,194 five- and six-inch shells, knocking out thirty tanks. The Italian *Livorno* Division was also badly mauled. Meanwhile, the British Eighth Army occupied the ports of Augusta and Syracuse without a shot being fired; their garrisons had already been evacuated.

On 14 July, the airfields at Comiso and Ragusa were taken and rapidly put back into commission, and the British Eighth

Army and American Seventh Army met up. Montgomery then planned a dash up the east coast to Messina, trapping the defenders on the island and forcing a surrender, but Field Marshal Albert Kesselring, the German commander-in-chief in Italy, pre-empted him. He sent in the 29th Panzergrenadier Division and two parachute regiments. On 17 July, General Hans Hube and the staff of XIV Panzer Corps took over command of all German fighting forces in Sicily. Resistance stiffened, and Montgomery was stopped at Catania. He then turned inland, switching his attack to the west of Mount Etna. This stepped on the Americans' toes and yielded little further progress.

Patton pushed westwards and captured Sicily's capital, Palermo, on 22 July. He, too, planned a dash on Messina along the north coast. But Hube stopped him at the little town of Santo Stefano, halfway down the coast road. Meanwhile, the 1st Canadian Division bypassed Enna and pushed north-west, confining the defenders to the north-east corner of the island. The British were now landing the 78th Division at Syracuse, while the American 9th Division landed at Palermo. This brought the Allies' strength up to eleven divisions. Totally outnumbered, Hube pulled back. The Italians had already suffered a series of defeats in North Africa and, with the mainland of Italy now under threat, they were eager to make peace with the Allies. On the night of 24 July 1943, Mussolini told his Fascist Grand Council that the Germans were thinking of evacuating southern Italy. Many party members had been suspicious about the Germans' intentions from the start. Hitler was clearly more interested in defending Germany than in defending Italy and, after the reverses on the Eastern Front, some believed that the defeat of the Third Reich

Troops in Messina *US soldiers walk warily through the ravaged streets of Messina, as the war on Sicily came to its conclusion, 24 August 1943.*

was inevitable. Their priority was to prevent Italy from becoming a battleground. They voted against Mussolini, effectively ousting him from power.

Believing himself to be indispensable, Mussolini turned up at his office as normal the following day. That afternoon he was arrested on the orders of the king. He was imprisoned on the Island of Ponza, then moved to a remote island off Sardinia. After that he was moved to Campo Imperatore high in the

Abruzzi mountains, where it was thought rescue was impossible. Meanwhile the new Italian government began secret peace talks with the Allies, while assuring the Germans that they were doing nothing of the sort.

A few days after the fall of Mussolini, Kesselring was ordered to withdraw the four divisions of the XIV Panzer Corps from Sicily. The Strait of Messina was bristling with anti-aircraft guns and Hube managed to get two-thirds of his force across before, at 0530 hours on 17 August 1943, he boarded the last assault boat to leave for Calabria. Three hours later, the British and Americans met in the ruins of Messina, leaving just two miles of clear water between the Allied army and the mainland of Italy. The cost of Operation *Husky* was 5,532 Allied dead, 14,410 wounded and 2,869 missing. The Italians lost 4,278 dead and the Germans 4,325. The Allies had taken 132,000 prisoners, with 520 guns and 260 tanks. But, the US destroyer *Maddox* had been lost and the cruisers *Cleopatra* and *Newfoundland* badly damaged by torpedoes.

CHAPTER 9

The Italian Mainland

On 2 September 1943, a small Allied force landed on the 'heel' of Italy, quickly taking the ports of Brindisi and Taranto. The following day, Montgomery's Eighth Army crossed the Strait of Messina and landed in Calabria, on the 'toe' of Italy. The invasion had begun.

That same day, the new Italian government agreed to the Allies' peace terms, though their capitulation was not announced until 8 September. Under the agreement, the Italian navy was to surrender in Malta. On its way there, it was bombed by the Germans. German units also turned on the Italians in Greece and the Balkans and disarmed them. On the Greek island of Cephalonia and in Croatia, two Italian divisions were massacred. Survivors joined the Greek resistance or Tito's partisans in Yugoslavia.

Under the peace agreement, the Americans had promised to land the 82nd Airborne Division on the outskirts of Rome and take the city, but the 3rd Panzergrenadier Division got there first.

THE SALERNO LANDINGS

On 9 September, an Anglo-American force under General Mark Clark landed at Salerno, thirty miles south of Naples. Kesselring had anticipated this and managed to hold the Allies back in their bridgehead for six days.

Hitler had anticipated the fall of Mussolini and put into action Operation *Alarich*. Seventeen more divisions were sent into Italy under the command of Rommel, who established his headquarters in Bologna. Several Italian units melted away, but Rommel managed to take over ten divisions and add them to his command. Effectively Italy had been invaded by Germany and Hitler even threatened to arrest the King.

To give his hold over Italy some sort of legitimacy, Hitler hatched a plot to rescue Mussolini. On 12 September 1943, German commandos under the command of SS officer Otto Skorzeny crash-landed gliders on the slopes behind Campo Imperatore and freed him. Mussolini was flown to Munich, where Hitler suggested he set up a new Fascist republic in northern Italy. The Repubblica Sociale Italiana was established on 18 September at Salò on Lake Garda. Members of the Fascist Grand Council who had voted against him, including his own son-in-law, former Foreign Minister Count Ciano, were arrested and executed. But otherwise, as Mussolini himself admitted, he was merely a puppet. None of the neutral countries – not even Fascist Spain – would recognize Mussolini's new republic. In Rome Marshal Ugo Cavellero committed suicide after Kesselring offered him command of a new Fascist army. Before the snows made the Alps impassable, 18,400 Italians crossed the border and had themselves interned in Switzerland. Others opposed Mussolini's new regime with strikes and sabotage; some took up arms.

On the same day as Mussolini was being rescued, Kesselring

counterattacked. He concentrated his attack between the British 56th Division on the right and the American 45th Division on the left, which had made quicker progress. The German forces attempted then to encircle the Americans and crush the beachhead at Salerno. The battle hinged around Ponte Bruciato. Clark threw every man he had into the fight, including a regimental band and the headquarters orderlies and cooks. The German advance foundered when Hitler refused to reinforce Kesselring's Tenth Army after Rommel had advised him that Italy could not be defended south of a line from La Spezia to Rimini.

At Salerno, the Germans were stopped five miles from the beach, where they were pinned down by Allied naval bombardment from ships close in to the shore. New German radio-controlled bombs hit the American cruiser *Savannah* as well as the British cruiser *Uganda* and the battleship *Warspite*. The Americans were eventually relieved when Montgomery broke through at Agropoli. The German Tenth Army had been defeated at a cost of 5,674 American casualties, including 756 killed and 2,150 missing.

On 1 October 1943, the American Fifth Army entered Naples, while more British forces landed at Bari and Termoli on the Adriatic coast. On 13 October, the Italian government in Rome declared war on Germany. This did not bother Kesselring unduly as German reinforcements were already consolidating their hold on north and central Italy. Rommel's Panzers managed to check the American Fifth Army on the Volturno River, just twenty miles north of Naples, then held them on the Garigliano. However, Rommel was still urging that Germany abandon

Rome and withdraw to the north. On 21 November he was relieved and Kesselring was left in sole command.

THE ROAD TO ROME

On the east coast, the British Eighth Army was stopped on the Sangro River. The advance had run out of steam because the roads through the mountains were jammed with vehicles. According to General Alphonse Juin of the French Expeditionary Corps: 'The mechanization of the British and American armies could actually hinder our rapid progress up the Italian peninsula.'

Reinforcements were required, so the 2nd Moroccan Division and the 3rd Algerian Division were landed with 65,000 men and 2,500 horses and mules. On 18 December the 2nd Moroccan Division proved its worth the first time it came under fire, taking Mount Mainarde across difficult terrain and against fierce resistance. This earned the French Expeditionary Corps a place in the line on the right of the Fifth Army's VI Corps.

The Germans dug in along the Gustav Line, a defensive position that ran for a hundred miles across the Italian peninsula, which pivoted on the town of Cassino with the historic monastery of Monte Cassino on the mountain above it.

THE ANZIO LANDINGS

With the road to Rome now blocked, the Allies staged another amphibious assault, landing 70,000 troops at Anzio and nearby Nettuno just thirty-seven miles south of Rome and sixty miles behind the Gustav Line, on 22 January 1944. The landings were initially successful, but the American commander Major-General John P. Lucas did not seize the opportunity to make a dash across

Mortar Team *US soldiers with mortar, Anzio, January 1944. Initial successes were not followed up at Anzio, leading to a standoff lasting several months.*

the Colli Laziali, or Alban Hills, for Rome, cutting German communications on the way and forcing Kesselring to evacuate the Gustav Line. Instead, Lucas took the best part of a week to consolidate his bridgehead. This gave time for Kesselring to mount a counter-offensive, effectively trapping the huge Anglo-American force in their bridgehead.

The idea of the landing at Anzio had come from Churchill. He had convinced Roosevelt and Stalin that it was a good idea and he even volunteered the British force being assembled for a landing on Rhodes. In frustration, Churchill wrote to General

Harold Alexander who was in overall command in Italy: 'I expected to see a wild cat roaring into the mountains – and what do I find? A whale wallowing on the beaches.'

Churchill felt that if the landings at Anzio and Nettuno had worked, his whole 'soft underbelly' strategy would prove itself and Anglo-American forces would be able to drive up the Italian peninsula, through Austria and into Germany before the Red Army got there. It was not to be. Later, in his memoirs, Churchill wrote: 'The spectacle of 18,000 vehicles accumulated ashore by the fourteenth day for only 70,000 men, or less then four men to a vehicle, including drivers and attendants ... was astonishing.'

Unable to move, Lucas was forced to established a static defence, which was pounded by a 28cm rail gun, known variously as 'Anzio Annie' or the 'Anzio Express'. With a barrel 135 feet long, it could hurl a 564-pound shell 38.64 miles, or a rocket-assisted shell 53.75 miles.

According to the official US Navy account of Anzio: 'It was the only amphibious operation in that theater where the Army was unable promptly to exploit a successful landing, or where the enemy contained Allied forces on a beachhead for a prolonged period. Indeed, in the entire war there is none to compare with it; even the Okinawa campaign in the Pacific was shorter.'

But Major-General Lucien K. Truscott, who was commanding the 3rd Division at Anzio and would go on to head the Fifth Army, was less damning:

I suppose that armchair strategists will always labour under the delusion that there was a 'fleeting opportunity' at Anzio during which some Napoleonic figure would have charged over the Colli

Laziali, playing havoc with the German line of communications and galloping on into Rome. Any such concept betrays a lack of comprehension of the military problem involved. It was necessary to occupy the Corps Beachhead Line to prevent the enemy from interfering with the beaches, otherwise enemy artillery and armoured detachments operating against the flanks could have cut us off from the beaches and prevented the unloading of troops, supplies and equipment. As it was, the Corps Beachhead Line was barely distant enough to prevent direct artillery fire on the beaches ... On 24 January [D+2] my division, with three Ranger battalions and the 504th Parachute Regiment attached, was extended over a front of twenty miles ... Two brigade groups of the British 1st Division held a front of more than seven miles.

Lucas himself compared it to the Dardanelles, but Patton disagreed.

'John, there is no one in the Army I would hate to see killed as much as you, but you can't get out of this alive,' he told his comrade. 'Of course, you might be badly wounded. No one ever blames a wounded general.' He advised Lucas to read the Bible when the going got bad, then told one of his aides: 'Look here. If things get too bad, shoot the old man in the backside; but don't dare kill him.'

Hitler saw clearly the significance of the situation at Anzio, especially in the light of the worsening situation on the Eastern Front and the attack across the Channel by Anglo-American forces that he was by now convinced would come soon. On 28 January 1944, he wrote to Kesselring, saying:

In a few days from now, the 'Battle for Rome' will start: this will decide the defence of central Italy and the fate of the Tenth Army. But it has even greater significance, for the Nettuno landing is the first step of the invasion of Europe planned for 1944. The enemy's aim is to pin down and to wear out major German forces as far as possible from the English base in which the main body of the invasion force is being held in a constant state of readiness, and to gain experience for future operations. The significance of the battle fought by the Fourteenth Army must be made clear to each one of its soldiers. It will not be enough to give clear and correct tactical orders. The army, the air force and the navy must be imbued with a fanatical determination to come out victorious from this battle and to hang on until the last enemy soldier has been exterminated or driven back into the sea. The men will fight with a solemn hatred against the enemy to whom everything seems a legitimate means to this end, an enemy who, in the absence of high ethical intention, is plotting the destruction of Germany and, along with her, that of European civilization. The battle must be hard and without pity, and not only against the enemy but also against any leader of men who, in this decisive hour, shows any sign of weakness. As in Sicily, on the Rapido and at Ortona, the enemy must be shown that the fighting strength of the German Army is still intact and that the great invasion of 1944 will be an invasion which will drown in the blood of the Ango-Saxon soldiers.

MONTE CASSINO

The landings at Anzio and Nettuno had failed to outflank the Gustav Line. This made a breakthrough there imperative. The

New Zealand Corps was ordered to lead an attack up the Liri Valley. Its commander, Lieutenant-General Freyberg, insisted that the historic monastery of Monte Cassino, which overlooked it, be bombed before his men advanced. He claimed that the Germans were using it as an artillery observation post and that heavy weapons were stored there. In fact, on the night of the attack, the only soldiers anywhere near the monastery were three military policemen stationed there to keep troops out. However a misleading radio message was intercepted. It said: '*Wo ist der Abt? Ist er noch im Kloster?*'

'*Abt*' is the military abbreviation for *Abteilung*, a section or squad. So the message was translated as: 'Where is the squad? Is it still in the monastery?' However '*Abt*' is also German for 'abbot'. But while '*Abt*' is masculine '*Abteilung*' is feminine, so it is clear that the message actually translates as: 'Where is the abbot? Is he still in the monastery?' But Freyberg was taking no chances and on the morning of 15 February 1944, 229 American bombers dropped 453 tons of incendiaries and high explosives on the monastery, reducing it to rubble. However, this did not lead to the breakthrough the Allies craved. So, on 15 March, 775 planes dropped 1,250 tons of bombs on the small town of Cassino, which was also shelled for two hours. The town was completely destroyed, but this proved to be self-defeating. The rubble provided excellent defensive positions, and the bomb craters hampered the deployment of armour. The fighting that developed in the streets of Cassino resembled the ferocious battle of Stalingrad, while on the slopes of Monte Cassino the Ghurkas fought hard for a few feet of ground. On 23 March, Freyberg called off the attack.

It had cost over two thousand men and had achieved none of its objectives.

General Alexander then shifted the British Eighth Army from the Adriatic to increase the pressure around Monte Cassino. A combined assault began on the night of 11 May. They broke through between Cassino and the coast. Monte Cassino eventually fell to the Polish Corps of the Eighth Army on 18 May. For his defence of Monte Cassino, General von Senger und Etterlin received the Oak Leaves to his Knight's Cross from Hitler. It was clear that by then the war had taken its toll on the German Führer. Von Senger wrote of the ceremony that it was:

...far from impressive. Hitler made a really horrifying impression and, in spite of myself, I wondered how the young officers and sergeants who were being decorated with me would react. His unattractive figure, with his short neck, appeared more slovenly than ever. The look in his blue eyes, said to have completely fascinated so many people, was vacant, possibly as a result of the stimulants that he was given constantly. His handshake was floppy. His leg and arm hung limp and trembling...

THE GOTHIC LINE

To defend the Gustav Line, Kesselring had had to take men away from Anzio, allowing the Allied forces there to break out. The Canadian Corps of the Eighth Army took the Liri Valley, and the Gustav Line began to collapse. General Mark Clark then made a dash for Rome. Assessing the situation, Kesselring declared Rome to be an 'open city' and evacuated his troops. Mark Clark entered the city on 5 June. It was a tremendous propaganda boost the day before D-Day. The capital of one of the enemy

Mozzano, Porretta, the Vernio pass north of Prato, and the Futa and Il Giorgo passes north of Florence. Every road between Casaglia and Bagno and the Mandriolo pass was blocked. The defensive line then ran down the valley of the Foglia, then across the narrow coastal plain to Pesaro.

Along that plain ran Route 16, the only road the Allies could use that did not entail climbing the great mountain barrier of the Apennines. However, it was cut by numerous rivers that often flooded, turning the soil in the surrounding area into a sea of mud. And there were numerous ridges that made good defensive positions.

The Germans built fortifications. They dug deep bunkers and anti-tank ditches, and laid mine fields. Todt engineers and conscripted Italian labourers built a series of positions to link the main strongholds in the mountains into one continuous defensive line and they built a belt of obstacles ten miles deep along the whole front. As the Allies approached they faced miles of anti-tank ditches, 120,000 yards of wire entanglements, 2,376 machine-gun nests and 479 antitank gun, mortar and assault gun positions. However, the defences were not quite finished. Only four of the thirty 7.5cm Panther tank gun turrets the engineers had ordered were in place.

Thanks to Mark Clark's dash on Rome, Kesselring had managed to withdraw ten divisions to the Gothic Line. At the height of the fighting in Normandy, Hitler sent a battalion of Tiger tanks from France and withdrew seven divisions from

Into Rome General Mark Clark becomes the first Allied officer to enter the city of Rome, 5 June 1944. The move was widely regarded as a propaganda victory, but a miltary blunder.

the Russian front, Hungary, Holland and Denmark to defend northern Italy. And three whole infantry divisions were being drawn up in Germany to replace those that had been practically wiped out in the Liri Valley.

While the Germans were reinforcing, the Allied strength in Italy was declining. Alexander had been warned as early as 22 May 1944 that he was going to have to give up seven divisions to Operation *Dragoon*. But it was not until 5 July that his pleas to be allowed to keep his force intact were finally turned down. By that time, the Polish II Corps had reached Ancona and a fierce battle was raging for Arezzo some thirty-five miles from the Gothic Line. Now Alexander had to fight on towards the Po without even the French Expeditionary Corps, whose North African mountain troops and proved invaluable in the fighting on the Gustav Line. And he could expect no reinforcements until the US 92nd (Negro) Division join him in September and a Brazilian division arrived in October.

Even so, with the battle of Caen under way, it was vital for Alexander to keep up the pressure. However, as it was unlikely that he was going to make a rapid breakthrough, Allied bombers took out all twenty-three road and rail bridges that crossed the river Po, on 12–15 July. This marked the beginning of the battle for the Gothic Line. Air attacks continued on railway lines across northern Italy and on the Brenner Pass, effectively isolating Italy from the rest of Europe. To keep supplies flowing to the front, fifty pontoon bridges had to be built over the Po each night, then broken up and hidden during the day.

CHAPTER 10

Beyond the Gothic Line

The Gothic Line, running through the Apennine Mountains across the Italian peninsula, was the last German line of resistance in Italy. Beyond the Line lay the open spaces of the northern Italian plain.

Alexander had twenty divisions, including four armoured divisions, under his command. Kesselring has twenty-six divisions, including six Panzer and Panzergrenadier divisions. However, the Allies enjoyed complete air superiority. The Luftwaffe in Italy had just 170 planes, most of which were obsolete. The Allies could call on seventy-five complete squadrons in Tactical Air Force alone. This allowed the Allies to harass the German supply lines, while the Germans had no chance to strike at the Allies' rear.

The Germans also suffered shortages of armour and artillery. And as Kesselring was very conscious of the Allies' skill at amphibious landings he held back six divisions to defend the Ligurian coast and the Gulf of Venice. Another two German-trained Italian divisions had to be held back to fight what was turning into a civil war in Mussolini's Repubblica Sociale Italiana, where partisans were attacking military depots and disrupting lines of communication. Nevertheless, Kesselring was confident that he could hold the Gothic Line, especially after inspecting the defences at the eastern flank.

Alexander planned to attack the middle of the line, along the road that leads from Florence to Bologna. Preparations were already under way, persuading the Germans that the attack would come up Route 16, when Clark's Fifth Army was reduced to a single corps by Operation *Dragoon*. Alexander's plan was then abandoned in favour of an alternative proposed by the commander of the Eighth Army, Lieutenant-General Sir Oliver Leese. He wanted to attack up the coastal plain where his superiority in tanks and guns could be used to great effect. This also left the US Fifth Army freedom of action to deliver another blow further to the west. The attack would have to be delayed to 25 August to give the Eighth Army time to cross the mountains to the Adriatic coast. The cover story would also have to be reversed, so the Fifth Army were told to make 'ostentatious preparations' for their attack against the mountain positions.

It took just fifteen days to transport two complete corps headquarters, a mass of corps troops, eight divisions and 80,000 vehicles across the Apennines, even though the roads had to be completely rebuilt in places after being destroyed by the retreating Germans. More than forty bailey bridges had to be constructed. Meanwhile, three British divisions under Lieutenant-General Sidney Kirkman joined the American Fifth Army for their thrust towards Bologna.

ASSAULTING THE LINE

The attack was going to be made on a narrow front, with the Polish making for Pesaro and the Canadians for Rimini, but the main assault would come through the hills a little inland. Everything went well to start with. German front-line troops were being relieved at the time and it was thought that the British advance was simply a response to that, rather than a full-out assault. Kesselring's Panzer commander Colonel-General Heinrich von Vietinghoff-Scheel was away at the time and it was only after he returned on 28 September that the Germans realised what was going on. Allied infantry had already reached the Folgia and the Gothic Line had been penetrated.

On 1 September, the Ghurkas of the Fourth Indian Division took the heavily fortified town of Tavileto using just kukris and grenades. On the plain, the Canadians had suffered heavy losses crossing the River Conca, but by dawn of 3 September they had established a bridgehead alongside Route 16. When the 26th Panzer and 98th Divisions had arrived on the scene, they were badly damaged.

However, the attack through the hills was not going so well. The track followed 'razor-backed mountain ridges'. Sometimes it was so narrow that it took several attempts to turn a corner. Drivers spent as many as fifty hours at the wheel. Crawling along in a low gear meant that many of the tanks ran out of petrol. Twenty were lost before reaching the assembly area and those at the back of the column had to put up with choking white dust.

In the midst of this, the German 162nd Division turned up, supported by 29th Panzegrenadier Division. The British lost another sixty-five tanks in a hail of shot and shell. To make things worse, as German reinforcements arrived, it began to rain, turning the track into a mud bath. Since it was now overcast, the British lost their air cover and Alexander pulled back to regroup.

The air cover provided by the British Desert Air Force was switched to support the Fifth Army whose attack started on 13 September. Two American divisions advanced on the pass at Il Giogo. It was held by the 4th Parachute Division who held out for four days.

Meanwhile General Kirkman's XIII Corps was advancing on Clark's right flank towards Faenza and Forli. On 14 September it cleared the watershed, and the following day it took Monte Preffeto. XIII Corps then turned to help the Americans, taking Monte Pratone.

Over the next four days, Monti Altuzzo and Monticelli and the neighbouring strongholds fell, giving the Allies a sevenmile stretch of the Gothic line on either side of the pass at Il Giogo.

Kesselring rushed in reinforcements, even taking men from the front at the Adriatic. On 27 September, Clark was halted by four divisions ten miles short of Route 9 at Imola. Kesselring's aim was to retake Monte Battaglia. The battle there lasted over a week before Kesselring gave the German infantry the order to dig in.

The Eighth Army began its offensive again on 12 September. After three days of bitter fighting it took the Coriano and Gemmano Ridges that guarded the entrance to the valley of the Foglia and overlooked the plain. The Third Greek Mountain Brigade took Rimini on 20 September. The following day, Allied patrols crossed the River Marecchia. The way was now open for Freyberg's 2nd New Zealand Division to move up along Route 16.

The Allies were now entering the Romagna, which is essentially a flat, alluvial flood plain that turned into a swamp when it rained. It was criss-crossed by rivers and drainage ditches. Stone farm houses, rows of fruit trees and vineyards provided ready-made defensive positions.

By 29 September the New Zealanders had reached the River Fiuminico. But torrential rain meant the river was in flood. The bridges had been swept away and the river was too deep to ford, so the advance was halted. Inland, X Corps fought on and were within ten miles of Cesena.

General Leese had been given command of Allied land forces in South-East Asia. He had been replaced by General Sir Richard McCreery, who sent the Polish Corps and the 10th Indian Division through the mountains. By 21 September they had taken Cesena and established a bridgehead over the Savio river, where the Germans held them for four days before falling back on the Ronco.

To the west, Clark struck out along Route 65 towards Bologna. Initially resistance was light due to heavy bombing and the fighting to the east. But by the time they reached the Livergano escarpment, the two divisions they had been facing had been bolstered to five, including the 16th SS Panzer Division, along with elements from three other divisions. A spell of clear weather allowed air strikes that helped II Corps drive the Germans off the escarpment on 14 October. Resistance stiffened. It took more air strikes and 8,600 rounds of ammunition for the 88th Division to take Monte Grande on 20 October. Meanwhile, the Americans were beaten back from the small village of Vedriano for three nights running by ferocious counter-attacks. Since 10 September, II Corps had lost 15,716 men. The 88th alone had lost over five thousand. Clark, too, gave the order to dig in.

The advance was stalled. Clark himself would share some of the hardships of his men, passing the winter months in a caravan on the Futi pass, high up in the Apennines.

Alexander's advance along the coast was halted too. He wrote: 'Rain, which was at the time spoiling the Fifth Army's attack on Bologna, now reached a high pitch of intensity. On 26 October all the bridges over the Savio, in our immediate rear, were swept away and our small bridge heads over the Ronco were eliminated and destroyed.'

Since July, the Eighth Army's battle casualties totalled 19,975 and every infantry battalion had to be reformed. Over four hundred tanks had been lost and the 1st Armoured Division had to be disbanded.

For the Germans, the situation was much worse. LXXXVII Panzer Corps alone had suffered 14,500 battle casualties. Eight thousand had been taken prisoner. Only ten of Kesselring's ninety-two infantry divisions could muster more than four hundred men, and a third could only muster two hundred.

Kesselring proposed shortening the line by withdrawing to the Alps. Hitler told him to fight where he stood. Meanwhile, Alexander proposed a landing in Croatia to attack Kesselring's rear. This too was turned down as the Allies' main concern at the time was the setback at Arnhem. There was also a shortage of certain types of artillery shell, and the bad weather robbed the Allies of air support.

Nevertheless, the Allies inched forward. In early January the Canadians took Ravenna. Soon after that they reached the southern shore of Lake Comacchio. After a ferocious battle, they forced the Germans back behind the Senio river. Meanwhile, V

Corps headed westwards and captured Faenze, while the Poles advanced on the upper reaches of the Senio.

THE ROAD TO BOLOGNA

On 22 December the Fifth Army concentrated ready for a planned attack on Bologna two days later. But the weather broke and, in a last desperate roll of the dice, Mussolini sent two newly formed divisions against Clark's left flank. The Monte Rosa Division and the Italia Bersaglieri Division, led by the German 148th Division, headed down the Serchio Valley with the aim of capturing the port of Livorno. The only unit in their way was the 92nd (Negro) Division, stationed at Bagni di Lucca. They defended stoutly, but leading German units were just about to overrun the two main defensive lines on 25 December, when the 8th Indian Division arrived and drove them back. In response to this threat to his main supply base, Clark had to divert two divisions from the main battle area and, as heavy snow began to fall, Alexander ordered both armies to switch to the defensive.

During the winter, there was a change of command on both sides. Kesselring was promoted to commander of all German forces in the west and was replaced by Vietinghoff, who had orders from Hitler not to cede any more ground. Kesselring had already been building up defences along the River Reno and the Po itself. Although some of his men had been transferred to other fronts, he still had nineteen divisions deployed along his 130-mile front, with another five German, four Italian and one Cossack division held back in case of an amphibious assault and to guard the Italian border.

Alexander was made Supreme Allied Commander

The Brenner Pass *German Tiger tanks defending the Brenner Pass against the advancing Allies, April 1945.*

Mediterranean and promoted to Field Marshal. Clark took over as commander of the Fifteenth Army Group, which was weaker than ever after three British divisions had been sent to fight in the civil war that had broken out in Greece. He had just seventeen divisions, including the newly deployed American 10th Mountain Division. Command of the US Fifth Army was given to General Truscott, who had been recalled from France.

Supply on both sides was becoming a problem in the winter snow. On the Allied side, the supply routes were kept open with the help of thousands of civilians, along with all the units not directly manning the front. However, they were well supplied with the specialized amphibious vehicles that had been used on D–Day, as well as tanks fitted with bridge-laying equipment and flame throwers ready for a spring offensive. The Germans, on the other hand, increasingly suffered from the work of partisans behind their lines. They had to horde their meagre stocks of ammunition. And as spring approached, Allied bombers began pounding their supply lines. On 6 February alone, 364 missions were flown against the Brenner Pass and the Venetian plain, virtually unopposed, and four thousand aeroplanes were massed to support ground operations.

Alexander prepared for the final assault on the German forces in Italy by playing on German fears that there would be an amphibious assault on the shores of the Gulf of Venice. British Commandos would clear the shores and islands of Lake Comacchio, while the 56th Division attacked across the shallow waters of the lake using amphibious tanks and four hundred 'Fantail' tracked vehicles. But this would be a diversionary attack that would protect the flank of the Eighth Army's main force, which would attack further inland up Route 9. The aim of this attack was to cut the German line at Argenta, halfway between the coast and Bologna, thereby splitting the German forces in two and cutting their lines of retreat to the east. Meanwhile, the American Fifth Army would move on Bologna.

Shortly after noon on 9 April, Allied medium bombers with close air support went to work on the defences along the Senio and beyond, taking out strongpoints, command posts and gun positions. Ninety minutes later, smoke shells were fired to mark a bombing line. The heavy bombers moved in and dropped 125,000 fragmentation bombs on the German troops along the Senio. This was followed by concentrated gunfire and low-level fighter-bomber attacks.

At 1900 hours, the Allied aircraft switched to dummy attacks to keep enemy heads down while the infantry crossed the river. They the used flame throwers that set the whole front on fire. After fierce fighting, a bridgehead was established on the western flood plains and bridges were laid for the armour to follow. On 10 April, 1,600 Allied heavy bombers renewed their air assault, and the following day the New Zealand Corps crossed the Santerno river at Massa Lombarda. The forward battalions of the German 362nd and 98th Divisions had been destroyed and some two thousand men taken prisoner.

The Eighth Army then turned northwards and moved on Argenta. The advance was led by a special strike force, called the 'Kangaroo Army', made up of the Irish Brigade and the 2nd Army Brigade, forward elements of the 78th Brigade. These men travelled on Sherman tanks that were converted to carry infantry called 'Kangaroos'. The 56th Division had suffered heavy casualties crossing Lake Comacchio and the 78th were slowed by huge minefields outside Bastia. But slowly, as reserves under General McCreery moved up, the pincers began to close on Argenta.

General Truscott was then supposed to have launched the Fifth Army's move on Bologna. However, poor flying weather meant that it had to be postponed until 14 April. Over the following four days the Allied air force would fly over four thousand sorties in support of Truscott's two divisions. During the first half hour of the Fifth Army's attack on German positions on Monte Rimici and neighbouring Monte Sole, some 75,000 shells were fired at the enemy strongpoints. Even so, the American II Corps advanced less than two miles in the first three days of the assault. However, the American 10th Mountain Division took Montepastore, and for two days the American 1st Armored Division and Vietinghoff's last reserves, the 19th Panzergrenadier Division, fought it out in the valley of the Samoggia.

The Germans were now exhausted. On 20 April, Vietinghoff ordered the retreat of his men to the north of the Po, in defiance of Hitler's orders. But it was too late. Every bridge was down and the new ones that had been hastily constructed were blocked by columns of burning vehicles. Shattered formations were trapped on the south side of the river where they fought on.

By then, the 29th Panzergrenadier Division, and the remnants of other units, were trying to hold back the advance of V Corps just fifteen miles from Ferrara. Along Route 9, the Polish Corps and the New Zealanders had fought three German divisions to a standstill, and at daybreak on 21 April a Polish brigade entered Bologna unopposed from the east.

The day before, a company of the American 86th Mountain Infantry had crossed Route 9 to the west of Bologna. The US II Corps and the 6th South African Armoured Division bypassed the city on Route 64. Lead elements made contact with the 16th/5th Lancers fifteen miles west of Ferrara on 23 April.

General von Senger, the commander at Monte Cassino, managed to escape across the Po at Bergantino on the 23rd on one of the four ferries that was still serviceable out of thirty-six in the area. Even then, they only operated at night because of the incessant air attacks on anything that moved in the vicinity. He was fleeing 'a scene of extraordinary desolation and fearful carnage'.

By this time there was no longer any coherent resistance and along the river lay the ruins of the Germany army. German losses ran to 67,000, including 35,000 taken prisoner.

On 25 April, Allied armoured columns crossed the Po. One week later, on 2 May 1945, the remaining German and Italian men of Army Group C – nearly a million men – surrendered to the Allied forces. The war, in Italy at least, was over. Mussolini was captured by partisans while trying to escape over the border into Switzerland disguised as a German soldier. On 28 April 1945, he and his mistress Claretta Petacci were shot and killed. Their bodies were hung upside down from lampposts in the Piazza Loreto in Milan.

SECTION THREE
THE WESTERN FRONT

Despite the heavy casualties suffered by the
Americans on Omaha Beach, and the general
failure to achieve first-day objectives, the D-Day
landings must be considered as an enormous
success. The Allies had a toehold in the west of
Europe; from now on, the German army would
have to fight the war on two fronts.

CHAPTER 11

The Liberation of France

*The success of the landings in Normandy had
given the Allies a secure beachhead in enemy territory.
The job that lay ahead of them now was to break
out of their beachhead before the Germans could bring
up reinforcements.*

The Allied planners had calculated that the greatest threat
to the operation was a swift German counter–attack. It
never came. This was partly because of Operation *Fortitude*. The
German High Command still expected an attack in the Pas de
Calais and initially believed that the landings in Normandy were
merely a diversion. With lines of communication cut by the
French Resistance and heavy Allied bombing, confusion reigned
on the German side. Rommel was in Germany for his wife's
birthday and his planned interview with Hitler. Because of the
Allies' control of the skies, he dared not fly back and had to make
the long journey back to France by road. This left the defenders
leaderless during the critical first few hours of the attack.

The man nominally in charge, Field Marshal von Rundstedt,
knew exactly what to do. He realized that the scale of the
airborne assault meant that the attack on Normandy was no
mere diversionary tactic and, two hours before the Allies first set

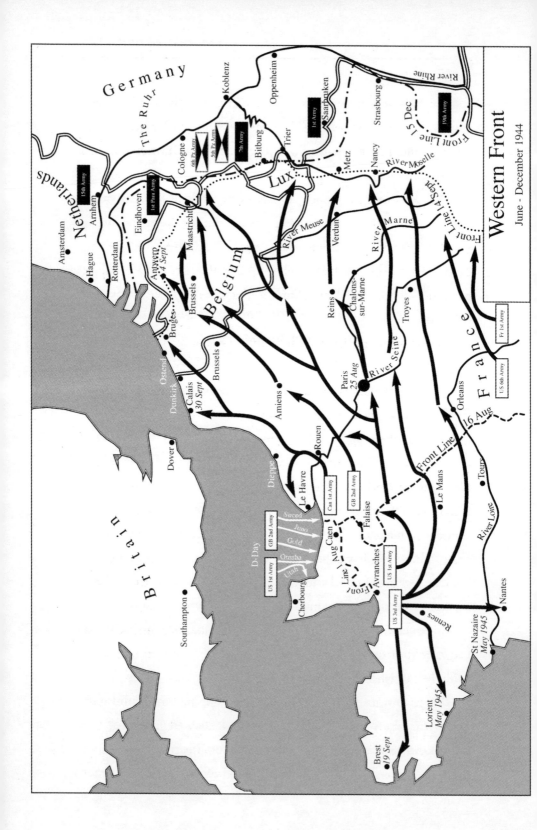

Western Front
June – December 1944

foot on a beach, he ordered a reserve Panzer division to move towards Caen. However, the Panzers were not under his control. They could not be moved without Hitler's authorization and Hitler was asleep. He slept until noon.

The skies that morning were overcast and the Panzers could have moved without much harassment from the Allied air forces. But by 1600, when Hitler finally gave his approval for them to be moved, the clouds had broken up and Panzers had to hide in roadside woods until dark. For the defenders, a whole day had been lost.

Nevertheless Hitler was jubilant. 'The news could not be better,' he said, when he heard of the Allied landings. 'As long they were in Britain we couldn't get at them. Now we have them where we can destroy them.' The Nazi propaganda minister Joseph Goebbels also expressed his delight. 'Thank God, at last,' he said. 'This is the final round.' For some time, the German High Command had watched in frustration as the Allies built their strength in Britain, untouched by the Luftwaffe or the Wehrmacht. Meanwhile, Allied bombing weakened Germany to the point where it was facing a serious petrol shortage, and the endless waiting sapped the Germans' morale. Now the enemy was within range of German guns.

However, the opportunity to drive the Allies back into the sea was quickly lost. By the end of 7 June, the invasion forces from all three British beaches had linked up to make one continuous front and British troops from Gold Beach had made contact with Americans from Omaha. Bayeux had been liberated, but the British had yet to achieve their DDay objective: the capture of Caen. However, 156,000 troops were now ashore at the cost of some 10,000 casualties. Losses were much lower than expected.

Hitler ordered that the German defenders should cede no more land. In some ways, this was a sensible decision. The bocage country inland from the invasion beaches favoured the defenders. The Allies had to fight hedgerow by hedgerow. However, for the Germans, fighting this way was not a winning strategy. They could inflict enormous casualties on the invaders, but they could not halt their advance. It also tied the hands of Rommel who, in the desert, had shown himself the master of fast, fluid, open warfare.

Rommel moved 2nd Panzer Division into the British sector and von Rundstedt finally got Hitler's permission to move the 1st SS Panzer Division *Leibstandarte Adolf Hitler* from Belgium and 2nd SS Panzer Division *Das Reich* from Toulouse in the south. These formidable forces would be used to defend Caen. However, due to Allied air superiority and harassment by the SAS, the journey from Toulouse took seventeen days instead of the five days von Rundstedt had anticipated.

Rommel pinned his hopes on holding the town of Carentan at the base of the Cotentin Peninsula, preventing the US VII Corps from Utah Beach joining up with V Corps from Omaha. He received a setback when the commander of 91st Air Landing Division, holding Carentan, was ambushed and killed by American troops. However, the German 6th Parachute Regiment put up stiff resistance and it was not until the morning of 10 June that the patrols from the two divisions linked up. Rommel moved the II Parachute Corps and the elite 17th SS Panzergrenadier Division into the area. But again their movement was hampered by the Allied air forces and the Resistance. The Panzergrenadiers only reached their positions south-west of Carentan on the evening of 11 June, by which time the situation was desperate. The Luftwaffe took to the air that night to drop eighteen tons of ammunition to 6th Parachute Regiment at Carentan. It was not enough to save them. Supported by a massive artillery bombardment from naval and field guns, the 101st Airborne Division attacked at dawn on 12 June and overran the town. A counter-attack by 17th SS Panzergrenadiers was repulsed as troops from Utah Beach arrived. The forces from all the Allied beaches then joined up to form one continuous front.

The US V Corps also began a sustained push southwards towards St Lô on 12 June, but found themselves facing stiff opposition in the bocage. On 15 June, the 29th Division found itself halted five miles from St Lô. Meanwhile, the British had exploited the gap between the German 352nd Division – which had eventually been driven back from Omaha Beach – and the Panzer Lehr, only to stall after the battle of Villers- Bocage which cost the British twenty Cromwell tanks.

VILLERS-BOCAGE

The battle was fought between 22nd Armoured Brigade reinforced by a lorried infantry battalion, the 1st/7th Battalion of the Queen's Regiment, and elements of the 101st SS Heavy Panzer Battalion. The British had pushed on from the town of Livry and were making in Villers-Bocage at around 0630 on 13 June, D+7, when everything came unstuck.

On D-Day, 101st SS Heavy Tank Battalion had been stationed at Beauvais, north-west of Paris. Hastily posted to Normandy, they arrived in the Villers- Bocage area on 12 June.

Due to regular attacks by the Allied air forces, 2 Company now consisted of just five Tiger tanks. But they were commanded by the legendary SS *Hauptsturmführer* Michael Wittmann, an ace with 138 enemy tank kills to his name. While the rest of his company were performing much needed maintenance in a small wood near the village of Montbrocq, around a mile north-east of Villers-Bocage, Wittmann went out on a reconnaissance mission. He was just south of the Villers–Caen road when he was stopped by a sergeant who told him that he had heard the unmistakable sounds of tanks coming out of Villers-Bocage, even though there were no German tanks in the area. Wittmann dismounted and crawled through the hedge that flanked the

Tiger Tank *Issued only to elite units, such as the 101st SS Heavy Tank Battalion (pictured), the Tiger tank was a formidable opponent for the Allies in France.*

road. He saw A Squadron and the infantry half-tracks making their way up the hill. The British Cromwell tanks, with their 75mm guns, were no match for the Tiger and its 88mm cannon.

At 0830, Wittmann emerged in his Tiger down the track from Montbrocq right into the middle of the British column advancing up the hill. The lead tanks turned their guns and depressed them to fire on the Tiger, but the movement of their turrets was too slow. Two shots from the Tiger knocked out two tanks, blocking the road and making it impossible for other Cromwells to come to the defence of the column. Wittmann then turned his tank down towards Villers-Bocage knocking out the infantry's half-tracks one by one as he worked his way down the line. A sixpounder anti-tank gun was trained on the tank by a crew of riflemen led by Sergeant Bray. The Tiger blew it to pieces. Further down the hill, in Villers-Bocage itself, the Tiger took out the Honey tanks of the Sharpshooters' Reconnaissance Troop.

The four Cromwell tanks of the regimental headquarters were in the centre of town. One of them, under Major Carr, the Sharpshooters' second-in-command, went to investigate. When he saw the Tiger advance out of the smoke towards him, he ordered his gunner to fire, but the shell simply bounced off the Tiger's armour. Its reply left the Cromwell a burning wreck and all the crew dead or wounded. The Tiger's next two shots took another two of the Regimantal HQ's Cromwells out. Captain Pat Dyas, in command of the fourth, backed it into a garden and waited. His idea was to knock out Wittmann's Tiger as it trundled past. A 75mm shell could not penetrate the armour-plating on the front or side of the Tiger, but it could jam the turret or knock a track off. But Dyas's gunner had got out of the tank to take a leak shortly before the Tiger appeared and the radio operator did not have time to climb into his seat before the Tiger had passed them. Nevertheless, once the new gunner was in place, Dyas ordered his driver to follow Wittmann's Tiger in the hope of damaging it with a shot at its more thinly armoured rear. However, when Wittmann reached the end of the street, he met a modified Sherman tank with a 17-pounder gun, under the command of Sergeant Lockwood. Wittmann loosed off a shot at him, demolishing a shop behind the Sherman. Lockwood replied, but his shell bounced off the angled facets of the Tiger's turret. Wittmann quickly turned and fled back up the main street, running into Dyas in his Cromwell. Dyas found himself facing not the Tiger's thinly armoured rear, but its heavily clad front. Two 75mm shells simply bounced off. Wittmann's reply – one 88mm – hit the Cromwell's turret, killing the wireless operator-turned-gunner and blowing Dyas out of the tank. The driver was cut down by machine-gun fire as he tried to make his escape.

Using a radio that was still functioning in another of the wrecked tanks, Dyas warned Cranley that the Tiger was coming back his way. Cranley replied that he too was under attack. But before they could continue their conversation, a burst of machine-gun fire from the retreating Tiger sent Dyas leaping for cover. After hiding briefly in a pigsty, Dyas was led by a small girl to B Squadron at the west end of the town. There he told Major Aird that, with Cranley cut off and Carr either dead or seriously wounded, Aird had better take over command of the regiment.

Half an hour later, the rest of Wittmann's company arrived

on the hill. The four Tigers destroyed the remains of A Squadron and machine-gunned anyone who moved. Then the infantry moved in to round up survivors and take them as prisoners of war. The only man to escape, other than Dyas, was Captain Christopher Milner of A Company, 1st Rifle Brigade. He had made a dash into an orchard. A German spotted him, but he gave his pursuer the slip by climbing a tree. He made good his escape under the cover of a British bombardment of the position. During the night he worked his way around Villers-Bocage, avoiding both Germans and Allied sentries with itchy trigger fingers. At dawn he met up with 5th Royal Tank Regiment to the south-west of the town.

Wittmann caught up with his company and returned to the centre of town with two other Tigers and a Panzer IV. This time the British were ready for him. The 1st/7th Queens had entered the town about 1000 and set up an anti-tank gun. Major Aird, now in command of the Sharpshooters, had sent Lieutenant Cotton off to the south to try and relieve Cranley, avoiding the main street. But he had run into some Germans and a tricky railway embankment and had been forced to return to the town centre. Aware of the danger his troops were in, he hid his tanks in side streets, hoping to get a flanking shot of the Tigers at short range. Knowing that each tank would have only one chance, he ordered his men to sight their guns down the barrel using a mark on the wall on the opposite side of the main street. Then he waited.

Driving straight into this ambush, Wittmann's Tiger was put out of action by the Queens' anti-tank gun, though Wittmann and his crew escaped. A modified Sherman with a seventeen-pounder gun, under the command of Sergeant Bramall, knocked out a second Tiger. The third was caught in a small street to the south, and destroyed. Having missed the Mk IV with its first shot, Corporal Horne's tank pulled out into the main street and disabled the tank with a shot up its vulnerable back end.

But this was by no means the end of the battle. The Tiger tanks of 1 Company of 101st SS Heavy Tank Battalion turned up, along with a few Mk IV tanks from Panzer Lehr and infantry from 2nd Panzer Division. Villers-Bocage became the site of a ferocious battle. As the afternoon wore on, it became clear that the Germans were happy to pour more men in to take the town. The British fell back to the high ground near Amayé to the west of the town and did not reenter Villers-Bocage for two months.

The following dawn the Germans attacked, but were held off by artillery fire, then fled when the Queens counterattacked. However, that night it was decided that the 22nd Armoured Brigade should withdraw. To cover their retreat, Villers-Bocage was bombed flat.

THE COTENTIN PENINSULA

While the Allied advance to the south and east had been halted, General Joseph 'Lightnin' Joe' Collins struck out westwards across the foot of the Cotentin Peninsula, reaching the west coast at Barneville on 17 June. Rommel wanted the German units in the area to save themselves by retreating to the south, or at the very least to fall back on Cherbourg. Hitler countermanded this and ordered them to stay where they were. As a result they were destroyed as the Americans fought their way up the peninsula. The success of this operation enabled the

US Sherman tanks and troops move through the bombed town of Flers as they move inland from the Normandy beachheads.

entire Allied army in Normandy to turn and face southwards. By 17 June, 557,000 Allied troops had been landed, along with 81,000 vehicles and 183,000 tons of supplies. Already they outnumbered the German troops they faced, though the British in the east were confronted by a greater concentration of armour. Fresh Allied troops coming in outnumbered the casualties being sent home. Casualty rates could still be high, though; the US 82nd Airborne had lost 1,259 on D-Day alone and sustained a casualty rate of forty-six per cent before they were relieved in early July. The Allies were now in a position where exhausted units could be withdrawn and replaced. There was no shortage of ammunition and supplies and, although the

Allies had failed to make a decisive breakout, the odds were very much in their favour.

Having put all their effort into fighting the invaders on the beaches, the Germans had squandered a lot of their strength. They had lost 26,000 men, including one army corps commander and five divisional commanders. Casualties outstripped their replacement rate and their armoured strength was being inexorably whittled away by air and artillery bombardment. Ninety per cent of the railways in Normandy had been knocked out by the Allied air forces and the Resistance, and the German front line troops soon grew short of fuel and ammunition.

While Hitler still held his Fifteenth Army in reserve, ready to repel any attack on the Pas de Calais, he brought in 9th and 10th SS Panzer Divisions from the eastern front. Two more divisions were moved up from the south of France and elements of the Fifteenth Army were moved into Normandy to be replaced by units brought in from Scandinavia. Seven armoured divisions would now be readied for the counter-attack, while the troops already engaged held the invaders where they were. While on paper, this strategy looked as if the Germans would have no trouble pushing the Allies into the sea, von Rundstedt and Rommel were far from convinced. They knew from experience that the new units would arrive late and understrength, and Allied firepower would quickly cut them down to size. When they expressed their doubts, Hitler flew to France from his Wolf's Lair headquarters in East Prussia. The meeting took place at Soissons, north-east of Paris, on 17 June. Again Hitler refused to hand over control to his officers on the spot and ordered no further retreats, no matter how dire the situation. Typically, he made the entire 1,200-mile round trip without once bothering to visit the battlefield.

Even so, the plan might have worked. With their advance halted, the Allies had, momentarily, lost the initiative. The landings were running about two days behind schedule and, when the great storm blew up on 19 June, it put the Allies even further behind. Montgomery ordered the Americans to take Cherbourg urgently. Although it fell on 27 June, sporadic resistance continued until 1 July, and the Germans had so thoroughly sabotaged the port facilities that it was not up to capacity until the end of September.

Even more serious was the failure of the British to take Caen with its airfield at Caripiquet. This meant that only one fighter-bomber group could be deployed in Normandy. The situation became all the more urgent after 13 June, when V-1 rockets started falling on London. They were being launched from sites in the Pas de Calais, which could be attacked more easily if the Allies had an airbase at Carpiquet.

Montgomery gave orders for the British to take Caen. Again the plan was to outflank Caen to the west and take a high point – Hill 112 – to the south. Operation *Epsom* began on 26 June with a bombardment by over seven hundred guns. But bad weather robbed them of any air support from England and only limited sorties could by flown by 83rd Group of the Second Tactical Air Force stationed in Normandy. Progress slowed to two thousand yards a day. Eleventh Armoured Division reached the slopes of Hill 112 on 29 June, but the Germans committed three Panzer divisions to the action, forcing the British to withdraw. However, the weather began to improve, leaving the Panzers vulnerable to air attack. They were unable to take advantage of the situation with a cohesive counter-attack and the British were left with much of the ground they had gained.

With the improvement in the weather, the Allied build-up picked up speed again. By the end of June, 875,000 men had landed in Normandy, along with 150,000 vehicles. The British had taken 24,698 casualties and the Americans, 37,034. Between them they had received some 79,000 replacements. But while the Americans had a further nine divisions waiting in England, along with another thirty-nine ready for a second invasion in the south of France, the British were running out of men. Only four British and Canadian infantry divisions and two Canadian armoured divisions remained in Britain.

This gave Montgomery a grave problem. It was vital to take Caen, but this meant that the fiercest fighting fell on the weaker of the two armies under his control. Already heavy losses were causing a breakdown of the British army's renowned regimental system. He could not afford to waste men and despite the urgings of the Americans and the Air Force to launch an all-out offensive, he proceeded cautiously. By early July the Allied armies had not advanced more than fifteen miles from the beaches and occupied less than a fifth of the territory envisioned in Montgomery's original plan. General George Patton, commanding officer of the American Third Army, and General Henry Crerar, commanding officer of the First Canadian Army, were ashore, but the beachhead was too small to deploy two new armies.

Around half of the US Ninth Air Force had joined 83rd Group in Normandy, but the air forces had only nineteen out of the twenty-seven airfields they had been promised. With such a narrow beachhead they risked enemy shelling on take-off and landing, and mid-air collisions. Allied commanders began to fear that the whole invasion might result in a stalemate. However, the German commanders were even more depressed than those at SHAEF. General Dollmann committed suicide. Rommel and von Rundstedt went to the Wolf's Lair in another attempt to be allowed to control the battle on the ground. Again permission was refused. When they returned, junior officers asked for permission to give up some ground to regroup. Von Rundstedt passed their request up the chain of command and the next day he followed this up with a phone call suggesting that Hitler sue for peace. Von Rundstedt was replaced by Field Marshal Gunther von Kluge and there was a general shakeup of German command in the west.

General Bradley tried to break out, pushing south down the west coast of the Cotentin Peninsula on 7 July, then turning eastwards toward St Lô. But, again, bocage fighting kept progress down to two thousand yards a day. By 11 July the push had run out of steam, leaving Bradley demoralized. The only person who seemed remotely optimistic about the way things were going was Montgomery. He had a new plan to take Caen, suggested by Air Marshal Leigh-Mallory. Earlier that year a similar stalemate at Monte Cassino in Italy had been broken by the carpet-bombing of the defenders.

Starting at 2150 hours on 7 July, Bomber Command dropped 2,300 tons of bombs on Caen, destroying much of the city. Although they largely missed the German defensive positions, the raid raised the British troops' morale. Many of the bombs had time-delay fuses that were set to go off as the British and

Canadians attacked at 0420 hours the following morning, supported by another huge bombardment. As a result, 12th SS Panzer Division was practically wiped out. Fighting was ferocious and the Germans sustained casualty rates of up to seventy-five per cent. By the morning of 9 July, Caen north of the River Orne was in Allied hands. The next day the British pushed towards Hill 112 to threaten the southern part of the city.

Montgomery then ordered Bradley to push on to the south, so that Patton could break out into Brittany to the west, and the First Army under General Courtney Hodges was to swing eastwards through Le Mans and Alençon in Operation *Cobra*. However, first they had to take St Lô. This took eight days and was enormously costly in casualties. The liberation of St Lô was followed by torrential rain which halted any further American advance, and Operation *Cobra* had to be postponed. Meanwhile, the British started Operation *Goodwood*. Following another carpet-bombing, they would take the rest of Caen, then engage the German armour in the open 'tank country' to the east of the city to keep them away from the American breakout. With the battle underway, Rommel was removed from the battlefield once again, this time because he had been badly wounded when an Allied plane attacked his staff car. On 18 July, Caen was liberated by the Canadians. The British armour moved on to the east only to find the German defences there much heavier than expected. On 20 July, while Montgomery was announcing the success of Operation *Goodwood* to the world, the British armour was halted by German anti-tank guns. In the ensuing battle, 413 tanks – thirty-six per cent of the British Second Army's armour – was lost. They had progressed just seven miles at a rate, Eisenhower said, of a thousand tons of bombs a mile.

According to Montgomery's initial plan, Eisenhower should take over command on the ground in Europe on 1 August. Churchill had given Eisenhower permission to sack any British officer he found unsatisfactory and many people, including Air Marshal Tedder, were calling for Montgomery's head. But Eisenhower felt that sacking Britain's most famous general would damage morale and put a dent in the Anglo-American coalition. He visited Montgomery and, later, in a letter, urged him to abandon his customary caution as the enemy was now too weak to mount an effective counter-attack.

In Germany, more robust methods were being employed in an attempt to remove the commander seen to be responsible for the latest military failure. In the Wolf's Lair, a bomb went off under the table in Hitler's headquarters. Hitler himself was shielded from the blast by a solid oak table leg, and survived. None of the senior commanders in Normandy were implicated in the plot, with the single exception of Rommel. But as a great military hero he was allowed to commit suicide rather than face a trial that might have been damaging to the regime.

OPERATION COBRA

Despite the catastrophic consequences of Operation *Goodwood* for the British armour, Montgomery's overall strategy worked. The Germans committed the Fifteenth Army's last armoured division, 116th Panzer, to the Caen section, leaving four US armoured divisions and thirteen infantry divisions facing weakened German forces comprising two armoured divisions and seven infantry divisions – a superiority of two to one.

Everything was set for Operation *Cobra* to go ahead on 24 July.

It began, like *Goodwood*, with saturation bombing along a seven-thousand-yard front. The 1,500 bombers of the US Eighth Air Force were to take out the Panzer Lehr Division which was deployed to the west of St Lô. At the last minute the operation was postponed due to bad weather, but the message did not get through to 335 planes which, in the poor visibility, bombed their own frontline troops. *Cobra* went ahead again the next day. On the same day, General Crerar decided to start his advance down the Caen–Falais road in Operation *Spring*. This met fierce opposition from 1st and 9th SS Panzer Divisions, and had to be called off after twenty hours. However, the Germans assumed that *Spring* was the main offensive and they thought that the minor attack in the west the day before had been halted by their own artillery. But on 25 July, *Cobra* started up again with another saturation bombing. Again the Americans managed to bomb their own front line, killing the chief of the US ground forces, Lieutenant-General Lesley McNair, who was the highest-ranking Allied officer killed in Europe. However, the bombing also had a devastating effect on the enemy: Panzer Lehr lost two-thirds of its men and all its tanks. On the first day, the Americans advanced four thousand yards; on the second, eight thousand yards; and on the third, the 2nd Armored Division ('Hell on Wheels'), broke through into open country. The next day, VII Corps captured Coutances, opening the door to the west. Two days later, on 30 July, VIII Corps, now under the command of General Patton, seized Avranches at the base of the Cotentin Peninsula, and there was nothing in front of him. On 1 August, the Third Army became officially operational. In twenty-four

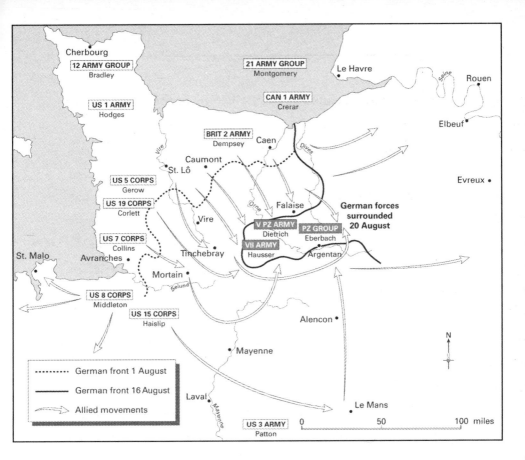

Cherbourg
12 ARMY GROUP Bradley
21 ARMY GROUP Montgomery
Le Havre
Rouen
US 1 ARMY Hodges
Elbeuf
BRIT 2 ARMY Dempsey
Caen
CAN 1 ARMY Crerar
Caumont
St. Lô
Evreux
US 5 CORPS Gerow
US 19 CORPS Corlett
Falaise
German forces surrounded 20 August
Vire
V PZ ARMY Dietrich
PZ GROUP Eberbach
US 7 CORPS Collins
Tinchebray
VII ARMY Hausser
St. Malo
Avranches
Argentan
Mortain
US 8 CORPS Middleton
US 15 CORPS Haislip
Alencon
N
Mayenne
········· German front 1 August
——— German front 16 August
⇢ Allied movements
Laval
Le Mans
US 3 ARMY Patton
0   50   100 miles

hours, Patton pushed three divisions through a five-mile gap at Avranches, out of the bocage country of Normandy and onto the open roads of Brittany.

The Germans soon realized that Operation *Cobra* was the Allies' main thrust, not *Spring*. Panzers were pulled out of the Caen area and sent to close the gap, but they could only move slowly due to lack of fuel. By this time, Operation *Fortitude* was failing. The Germans were slowly coming to doubt that an attack was coming on the Pas de Calais. The real attack had already arrived in Normandy and they began moving their forces westwards.

On 3 August Hitler ordered that the armoured divisions holding the line between the River Orne and the town of Vire be replaced with infantry divisions, freeing the armour to push westwards to Avranches and cut Patton's forces in two. That same day, Patton was given new orders too. Operation *Cobra*, in the original plan, had been designed to secure the ports of Brittany. Now Bradley ordered Patton to send only a small force into Brittany. As a consequence, some of the Brittany ports were not liberated until September. Instead, Patton was to circle to the south and east, outflanking the Panzers that Hitler was sending against Avranches. Meanwhile, Bradley's V Corps and the British VIII Corps began to push towards Vire. It was tough going. VIII Corps was halted two miles outside Vire. The British XXX Corps pushed on, but made such slow progress that Montgomery replaced its commander, Major-General Bucknall, with Lieutenant-General Brian Horrocks, who had commanded XXX Corps in North Africa. Vire eventually fell to America's XIX Corps on 6 August.

By this time the German forces were disintegrating. Although unit names and numbers remained, on the ground men fought in battle groups that had been reduced to the size of a battalion. Men often did not know where they were, and commanders were changed so often that no one knew who was in charge. This did not mean they were a pushover. When the Germans turned and fought they often showed a tactical superiority that, together with the technical superiority of their tanks, could bring an Allied advance to a sudden halt. However, as the fighting became more mobile, the German commanders became more dependent on orders conveyed by radio. This gave the Ultra codebreakers at Bletchley Park a clearer idea of what was going on. Vehicles – even tanks – had to be abandoned due to lack of fuel. Ammunition was running low, particularly for anti-tank guns. The weather was also improving, allowing Allied air forces to attack slow-moving horse-drawn German columns. By 6 August, the German Army Group B had suffered 144,261 casualties and had only 19,914 replacements.

COUNTER-ATTACK AT MORTAIN

Hitler mustered 185 tanks and threw them at Mortain, which was held by the American VII Corps, in the kind of armoured attack that Rommel had said was doomed against Allied air power. No one, with the exception of Hitler, had any faith in the plan. The commander of 116th Panzer Division had to be replaced when he refused to join the attack.

Although Ultra gave the Allies a few hours warning of the attack, the Germans managed to take Mortain and, briefly, held the high ground to the east of the town. Forty of the seventy German tanks spearheading the attack were destroyed by the evening of 7 August and the armoured column ran out of fuel after just five miles. Meanwhile, Patton was making rapid progress, and by 8 August he had taken Le Mans.

On 9 August Hitler ordered the stalled Panzers to hold their position, and two days later the Seventh Army was ordered to push westwards on Avranches. By then, no one on either side thought the Germans could win the battle of Normandy.

Through Ultra, the Allies knew Hitler's plans. A stubborn man, he was not about to order a retreat. This left his entire army in Normandy liable to be encircled. While the British and Canadians pushed south-east and eastwards, cutting off his retreat to the Seine, Patton was told to turn northward, closing the trap.

The Canadians, who were to head first for Falaise, made slow progress against stiff opposition and were halted after nine miles on 11 August, only halfway to their objective. However, the following day, the American XV Corps, driving up from the south, reached Argentan. This gave new heart to the Canadians who pushed on, reaching Falaise on 16 August. The German Seventh Army and their Panzer support were now caught in a pocket. Their only way out was through the twelve-mile gap between Falaise and Argentan. Patton begged Bradley to push on northwards to close the gap but Bradley refused, fearing that he did not have enough men in place to resist any counter- attack that such a move was bound to provoke. The Germans were not unduly worried by their encirclement. They had been surrounded before on the eastern front. However, the Soviets had not enjoyed the overwhelming air superiority that the Allies could call upon to pound their dwindling numbers.

Hitler assembled his Panzer Group Eberbach, under General Eberbach, to make a decisive counter-attack against XV Corps in Argentan. But by the time it was in place, it amounted to no more than four thousand men and forty-five tanks. Field Marshal von Kluge, commander of Army Group B, went missing after his car was attacked by a fighter-bomber. SS General Paul Hausser, recently promoted head of the Seventh Army, temporarily replaced him.

OPERATION DRAGOON

Even Hitler began to lose confidence when the Allies launched Operation *Dragoon*. On 15 August, the Allies began their invasion of the south of France with amphibious landings on the Côte d'Azur. Hitler said it was the worst day of his life. Originally designated Operation *Anvil*, the name had been changed to *Dragoon* by Churchill, who, favouring an attack in the Balkans, felt he had been dragooned into the attack on the south of France by the Americans.

Like the D–Day landings in Normandy, the invasion of the south of France began with an airborne assault. Early in the morning of 15 August, a handful of planes dropped dummy parachutists west of the port of Toulon to confuse the enemy. Meanwhile, to the left of the beach, near St Tropez, Allied craft towed radar-reflecting balloons to make it appear that a huge assault force was arriving to support the airborne assault on Toulon. A French commando team came ashore and cut the road to Toulon, while another team under the movie star Douglas Fairbanks Jr, now a Lieutenant-Commander in the US Navy, landed near Cannes. They came ashore in a minefield, setting off explosions that drew German gunfire. They fled back to their boats, but were mistakenly strafed by Allied planes. Swimming back to the shore, they were then captured by the Germans. But within twenty-four hours they were freed by the Allied invasion.

The 'Devil's Brigade', a Special Services unit made up of Americans and Canadians under Colonel Edwin A. Walker, landed on the Iles d'Hyères to silence the guns there that overlooked one of the beaches, but found they were dummies. However, they met stiff resistance when they moved on Port Cros, the harbour on the western island. This was overcome with the help of salvoes from the fifteen–inch guns of HMS *Ramillies*.

At 0430, the first of 396 Dakotas that had taken off from ten airfields in Italy was over the drop zone – the fields and vineyards around the town of Le Muy, forty miles north-east of Toulon and ten miles inland from the invasion beaches. A low-lying fog convinced some of the paratroopers that they were landing in the sea and they jettisoned heavy equipment and their weapons. It also caused navigational problems for the pilots and one battalion landed ten miles from the drop zone.

At 0920 the first wave of gliders arrived. Two had already been lost on the way. The right wing of one of them had snapped off. As it rolled it broke the tow rope and disintegrated, scattering men and equipment across the sea. No one survived. Another broke its tow rope over the sea, but ditched safely near an Allied ship. Everyone was rescued. The remaining seventy-one dropped into the landing zone at ninety miles per hour. The paratroopers had cleared some of the 'Rommel's asparagus' in the area, but there was nothing they could do about the trees, which caused a great deal of damage and loss of life.

The enemy coastal defences were pounded by naval gunfire. Minesweepers went in to clear a path close to shore. Then radio-controlled boats packed with explosives were sent in to blast a way to the beaches. They were followed by landing craft firing wave after wave of rockets. The 3rd and 45th Infantry Divisions got ashore with little trouble, but the 36th ran into an unexpected minefield on the section of the beaches code-named Camel and withering fire in the Camel Red sector that no amount of naval gunfire could suppress. The fighting was so intense that further waves were diverted further down the beach.

A further 332 gliders arrived at dusk and by the end of the

day some nine thousand British and American soldiers were in position, along with 221 jeeps and 213 artillery pieces. The airborne operation thus far had cost 434 killed and 292 injured. The following day the airborne troops took Le Muy. Further inland they took Draguigan, with the help of the Resistance, and freed members of the *Maquis* the Germans were holding there. They also captured Lieutenant-General Ludwig Bieringer, a corps commander, and his headquarters staff. When the lost battalion rejoined its regiment, they pushed out towards Les Arcs in the west.

On the beaches, the 36th Infantry attacked the defenders of Camel Red beach from the flank and the Allies consolidated their hold. By dusk, forward elements of the amphibious force joined up with the airborne force. By midnight on 17 August the Seventh Army under Lieutenant-General Alexander M. 'Sandy' Patch, a veteran of Guadalcanal, had landed more than 86,500 French and American troops, 12,500 vehicles and 46,100 tons of supplies.

The Allies were also masters of the air in the south of France. Between 16 and 18 August, the Luftwaffe flew only 141 sorties. A landing craft was sunk and at dusk on 18 August five Junkers Ju 88s bombed the American command ship USS *Catoctin*. The attack killed six and wounded forty-two, but did only minor damage to the ship. After that the Luftwaffe withdrew from southern France, leaving the skies to the USAAF, who bombed bridges and strafed road and rail traffic to devastating effect.

The invaders were helped by the Resistance who were strong in the south. They had harassed Panzers moving north for the defence of Normandy, but a premature call for an armed uprising, issued by mistake by de Gaulle's headquarters in London, led to lightly armed guerrillas facing armour and aircraft. The Germans also took their revenge on the civilian population, burning villages and massacring the inhabitants.

The invasion force received invaluable information through Ultra. Bletchley Park decoded a message from General Johannes von Blaskowitz, whose Army Group G held the area from the Italian border to the Pyrenees, ordering the withdrawal of mobile forces and leaving the ports of Toulon and Marseilles defended by garrison troops. Patch gave chase with his main force, while the airborne infantry liberated Cannes and Nice and the French II Corps headed for Toulon and Marseilles.

CLOSING THE FALAISE POCKET

On 16 August, von Kluge reappeared at his headquarters in Normandy. He reported that the Falaise pocket could not be held and that they had to withdraw. Finally, Hitler agreed, but it was too late. The following day a renewed push by the Canadians and the US V Corps, which had taken over from XV in the south, closed the Falaise gap to just a few hundred yards and, despite fierce fighting, on 20 August it was closed altogether. Von Kluge was sacked and summoned to the Wolf's Lair under suspicion of treason. Having a good idea of what was in store there for him, he committed suicide. Field Marshal Walther Model replaced him, but there was little he could do. General Eberbach managed to get some of his formations out of the Falaise pocket, but he was captured on 30 August. SS General Hausser was badly wounded and lost an eye. He escaped from the pocket, but found himself without a command. The Seventh

Army was no more. Those left in the pocket were pulverized by Allied bombing. The stench of rotting flesh was so bad it could be smelt in the planes overhead. Resistance ceased on 22 August.

Visiting the battlefield two days later, Eisenhower said:

The battlefield at Falaise was unquestionably one of the greatest killing grounds of any of the war areas. Roads, highways and fields were so choked with destroyed equipment and with dead men and animals that passage through the area was extremely difficult. Forty-eight hours after the closing of the gap, I was conducted through on foot, to encounter a scene that could be described only by Dante. It was quite literally possible to walk for hundreds of yards at a time, stepping on nothing but dead and decaying flesh.

Some 10,000 Germans were killed in six days in the Falaise Pocket and 50,000 prisoners were taken. Of the 20,000 to 50,000 who escaped, many more were killed before they reached the Seine. Thousands more who were cut off elsewhere gave themselves up. The Allies found 7,700 wrecked or abandoned vehicles in the pocket, not including 567 tanks or self-propelled guns, along with 950 abandoned field guns. Two Panzer divisions and eight divisions of infantry were captured almost complete: the remnants of the eight battle groups of Panzers who had escaped could only muster seventy tanks and thirty-six field guns between them. The destruction was so complete that it was difficult to calculate the scale of the victory. What remained of the German army in western Europe ran headlong for the German border.

THE LIBERATION OF PARIS

While the Allied air forces had been finishing off the Germans in the Falaise pocket, Patton's Third Army had been racing eastward. He crossed the Seine on 19 August. The British and Canadians turned eastwards, reaching the Seine on 25 August. Eisenhower decided that the advancing Allies should bypass Paris to avoid the destruction and loss of life a battle for the city would entail. Hitler had intended to turn the city into a fortress but, given the hopelessness of the German position in France, decided to have the city burnt down.

It was the people of Paris themselves who decided the outcome. For more than four years they had suffered the humiliation of occupation. As if to rub salt in their wounds, every day for the 1,500 days of the occupation, German troops had paraded around the Arc de Triomphe and marched down the Champs Elysées to the Place de la Concorde. Now, with the Allies on French soil, Parisians grew restive. On 10 August, French railwaymen staged the first real strike of the occupation, calling for better food in Paris and higher wages. In response, the Germans shipped their political prisoners out of the city and sent them to concentration camps where most of them died. However, 1,500 Jews found they had been granted a short reprieve when the buses assigned to transport them were sabotaged.

Electric and gas supplies in the city became sporadic and the Metro stopped running. Sensing that trouble was brewing, on 13 August the Germans started disarming the city's 20,000 gendarmes. The policemen responded by going on strike. The Resistance called on them to put aside their uniforms and keep their guns. Otherwise they would be considered traitors. 'The hour of liberation has come', they were told.

Sporadic gunfire began to be heard on the streets of Paris. The Germans reacted swiftly. The SS machine-gunned thirty-five French youths at the Carrefour de Cascades on the night of 16 August. With Paris near to insurrection, Hitler issued an order: 'Paris must not fall into enemy hands, but, if it does, he must find nothing but ruins.' The city's new commandant, Lieutenant-General Dietrich von Choltitz, was instructed to wreck Paris's industrial capacity, blow the bridges over the Seine and destroy the city's famous monuments. All its significant buildings were mined ready for demolition, but von Choltitz stayed his hand. However, when German soldiers were shot at, he threatened to raze entire city blocks and kill the inhabitants in reprisal.

Swedish consul Raoul Nordling intervened to calm the situation and Field Marshal Model gave von Choltitz permission to delay destroying the bridges, which might still be needed in his withdrawal from France. And there seemed no point in inflaming the citizenry, if the city was still to be defended. Von Choltitz still had fifty tanks and a garrison of 22,000 troops. He had been promised another division, which would have made the city a costly objective to take.

The Communists planned an uprising. To pre-empt this the Gaullist Resistance organized two thousand striking policemen to seize the Préfecture de Police near Notre Dame. They hoisted the Tricolor and sang the 'Marseillaise'. Next, they took the Palais de Justice and, when German tanks appeared in the Boulevard de Palais, they were fired upon.

The following day, 20 August, the Gaullists seized the Hôtel de Ville. Nordling had an urgent meeting with von Choltitz in which the commandant granted the Resistance fighters combat status. They would be allowed to hold the buildings they occupied, provided they did not attack the German stronghold in the centre of the city. But the truce could not hold. On the left bank and in other areas no longer under German control the revolutionary cry 'Aux barricades!' went up. The cobblestones were torn up and hundreds of barricades, made from overturned vehicles and felled trees, were manned by Parisians in makeshift uniforms.

The Germans fought back half-heartedly. While tanks machine-gunned buildings, no high-explosive rounds were fired. Their tactics were largely defensive and they never pressed home their attacks. Only the SS seemed to be spoiling for a fight. While the French took prisoners, they murdered theirs.

By 22 August there was open warfare on the streets of Paris in at least three areas. The Resistance begged the Americans for help. Eisenhower ordered Bradley to take the city, fearing that the Germans would use aircraft and tanks against the populace with huge loss of life. By the night of 23 August, the Grand Palais was on fire, hit by an incendiary round, and five hundred Parisians were dead. The Resistance seized the mairies, the borough town halls. The Germans responded by using tanks to machine-gun them. Nevertheless, aside from the Germans' central stronghold, the city appeared to be almost entirely in the hands of the Resistance.

For political reasons, Eisenhower had already ordered that the first unit into Paris was to be the 2nd Free French Armoured Division under Major-General Philippe Leclerc. He sent a message dropped by plane to the Préfecture saying, 'Hold on we are coming'.

However, he made slow progress, losing three hundred men, forty tanks and over a hundred other vehicles in the first day. V Corps commander Major-General Leonard Gerow asked Bradley for permission to send his 4th Infantry Division, which had landed at Utah Beach, to join the assault on Paris. Bradley said, 'To hell with prestige, tell the Fourth to slam on in and take the liberation.'

On the night of 24 August, Leclerc sent an advance party into the city. At 2122, six half-tracks and three tanks arrived at the Hôtel de Ville. Their presence was announced by the ringing of church bells. Von Choltitz called Field Marshal Model's headquarters and held the phone to the window so that he could hear the bells announcing the liberation.

The following morning – D+80 – Leclerc's main force swept into the city from the south-west, while the US Fourth Infantry liberated the east. By 1000 only a few pockets of German resistance remained. Von Choltitz did nothing to further the fighting. On hearing that the Allies had entered the city, Hitler asked, 'Is Paris burning?' Von Choltitz gave no orders to fire the demolition charges and signed documents surrendering the city to Leclerc, then jointly to Leclerc and the Resistance, who had sustained over 2,500 casualties with around 1,000 dead. Some ten thousand Germans were taken prisoner, along with thirty-six tanks.

By noon, Tricolors fluttered from the Arc de Triomphe and the Eiffel Tower. The next day the Free French leader General Charles de Gaulle, who had set up a new administration in Bayeux in June, made a triumphal entry to the city to take control. But Hitler still wanted Paris to burn. That night the

Luftwaffe dropped incendiaries, burning down five hundred houses, killing fifty and injuring five hundred. For Paris it was the worst air raid of the war. Later, on 6 September, the first V-2 rocket would be fired against Paris.

On 27 August, Bradley and Eisenhower entered the city, and on 29 August the US 28th Division made a triumphal march through the city. Meanwhile to the south there had been heavy fighting. Although Toulon and Marseilles were lightly defended by Normandy standards, the Free French faced stiff resistance there. Only the use of heavy naval bombardment allowed them to overcome the Germans, and on 28 August both ports fell into Allied hands. By then the Allies had caught up with Montgomery's original invasion schedule.

During the battle of Normandy, thirty-eight Allied divisions had seen off fifty-one German divisions, though SHAEF computed the Germans' actual combat strength to be equivalent to thirty-three divisions. The cost to the Allies was 209,672 casualties, including 36,976 dead. Another 16,714 aircrew had been lost in the 4,101 aircraft downed over the battlefield. German dead and wounded amounted to some 240,000, along with 200,000 missing or captured. They lost over 3,600 aircraft, 1,500 tanks, 3,500 guns and 20,000 vehicles. Meanwhile, as the Germans fell back in disarray, the Allies grew stronger. By the end of August, they had landed 2,052,299 men, 438,471 vehicles and 3,098,259 tons of stores. A further 380,000 men, 69,000 vehicles, 306,000 tons of supplies and 18,000 tons of fuel had been landed on the *Dragoon* beaches.

VENGEANCE WEAPONS

Until the very end of the war Hitler believed that new weapons could win it for him. And even if they could not, they could be used to revenge himself on his enemies. They became known as vengeance weapons and took the designation 'V'.

The first of these was the FZG-76 – renamed the V-1, a jet-propelled flying bomb and a forerunner of today's cruise missile. They were also known as buzz bombs or doodlebugs. About twenty-five feet long, they carried a 1,870-pound explosive warhead. The wingspan was 17ft 6in and they were launched from fixed ramps around fifty feet long. A piston mechanism propelled them up to a speed of two hundred miles per hour where the jet engine cut in. The simple guidance system was set before launch, so they could not been diverted by jamming or radio interference.

Carrying 150 gallons of fuel, the maximum range was about 130 miles. At that range some eighty per cent would land within eight miles of the designated target, so they were only effective against a big target such as London.

The top speed was about 360 miles per hour and they flew at an altitude of 3,500 to 4,000 feet, making them very difficult for anti-aircraft fire to hit; they were too low for heavy guns and too high for light ones. It was only when automatic power control was applied to British guns that they had any success. Before that the Allies depended on bombing their portable ramps or tipping them off course with the wing of a fighter.

Development of the V-1 began in June 1942 at the research station at Peenemünde on the Baltic. Made from wood and steel, they were designed to be cheap and simple to mass produce,

using little scarce material. Mass production began in March 1944 and about 3,500 were produced before the war's end.

V-1s were first fired against London on 13 June 1945. In all, 9,251 were fired against England, of which 4,621 were destroyed. Another 6,551 were fired at Antwerp after it had fallen into Allied hands, of which most were destroyed.

The research station at Peenemünde also developed a super gun. In 1943, aerial photographic interpreters spotted early signs of construction of batteries of the Hochruckpumpe, Taudendfusil or 'London Gun' in the Pas de Calais. This was a gun with a barrel over 120 metres long that would blast twenty-five kilograms of high explosives over a hundred miles. There were to be two batteries of twenty-five guns, each of which would rain down ten shells a minute on central London. However, in the run-up to D-Day, the United States Ninth Army Air Force destroyed the site and the project was abandoned.

Then came the V-2, which was the forerunner of the space rockets and ballistic missiles we know today. Originally called the A-4, it was one of a series of rockets begun in the early 1930s by Werner von Braun and Walter Dornberger, who both ended up working on the American space programme.

Work on the A series started at the Artillery Proving Ground at Kummersdorf and was later transferred to Peenemünde. The A-2 was the first rocket to fly successfully using liquid fuel. Two were fired from the island of Bokum in December 1934. It was succeeded by the A-3, the first rocket to have a control

Opposite: V-2 Rocket The world's first successful rocket, the V-2 could have turned the war in favour of the Germans, had their launch sites not been targeted by the RAF and the USAAF.

system to maintain its attitude. This made use of a gyroscope. Its design was based on the shape of the German army's standard 7.92mm bullet.

The A-3 was a test vehicle for features of the A-4 and was only fired once. An A-5, powered by hydrogen-peroxide engines and sixteen feet long, was also developed as a test vehicle.

In 1936, work began on the A-4. Forty-seven feet long and weighing 13.6 tons at launch, it was originally designed as a rocket to supplant heavy artillery. The engine burnt alcohol in liquid oxygen, developing 60,000 pounds of thrust. This hurled the rocket over sixty miles into space with a range of 220 miles.

Programmed controls turned the missile onto a predetermined trajectory after launch. Once this had been achieved, the motor shut off, usually after about seventy seconds. It carried around a ton of high explosive, which had simple impact fuses to set off the payload when it hit the ground. The warhead was filled with Amatol, a mixture of ammonium nitrate and TNT. It is a relatively weak explosive, but other mixtures would explode prematurely, usually several thousand feet above the earth. This was caused by air friction heating up the warhead.

The first successful flight took place on 3 October 1942 at Peenemünde where, after some delays, it went into production. After a devastating Allied air raid in August 1943, production was moved to an underground factory at Nordenhausen in the Harz Mountains, where production peaked at nine hundred a month.

The first operational use took place on 6 September 1944, when two were fired at newly liberated Paris. The following day, the bombardment of London began. Some 1,800 V-2s had been stockpiled and it was thought that production would keep up with their use, though Allied air attacks on Germany's railways frequently interrupted supplies.

There was no defence against V-2s. Travelling at supersonic speeds, they were too fast to be detected or destroyed by gunfire. They could be fuelled and prepared for firing under cover and could be launched from any clear space a few yards in diameter. Transported to the launch site by a Meillerwagen, the missile was erected until it stood on its fins on the launch platform. This could be revolved to orientate the gyroscope guidance system. The Meillerwagen was then removed and the firing site cleared. The missile was fired by a simple electrical connection. The whole procedure took only a few minutes, leaving Allied aircraft with no opportunity to locate and bomb the launch site. By the end of the war, the British had failed to come up with any defence against it.

Some ten thousand V-2s were produced. Of these, 1,359 were fired against London, killing some 2,500 people and injuring a further 6,000. Antewerp was hit by 1,351, Liège by 98, Brussels by 65, Paris by 15, 5 were fired at Luxembourg and 11 were fired at Remagen Bridge. The V-2 was the only rocket of the A series to see service during the war, but the A-4b was also developed. This was a winged version which would glide to its target, increasing its range to 280 miles. Two were built but failed their flight tests.

The A-9 was designed, using a motor fuel composed of hydrocarbons and sulphuric acid that would give it a range of four hundred miles. But it was dropped in favour of the A-4, which was easier to manufacture. In 1940, preliminary design

Jet Fighter *The Messerchmitt 262, the most effective fighter of the war. Only the limited numbers produced kept their contribution to the German war effort to a minimum.*

work began on a two-stage rocket. The first stage was the massive A–10, which would carry an A–4 or A–9. The second stage would be launched high in the stratosphere. With a range of 2,800 miles, this could have been used to bombard the eastern seaboard of Canada and the United States.

It could have also been used to carry the atomic bomb the Germans were thought to have been working on. Other teams were developing superbombers with sufficient range to carry out bombing raids across the Atlantic.

While teams of engineers worked on fanciful designs, Messerschmitt managed to develop a practical jet fighter, the Me 262. This might have been the first fully operational turbojet aircraft, instead of Sir Frank Whittle's Gloster Meteor, had its development not been interfered with by Hitler.

The project began in 1938. The first piston-engined prototype flew in April 1941 and the third prototype, using jet power only, took to the air in July 1942. However, development slowed because Nazi leaders saw no need for such an advanced aircraft. It was only when Hitler saw it at an air display in November 1943, that production went ahead. But he did not see it as a fighter. 'That's just what we need for our Blitz bomber,' he said.

The only version given the official go-ahead was the Me 262A-2a *Sturmvogel*, with pylons under the fuselage for two 1,100-pound bombs. However, Messerschmitt continued working on a fighter version called the Me 262A-1a – or *Schwalbe* (Swallow) – in secret. One or two were used by Luftwaffe test pilots on combat missions in July 1944, but the first operational unit was not formed until the end of September.

With a top speed of 540 miles per hour, the Me 262 was powered by two Jumo 004 turbojet engines, each developing 1,980 pounds of thrust. Though powerful, these were unreliable and engine failure and a lack of proper training resulted in high casualties. The standard fighter had four 30mm cannons. By the end of 1944, other versions were flying. There were night-fighters equipped with radar, two-seater bombers, reconnaissance versions, trainers and versions carrying huge 50mm MK 114 guns or R4/N rockets to destroy bombers. One version carried the *Jagdfaust*, an array of twelve mortars that could fire diagonally up at Allied bomber formations. These could have seriously hindered the Allied bombing campaign.

By the end of the war, 1,433 Me 262s had been built, but due to shortages of fuel and pilots, few were actually flown. This was fortunate for the Allies since the Me 262 was the most formidable fighter of the war. In one month in 1945, one unit with just six serviceable Me 262s shot down forty-five of the Allies' newest warplanes. Thanks to the delays in their production, however, there were too few to make a difference.

CHAPTER 12

The Low Countries

By September 1944, the Allied armies in Normandy had linked up with the armies pushing up from the south. Most of France had been liberated, and the Allies were looking to push through Holland and Belgium and on into the Reich itself.

On 1 September 1944, Montgomery formally relinquished command of the Allied forces in France to Eisenhower. And while US forces dashed across France and Belgium towards the German border, Montgomery and his 21st Army Group headed north-eastwards to clear the V-1 and V-2 sites which were raining down flying bombs and ballistic missiles on London, liberate the port of Antwerp and drive into northern Germany.

OPERATION MARKET GARDEN

Normally chided for his caution, Montgomery now planned a bold move. He wanted to use airborne troops to capture five bridges on the road from Eindhoven to Arnhem. He would then drive his Second Army down this corridor across Holland through the German border defences and into the Ruhr, Germany's industrial heartland. The airborne part of the operation was codenamed *Market*, and the infantry and armoured part, *Garden*. So the combined operation became known as Operation *Market Garden*.

The operation was to be mounted within a week. Although he gave the go-ahead, Eisenhower had misgivings. So did Lieutenant-General Frederick Browning, deputy commander of the First Allied Airborne Army. In a planning meeting, he asked how long it would take for the Second Army to relieve the airborne troops holding the last bridge, the bridge at Arnhem. Montgomery said, 'Two days'. Browning studied the map and replied, 'Sir, I think we might be going a bridge too far'.

Five thousand aircraft were assembled for what would be the largest ever airborne operation. Three divisions – the British First Airborne and the US 82nd and 101st Airborne, plus the 1st Polish Parachute Brigade – would be dropped over three days, as there were not enough planes to drop them in one go. The 101st Airborne would land around Eindhoven at the southern end of the corridor. The 82nd would take the central section around Nijmegen. The 'Red Devils' of the First Airborne and the Poles, under Major-General Robert Urquhart, would take the final section at Arnhem. They would have the longest to hold out and, until the Second Army reached them, they would be on their own.

Aerial reconnaissance photographs and reports from the Dutch Resistance indicated that there were Panzers in the area of Arnhem, but the 1st Airborne were briefed to expect weak opposition from second-rate troops. The plan called for the 1st Airborne to take the defenders by surprise by being dropped near the bridge in close formation. But the pilots refused to fly slow, straight and level near the bridge, believing that it was defended by anti-aircraft batteries. Instead, the Red Devils would have to land on areas of open ground to the west of Arnhem, thereby losing the element of surprise.

The huge fleet of aeroplanes and gliders set off on the morning of 17 September. The landings in the early afternoon went well. However, the 1st Airborne soon found that the bunch of old men and boys they had been told they would be up against were actually two combat-hardened divisions of Panzers and a Panzergrenadier battalion armed with the new multi-barrelled, rocket-propelled mortars. But the 1st Airlanding Brigade fought off a German counter-attack and held the landing zone, while

A Bridge too Far British paratroopers, members of 1st Airborne Division, return from the disaster at Arnhem, September 1944. The Paras held out against SS Panzer troops for eight days, waiting in vain for the arrival of the British Second Army.

the 1st Parachute Brigade set out for the bridge. Their progress was hampered by Dutch civilians who treated them as liberators and wanted to ply them with drinks and food and the other spoils of victory. Later they discovered that their radio sets were not working.

The 1st and 3rd Battalions were stopped by heavy enemy fire on the main road, but the 2nd Battalion under Lieutenant-Colonel John Frost advanced quickly along a secondary road alongside the river. The Germans had blown up a railway bridge before they could get to it and a pontoon bridge upstream proved to be unusable. But the main road bridge, their objective, was still standing. As night fell, Frost and his men occupied houses overlooking the bridge's long northern approach ramp.

An attempt to take the bridge was repulsed by the Panzergrenadiers. However, Frost's men prevented the commander of II SS Panzer Corps, under Lieutenant-General Wilhelm Bittrich, sending one of his divisions across it to fight off the Allied attack at Nijemegen. Instead Bittrich tried to get his tanks across the river using a ferry upstream – a slow business – and sent his remaining troops to take the bridge. A fierce gun battle broke out between the SS troops and the paratroopers, the latter managing to destroy a column of twenty- two half-tracks and scout cars that tried to cross the bridge from the south. The Germans brought down artillery fire on Frost's position at the north end of the bridge. Soon the houses there were on fire and the cellars beneath were full of dead and wounded.

Unable to contact his men by radio, Major-General Urquhart left his divisional headquarters in the drop zone. He grabbed a jeep and went to try and find out what was going on. Eventually he caught up with his deputy, Brigadier-General Gerald Lathbury, commander of the 1st Parachute Brigade, who was advancing with the 3rd Battalion. It was then that fierce street fighting broke out. Lathbury was injured in the leg and was taken prisoner, while Urquhart had to hide in an attic overnight until he could make it back to British positions. He then discovered that divisional headquarters had been moved to the Hartenstein Hotel in Oosterbeek, three miles west of Arnhem, and headed there. On the way his jeep was fired upon. When Urquhart arrived, he learnt that, in his absence, he had been reported captured.

During the time he had been missing, the second wave of airborne troops had been delayed by bad weather and the Germans had found a copy of the plan for Operation *Market Garden* in a crashed glider at Nijmegen. They organized a rough reception for the rest of the 1st Airborne when it arrived at 1600 on 18 September.

Urquhart's forces on the ground were scattered and had only rifles, grenades and Sten guns to hold off Tiger and Panther tanks, and self-propelled assault guns. However, the 2nd Battalion was still holding on north of the bridge, though it was taking severe losses. If *Market Garden* had been going to plan, the Second Army should have been nearing the bridge by then. But there was no sign of them.

On 19 September, a renewed effort was made to join up with the 2nd Battalion, but this was halted a mile from the bridge by German reinforcements. The weather intervened again. Most of the 1st Polish Parachute Brigade was delayed. The glider force got through, but it landed in the middle of the battle zone and was caught in the crossfire. With the drop zones now in German hands, Urquhart radioed for supplies to be dropped near his headquarters at the Hartenstein Hotel. But the radio was still not working properly and the message did not get through. Of the 390 tonnes of food, medical supplies and ammunition dropped by the RAF, only thirty-one tonnes arrived in Allied hands.

By nightfall on 19 September, the Second Army had broken through and British tanks were only ten miles away, down the road they were now calling 'Hell's Highway'. But the 1st Airborne were taking terrible punishment and Urquhart took the reluctant decision to pull his scattered forces back into a box around the Hartenstein Hotel, leaving Frost's Second Battalion to fend for itself. Even in this defensive position his lines were only thinly defended and the crossroads at Oosterbeek came under such intensive fire that the 1st Airborne called it the Cauldron.

By the evening of the 20th, the Second Army had still not arrived. Colonel Frost was wounded. Ammunition was running low and he realized that their three-day stand was coming to a close. That night, they were overrun. At dawn on 21 September, Bittrich's Panzers crossed the bridge and went to confront the Second Army. Later that day, the Polish paratroopers were dropped at Driel, south of the river, straight on top of the Germans. Those who escaped headed for a small ferry across the river. When they got there they found it was not working. Some two hundred swam across the river to join Urquhart, while the remainder dug in on the south bank.

Early on the morning of 22 September, a detachment of armoured cars from the Second Army reached Driel and made contact with the 1st Airborne across the river. Over the next two days the British infantry came up, but the situation for Urquhart's men on the north bank was deteriorating. Their stores were running low and attempts to resupply them had failed. The 4th Battalion of the Dorset Regiment tried to cross the river, but failed. Eventually, at 0600 on 25 September, Urquhart was ordered to withdraw. That night, with muffled boots, they slipped down to the Rhine, where a few boats waited to ferry them across.

No one had expected so many men to escape and there was insufficient transport to carry them to the rear. So Urquhart's men, exhausted by eight days of fighting, had to march the eleven miles to the Second Army's main position at Nijmegen. They left behind 1,200 dead, 6,642 wounded, captured or missing. The German casualties were 3,300, of whom a third were dead. The people of Arnhem also suffered. For greeting the British as liberators, the Germans drove the entire population of Arnhem out of the town. They were only able to return the following spring. When they did, they found that their homes had been reduced to rubble.

THE BATTLE FOR HÜRTGEN FOREST

As the Allies raced across northern France, their extended lines of communication began to give them logistical problems. By the time they reached Lorraine in western France, General Patton's Third Army began to bog down. To the north, Lieutenant-General Courtney H. Hodges' First Army hit the defences of Germany's West Wall, which the Allies – not the Germans – called the Siegfried Line. Now defending their homeland, the Wehrmacht turned and fought.

Throughout most of October 1944, Hodges' forces besieged Aachen, finally capturing the city on the 21st. Having breached the West Wall at Aachen, Hodges intended to break out of the high ground east of the city, cross the Rhine River plain and advance to the river itself at Cologne. But first he had to secure his southern flank by clearing the Hürtgen Forest – fifty square miles of dank pine wood where trees grew up to a hundred feet tall. The lower limbs interlocked, keeping advancing troops stooped. The forest floor was devoid of any protective undergrowth and was in almost perpetual darkness. The weather did not make conditions any easier. That autumn it was cold and foggy, and rain, snow and sleet turned the ground into a sea of mud.

The Germans were delighted that the Americans wanted to attack there. Their troops were well dug-in. In the forest the Allies' superiority in artillery and command of the air would be of little use. Better still, the Hürtgen Forest was of little military value. If it was lost to the Americans, it could be flooded, since the Germans controlled the dams above the forest. It was a battle that the Germans could not lose.

The German defenders were battle-hardened veterans, while the Americans were largely teenagers, taken directly from high school and college.

The British General Sir Brian Horrocks was one of the few senior officers to visit the front line. He described the men of 84th Division as 'an impressive product of American training methods … splendid, very brave, tough young men'. But he thought it was too much to ask of green troops to penetrate strong defence lines, then stand up to counter-attacks from first-class German formations. He was also disturbed by the failure of American division and corps commanders and their staffs to ever visit the front lines. Even battalion commanders did not visit the front and had little idea what they were ordering their men to do. They worked from maps and gave orders over the radio and while company and platoon leaders had to be replaced every few weeks – sometimes every few days – due to battle fatigue and casualties, incompetent staff officers remained in place. Horrocks reported that the men were not even getting hot meals brought up from the rear – common practice in the British line.

The attack began on 14 September when the 9th Infantry Division took the town of Lammersdorf on the edge of the forest and the high ground around it. The next objective was Hill 554, which dominated the natural axis of advance through the forest known as the Monschau Corridor. On 19 September 1944, the 3rd Armored and the 9th Infantry Divisions moved into the forest, which was so dense that troops more that a few feet apart could not see each other. Officers soon learned that it was nearly impossible to stay in control of formations larger than a platoon. There were no clearings, only narrow firebreaks and trails, and maps were next to useless.

The Germans were secure in their bunkers. When they saw the GIs coming forward, they called down pre-sighted artillery fire with shells fused to explode on contact with the treetops. As the American dived to the ground for cover, as they had been trained to do, they exposed themselves to a rain of hot metal and wood fragments. The only way to survive was to hug a tree trunk. Then the soldier's steel helmet protected him from the lethal fragments from above.

With air support and Allied artillery almost useless, the GIs plunged on into the mud and minefields with only machine guns and light mortars as support. After several days of fierce fighting, the 39th Infantry Regiment finally took Hill 554. During the fighting, the 9th and 2nd Armored Divisions lost up to eighty per cent of their front-line troops.

On 6 October, the 9th Division resumed its attack up the Monschau Corridor. Its objective was Schmidt, a small town on the far side of the Kall River Valley that sat astride the major road junctions in that part of the forest. After ten more days of bloody fighting, the 9th Division had managed to push only about two miles into the woods. By this time the 9th had suffered some 4,500 casualties.

Despite the losses, the 28th Infantry Division under Major-General Norman 'Dutch' Cota were sent in on 2 November. Originally the Pennsylvania National Guard, the 28th was called the 'Keystone Division' because of their shoulder patch which showed a red keystone, the symbol of Pennsylvania. So many of the 28th fell in the Hürtgen Forest that the Germans called the patch *der blutige Eimer* – the Bloody Bucket. When the 28th tried to move forward, it was like walking into hell, survivors said. From their bunkers, the Germans sent forth a hail of machine-gun and rifle fire and mortars. The GIs were caught in thick minefields. Their advance bogged down. But for two weeks, the 28th kept attacking, as ordered.

On 5 November, division headquarters sent orders for tanks to move down a road called the Kall trail. As usual, no staff officer had gone forward to reconnoitre the situation in person. The trail was a river of mud, blocked by disabled tanks and felled trees. Casualties soared, and by 13 November all the officers in the rifle companies had been killed or wounded – most of them were within a year of their twentieth birthday. In the Hürtgen Forest, the 28th suffered 6,184 combat casualties, plus 620 cases of battle fatigue and 738 cases of trench foot. Virtually every front-line soldier was a casualty. The 28th Infantry Division had essentially been wiped out.

After the war, Wehrmacht General Rolf van Gersdorff said: 'I have engaged in the long campaigns in Russia as well as other fronts and I believe the fighting in the Hürtgen was the heaviest I have ever witnessed.'

When American veterans who had fought in Sicily, Italy, Normandy and Holland finally took the forest, they said they had never seen anything like it for the amount of shattered military equipment scattered throughout and the countless American dead. They named it Death Valley.

But Generals Bradley and Hodges were determined to take the Hürtgen Forest. They put in the 4th Infantry Division, which had come ashore on Utah Beach on 6 June. But it had gone through a score of battles since then, and not many D-Day veterans were still with the division. Most were either dead or in hospital.

Sergeant Mack Morris, who was there with the 4th, described the situation they found it:

Hürtgen had its fire-breaks, only wide enough to allow two jeeps to pass, and they were mined and interdicted by machine-gun fire. There was a mine every eight paces for three miles. Hürtgen's roads were blocked. The Germans cut roadblocks from trees. They cut them down so they interlocked as they fell. Then they mined and booby-trapped them. Finally they registered their artillery on them, and the mortars, and at the sound of men clearing them, they opened fire.

Between 7 November and 3 December, the 4th Infantry Division lost over 7,000 men – about ten per company per day. But still, replacements poured in. One company posted losses at 177 per cent of enlisted men. They had started with a full company of about 162 men and had lost 287.

But it was not just the Germans' stout defence that was to blame for the losses. It was also the fault of the commanders, as Captain John O'Grady of Ninth Army's Historical Section, who visited the forest in late November, outlined in a memorandum:

On 23 November the battalion was attacking a superior German force entrenched on an excellent position. The only thing that higher headquarters contributed to the debacle was pressure, and God only knows where the pressure started, perhaps Corps or perhaps Army. It had the effect of ordering men to die needlessly.

O'Grady was staggered at the commanders' sheer incompetence, saying:

Tactics and manoeuvres on battalion or regiment scale were conspicuous by their absence. It never seemed to occur to anyone that the plan might be wrong; but rather the indictment was placed on the small unit commanders and the men who were

doing the fighting. The companies went into battle against the
formidable Siegfried Line with hand grenades and rifle bullets
against pillboxes. The 84th Division walked into the most touted
defensive line in modern warfare without so much as the benefit
of a briefing by combat officers.

The First Army then put its 8th Infantry Division in. On 27
November, Lieutenant Paul Boesch, Company G, 121st Infantry,
was given orders to take the town of Hürtgen itself. At dawn the
following day, Boesch put one of his lieutenants on one side of
the road leading to the town while he took the other side. Then,
on his signal, Company G charged. Once out of the forest, he
said, the men went mad with battle lust.

Boesch said later of the attack:

It was a wild, terrible, awe-inspiring thing. We dashed, struggled
from one building to another shooting, bayoneting, clubbing.
Hand grenades roared, fires cracked, buildings to the left and
right burned with acrid smoke. Dust, smoke and powder filled
our lungs, making us cough, spit. Automatic weapons chattered
while heavier throats of mortars and artillery disgorged deafening
explosions. The wounded and dead – men in the uniforms of both
sides – lay in grotesque positions at every turn.

The 8th Division did not get far beyond the town before it was
halted. Eventually a regimental staff officer turned up to assess
the situation. 'The men are physically exhausted,' he reported.
'The spirit and will to fight are there; the ability to continue
is gone. These men have been fighting without sleep for four

days and last night had to lie unprotected from the weather in an open field. They are shivering with cold, and their hands are so numb that they have to help one another on with their equipment. I firmly believe that every man up here should be evacuated through medical channels.'

Many were suffering from trench foot. All had colds or worse, along with diarrhoea.

The 2nd Ranger Battalion was brought in. It had landed on Omaha Beach on D-Day. Since then it had taken one hundred per cent casualties. As it moved into the Hürtgen, it immediately began to take casualties from mines and artillery, and the men were left cowering in foxholes.

One of the major objectives in the Hürtgen was Hill 400 in the eastern edge of the forest. The Germans used it as an observation point to bring down artillery and mortar fire on anything that moved around it during the day. On 6 December, orders were given to attack Hill 400.

Under cover of darkness, Ranger companies A, B, C, D, E and F moved to the base of the hill and fixed bayonets. At first light, they charged. Sergeant Bill Petty, one of the few veterans of D-Day, said that what happened that day was worse than 6 June. When he reached the top of the hill with another Ranger named Anderson, they approached the main bunker and heard Germans inside. They pushed open the door and tossed two grenades inside. But before they could rush in and spray the place with bullets, a shell exploded a few feet away. The Germans were firing on their own positions. The shell blew Anderson into Petty's arms. Anderson was dead, killed instantly by a big piece of shrapnel in his heart. Less than an hour later, Anderson's brother – another Ranger – also died in Petty's arms after being hit by German fire.

The Germans were not willing to give up the hill and at 0930, the first of five counter-attacks that day began. Hand-to-hand fighting developed on top of the hill. Field Marshal Model offered Iron Crosses and two weeks' leave to any of his men who could retake the hill; the Americans, however, hung on against all odds.

'We were outnumbered ten to one,' recalled Lieutenant Lomell. 'We had no protection, continuous tons of shrapnel falling upon us, hundreds of rounds coming in.' At one point, Lomell saw his platoon sergeant, Ed Secor, 'out of ammo and unarmed, seize two machine pistols from wounded Germans and in desperation charged a large German patrol, firing and screaming at them. His few remaining men rallied to the cause and together they drove the Germans back down the hill.'

Lomell was already a legend among the Rangers for his bravery on D-Day. In 1995 he said: 'June 6, 1944 was not my longest day. December 7, 1944 was my longest and most miserable day on earth during my past 75 years.'

Ranger numbers dwindled and ammunition began to run out, but US artillery managed to keep the Germans at bay until nightfall. During the night, ammo bearers got to the top of the hill and brought down the wounded, including Lieutenant Lomell, on litters. Casualties were so great that the combined strength of the three companies left on top of the hill was five officers and eighty-six men.

At dawn, the Germans began shelling the hill so intensely that one explosion covered the sound of the next approaching shell. But when the Germans infantry attacked, US artillery and the Rangers' small arms fire drove them back. Eventually, late on 8 December, a tank-destroyer battalion and an infantry regiment relieved the Rangers, who had suffered ninety per cent casualties.

Nine days later, the Germans retook the hill and it was not until February 1945 that the Americans won it back. The battle had lasted ninety days and involved nine American divisions and their supporting units. More than 24,000 Americans lost their lives. There were another nine thousand casualties from trench foot, disease and combat exhaustion. But as the Germans still held the dams, it was a Pyrrhic victory.

THE BATTLE OF THE BULGE

Throughout the summer of 1944, the German army had been on the retreat on all fronts. By then Germany was so weak that even Hitler realized that victory by force of arms was no longer within his grasp. But he thought that if one decisive battle went in his favour the situation might still be turned to Germany's advantage.

A victory on the eastern front was out of the question as the Red Army was too strong. However, the failure of Operation *Market Garden* showed that the western Allies, with their over-extended supply lines, could still be halted; and the debacle in the Hürtgen Forest had shown just how much the Wehrmacht was still capable of. Hitler realized that they would be particularly vulnerable if he hit the Allies between the advancing British and American armies. A decisive victory there might force the Allies to the negotiating table – and they might even be persuaded to join their former enemy to take on Communist Russia together.

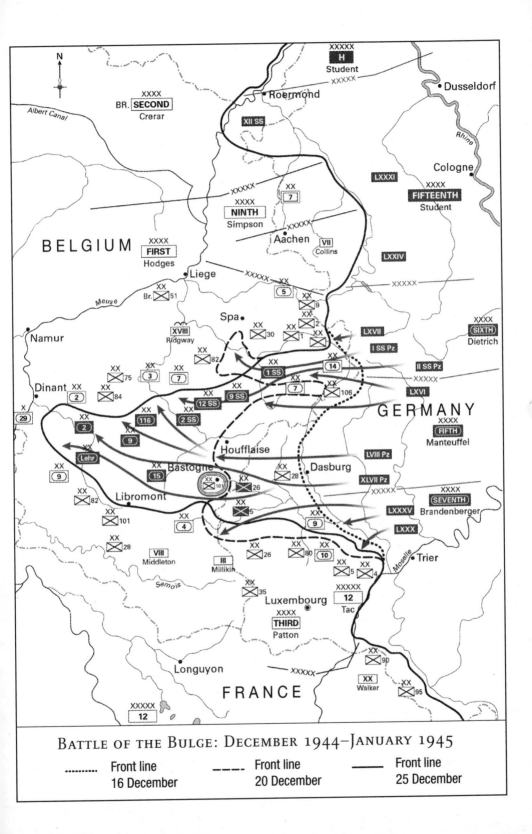

BATTLE OF THE BULGE: DECEMBER 1944–JANUARY 1945

.... Front line   ---- Front line   ——— Front line
16 December   20 December   25 December

On 16 September, while listening to a situation report on the Western Front, Hitler suddenly announced, 'I shall go on the offensive ... out of the Ardennes, with the objective, Antwerp'. An attack through the Ardennes had worked in 1940. As it fell between the British and US sectors, it was only lightly defended. A sweeping attack would sever the American supply lines and cut off the British in Belgium and Holland. The operation was called *Wacht am Rhein* – Watch on the Rhine – and it would put at risk 20 divisions. If it failed, there would be no stopping the Allies.

Hitler and his closest aides planned the operation in secret. When von Rundstedt, who had recently been reinstated as commander in the west, heard about it he was horrified:

> *It was obvious to me that the available force was far too small for such an extremely ambitious plan,* [Rundstedt said after the war.] *It was a nonsensical operation, and the most stupid part of it was setting Antwerp as its goal. If we had reached the Meuse we should have got down on our knees and thanked God, let alone try to reach Antwerp.*

Indeed, von Rundstedt pleaded for a 'little solution' – an offensive that stopped at the Meuse.

Von Rundstedt had sent 2,500 tanks into France on the Blitzkrieg in 1940. Now, against far superior forces, Hitler planned to send just 1,420, which would have to supply their own fuel by capturing American gasoline on the way. The Germans had enjoyed air superiority in 1940. That was now lost. They had had two thousand fighter-bombers back then. In

1944, they had just a thousand. And the Germans no longer had the overwhelming number of men they could call on in 1940. It was the Americans who had the limitless numbers now. By the fourth day of the offensive, US reserves had doubled the number of men in the Ardennes to 180,000. But, running true to form, Hitler ignored what the professional soldiers told him and decided to go ahead. However, he was persuaded to change the name of the operation from *Wacht am Rhein* to *Herbstnebel* (Autumn Fog) and delay the attack from 25 November to 10 December, then to 16 December to muster enough troops for the offensive.

Spearheading the breakout would be the Fifth Panzer Army under General Hasso von Manteuffel and the newly formed Sixth SS Panzer Army under *Oberstgruppenführer* Joseph 'Sepp' Dietrich. They would be supported by the Seventh Army under General Erich Brandenberger. The Panzers would attack on a ninety-mile front from Echtnernach in the south to Monschau in the north. The Fifth Panzer Army would be on the left, the Sixth on the right, while the Seventh Army would protect the armour's southern flank.

To blunt any counter-offensive, Hitler sent a hand-picked force of English-speaking troops behind the Allied lines carrying American weapons and wearing US uniforms. They would disrupt the Allied forces by misdirecting traffic and switching signposts. Their commander would be SS *Standartenführer* Otto Skorzeny, who had recently headed the daring raid to rescue Mussolini from his mountain prison, allowing Hitler to set up the Italian dictator in a new Fascist state in northern Italy.

Although Hitler was ill and exhausted, he switched his

headquarters from the Wolf's Lair in East Prussia to the Eagle's Lair near Bad Neuheim in the Rhineland, where he would direct the battle personally. He had been in the Eagle's Lair in 1940 when the German offensive had crushed the Allies in France. Those who accompanied him were increasingly of the opinion that he was rapidly losing touch with reality.

In November, while preparations were underway, the Allies had breached Germany's 'West Wall' frontier defences – the Siegfried Line – and had taken Aachen, the first German town of any size to fall to the Allies. However, the Allies were beginning to show signs of hubris. The front Hitler planned to hit was manned by just four divisions of the US VIII Corps, under Major-General Troy Middleton. They were spread thinly. The 4th and 28th Divisions had just been pulled out of the line to recuperate after heavy fighting, while the 9th Armoured and the 106th Division had never seen action before. On either side of the Ardennes front were the inexperienced and under-strength First, Third and Ninth Armies of General Omar Bradley's 12th US Army Group. This hardly seemed to matter as army intelligence ruled out a German offensive in this area, despite the lesson of 1940. These men were about to be hit by three German armies – twenty-five divisions in all, eleven of them armoured.

Eisenhower was taken completely by surprise when, at 0535 on 16 December, two thousand guns opened up in the Ardennes. The Germans attacked with a message from von Rundstedt ringing in their ears. It read:

Soldiers of the Westfront. Your great hour has arrived. Large attacking armies have started against the Anglo-Americans.

I do not have to tell you anything more than that. You feel it yourselves. We gamble everything. You carry the sacred obligation to give everything to achieve things beyond human possibilities for our Fatherland and our Führer.'

The offensive took place during a period of bad weather when the Allied air forces were grounded, and the Germans quickly developed a salient fifty miles deep in the American lines. Churchill quickly dismissed this as 'The Battle of the Bulge', a title he had first given to the 1940 Ardennes offensive. This time it stuck.

Skorzeny's troops in American uniforms went in first. They fooled no one and most of them ended up facing a firing squad. Seventh Army was held up not far from their starting point, but the Panzers did better. The Sixth SS Panzers struck through what was called the Losheim gap and made significant gains, which they could not exploit due to lack of fuel. The Fifth Panzer Army swept through the 28th and 106th Divisions, reaching Celles, six miles short of the River Meuse, where it was halted when the weather cleared and the Allied air forces took to the air again. The Fifth Panzers' supply route ran through the town of Bastogne, which was held by the 101st Airborne Division under Brigadier-General Anthony McAuliffe. He found himself completely surrounded in what was called 'the hole in the doughnut'. When called upon by the Germans to surrender, he famously responded, 'Nuts.' The 101st held out for six days, supplied by air drops.

By 19 December, the offensive was stalled, but Hitler refused von Rundstedt's suggestion that part of Manteuffel's Fifth

Panzers should be moved north to support Dietrich's Sixth SS Panzers who had done marginally better. Hitler wanted the SS to have all the glory. At a meeting at Verdun on the same day, Eisenhower told his generals, 'The present situation is to be regarded as one of opportunity for us and not disaster. There will be only cheerful faces at this conference table.' The outcome of the meeting was to shift Patton's Third Army 150 miles north to the left flank of the salient, while Montgomery, newly promoted to Field Marshal, would attack the northern side with some of Bradley's troops temporarily assigned to his command.

Although on 21 December the Fifth Panzers took the town of St Vith, von Rundstedt felt the advance had run out of steam. On 22 December, he asked Hitler's permission to withdraw. It was refused. On Christmas Day, the Sixth SS Panzers suffered a crushing defeat and the following day Bastogne was relieved, at the cost of 3,900 American dead and 12,000 Germans. The Americans lost 150 tanks in the action; the Germans, 450.

Hitler had no choice but to withdraw now as German atrocities had inspired the US troops to fight with renewed determination. In the advance guard of the German assault was *Standartenführer* Jochen Peiper, commanding 140 tanks and a battalion of motorized infantry. At Honsfeld, his men shot nineteen GIs and robbed their dead bodies. At an airfield near Bullingen, Peiper forced captured Americans to refuel his tanks. Afterwards, he shot them. Eight more prisoners of war were killed at Lignueville. A hundred American prisoners were machine-gunned in Malmédy. Twenty Americans who miraculously escaped hid in a café. It was set on fire and they were machine-gunned when they ran out. Hitler thought that news of these massacres would demoralize the American troops. In fact, it gave them a first-class incentive to fight back. By early January 1945, the front line was almost back where it had been before the Battle of the Bulge. Hitler claimed that *Herbstnebel* had been worth it, but the autumn fog had been dispersed by the crisp air of winter. The Germans had lost 10,000 men, the Americans 81,000 and the British, who played only a minor part in the action, 1,400. The Americans had also lost 733 tanks, the Germans 600, and an enormous number of guns and other equipment had been lost. However, the complete destruction of German cities by relentless bombing meant that the Germans could not replace their equipment. The Allies could. All Hitler had bought with the loss of his final strategic reserve was six weeks to prepare the defences on the Rhine.

THE CROSSING OF THE RHINE

By the time the Allied forces reached the frontier of Germany, the total defeat of Hitler's Third Reich was only a matter of time. But, for the British and American forces there was still one huge obstacle to overcome – the fast-flowing River Rhine which ran along much of Germany's western border.

In the early weeks of March 1945, the US First and Ninth Armies reached the Rhine, and a unit of the First Army, finding the railway bridge at Remagen only lightly defended, swept across on 7 March. On 22 March Patton's Third Army established a bridgehead near Nierstein, ready for a drive across southern Germany. To the north, Montgomery's 21st Army Group had also reached the Rhine and halted while the western bank was cleared. On the other side of the river were

Across the Rhine *US Seventh Army soldiers crossing the Rhine near Mannheim, March 1944.*

five divisions of Hitler's elite paratroopers, with one Panzer division and one Panzergrenadier division as a mobile reserve. They were a formidable force and it was feared that they would be highly motivated as they were now fighting for their home territory. After Arnhem, Montgomery had resumed his cautious demeanour, and he was determined to cross the Rhine with the minimum loss of life for his men.

Montgomery planned an airborne assault called Operation *Varsity,* using the US Seventeenth Airborne and the British Sixth Airborne, and an amphibious assault called Operation *Plunder,* using the British Second Army and the US Ninth Army under his command. The airborne troops would seize the high ground, overlooking the crossing points, on the other side of the river, to prevent the Germans deploying artillery there. To gain the element of surprise, he would reverse the normal order of things, with the airborne assault going in after the amphibious landings. First, bombers from the US Eighth and Ninth Air Forces would cut off the Ruhr on the other side of the river to prevent the Germans from bringing up reinforcements, while a thousand fighter-bombers of the Second Tactical Air Force would provide close air support.

At dawn on 24 March, the British Second Army crossed the Rhine. By that time, the British paratroopers had already left their bases in southern England. Meanwhile, the US troops, resting in Paris after the Battle of the Bulge, enplaned at seventeen bases around Rheims, Orléans, Evreux and Amiens. The two forces met up over Brussels. Between them they had 1,696 transport planes and 1,348 gliders, carrying 21,700 men, 600 tonnes of ammunition and 800 guns and vehicles. They were protected by a close escort of 889 fighters.

Airborne operations had been going on throughout the war, but there were still two schools of thought concerning tactics. The US forces liked to drop their airborne troops and release their gliders as low as possible to reduce the time they spent in the air, where they were particularly vulnerable. The British preferred to drop their airborne troops and release gliders high, to reduce the chances of the planes being hit by anti-aircraft fire. Both tactics worked in their fashion during Operation *Varsity*. The US suffered fewer casualties, but lost more planes. This was partly because they were using the Curtis C-46 Commando for the first time because it had two doors for the paratroopers to jump from, instead of the C-47 Dakota's one. But it also had a tendency to catch fire and was never used for paratroop drops again. However, flak suppression from the Allied artillery was so good that only forty-six transport planes and three per cent of the forty gliders were lost.

Both the British and American parachutists went in twenty minutes after the amphibious assault began. The British gliders followed three-quarters of an hour later, the American gliders forty-three minutes after that. The British 3rd Parachute Brigade landed on the left, to the north of the village of Bergen. They came under heavy fire from anti-aircraft guns, which were being used as ground support, but succeeded in taking the village of Schappenburg. The Fifth Parachute Brigade suffered casualties during the drop. They landed near the woods on the Hammiklen-Rees road and rapidly moved on to take their objectives. The Sixth Airlanding Brigade also sustained casualties in the air. They landed in open fields to the south of Hammiklen. Their objective was the village itself.

Even though the American paratroopers were dropped lower, when they hit the ground they were more dispersed. Two battalions of the 507th landed in the drop zone between Diersfordterwald and the Rhine. However the third battalion and the regimental headquarters landed well to the north. They found themselves just short of Diersfordt. A fierce firefight erupted and the Germans put up stiff resistance for most of the day until, at about 1500, they surrendered.

The 513th also landed north of their designated drop zone and found themselves alongside the right-hand battalion of the 6th Airlanding Brigade and 13th Devons. Together they secured the British objective, Hammiklen village, before the 513th moved on to take its own objectives.

During the airborne operation, the British lost 347 killed and 731 wounded; the Americans, 159 killed and 522 wounded. Some 3,789 German prisoners were taken and the 84th Division was practically annihilated. By dusk the airborne troops had joined up with the Second Army's amphibious forces. German resistance, initially stiff, was soon overcome, though the Allies took heavy casualties. Montgomery has been on occasion criticized for using such a great force to achieve so little. However, with the Allies now moving onto Germany's own soil, it was perhaps not unwise to think that the Germans might put up the fight of their lives. By this time, though, most Germans wanted to see the western Allies sweep through Germany as quickly as possible, rather than let it fall to the Russians. Having suffered terribly at German hands, the Soviets would be bent on revenge. And no one wanted to institute Hilter's scorched earth policy in front of the advancing Allies. On 25 March the German Fifteenth Army, containing the bridgehead at Remagen, collapsed. The American First Army then broke through. The Third Army crossed the River Main at Aschaffenburg and Hanau. Then the First and Third Armies used the Autobahn system, which Hitler had built to move his troops, to race across southern Germany. On 15 April 1945, near where the Rhine crossing had been made at Bergen, horrified British troops found a concentration camp: Bergen–Belsen.

THE LIBERATION OF BELSEN AND DACHAU

On 7 April 1945, the head of the Reich Security Office Ernst Kaltenbrunner, the highest-ranking SS officer after Himmler, sent an order directly to the commandant of the Bergen–Belsen concentration camp, Josef Kramer, that all the prisoners in the camp should be killed, rather than let them fall in the hands of the enemy. The order was said to have come from Hitler himself. When news reached representatives of the World Jewish Congress in Stockholm, they got a message to Himmler persuading him to reverse the order. When Hitler heard this, he flew into a rage.

The camp was situated between the villages of Bergen and Belsen, near Celle in Lower Saxony. It was not an extermination camp – there were no gas chambers there – but some 37,000 prisoners had died in the camp from starvation, overwork and disease, and their corpses had been flung into mass graves. Among them was fifteen-year-old Anne Frank, whose wartime diary would later become world famous. She had died of typhus in March 1945, while the Allied armies were massing only a matter of miles away.

The camp had been designed to house ten thousand, but throughout the war it had been hugely overcrowded. On 8 April 1945, around 25,000 to 30,000 prisoners arrived from other concentration camps in the area bringing the total population to over 60,000. Some had to be housed in the barracks of the adjacent army training centre. Up until this time, the Nazis had evacuated the concentration camps and destroyed them before they were overrun. Indeed, the Geneva Convention specified that civilian prisoners were to be evacuated from war zones. But this time it was not possible to evacuate all the prisoners from Bergen-Belsen for fear that the diseased inmates would spread an epidemic among the German soldiers. However, between 6 and 11 April 1945, three transports of Jews carrying foreign passports were evacuated, leaving behind 41,000 people in a pitiful state.

The British heard about the camp soon after they crossed the Rhine in March 1945, and opened negotiations for the transfer of its control. This took several days, and on the night of 12 April a cease-fire was signed between the local Germany military commander and the British chief of staff, Brigadier General Taylor-Balfour. An area eight kilometres long and six kilometres wide around the camp was declared a neutral zone. Until the British troops could take over, the camp would be guarded by a unit of Hungarian soldiers and soldiers from the German regular army. They would be given free passage to the German lines within six days of the British arrival.

The SS guards were also to remain at their posts until the British took over. In fact, most donned civilian clothes and prepared to escape. However, eighty SS men and women remained behind. They tried to fix up the camp and dispose of the thousands of bodies that lay in various stages of decomposition all over the camp. A mass grave was dug around a kilometre from the barracks and, between 11 and 14 April, all prisoners in the camp who could still work were conscripted to bury the corpses. While the camp's two orchestras played dance music, two thousand inmates used leather straps or strips of cloth tied to the wrists or ankles to drag the corpses to the grave. This went on from six in the morning until dark for four days. But when the British arrived, there were still ten thousand rotting corpses littered around the camp.

On the night of 14 April 1945, Rudolf Küstermeier lay awake in his bunk in Bergen-Belsen, only falling asleep in the small hours. Küstermeier, a Social Democrat, had been arrested in 1933 for illegal activities against the Nazi regime and sentenced to ten years in prison. After serving his sentence, he was sent to a concentration camp as an enemy of the state and had been transferred to Bergen-Belsen from Sachsenhausen near Berlin in early February. Küstermeier later recalled:

> *Suddenly I was woken up by one of the Russian workers in our block. He said: "Come, come, quick! There are tanks on the street." I heard the unmistakable clanking, rumbling noise...From far I heard the tanks pass through the camp entrance and a voice call from a loudspeaker van. I knew we were free. I lay there musing. Incessantly I had to fend off fleas and bugs who did not stop torturing me for a minute. I was feverish and my head was heavy and stupefied, but I was aware of the fact that we were free. More than eleven years of imprisonment were over. I lived. I would have a chance to recover. I would be able to participate in the tasks of reconstruction. I did not think of revenge but I knew that the most devilish tyranny the modern world had seen had lost its last footing, and that there would be a chance now for new men and a new life. I was filled with a deep sense of gratitude.*

On the afternoon of Sunday 15 April, British soldiers arrived at the German army training centre and the camp was handed over. Soon after, a party of British officers entered the concentration camp. They were accompanied by a loudspeaker van from Fourteen Amplifier Unit, Intelligence Corps and men of the 63rd Anti-Tank Regiment, Royal Artillery. Among them was Chaim Herzog, a young Jewish officer with the Intelligence Corps; he later became Israel's Ambassador to the UN.

In freshly pressed uniforms, Commandant Kramer and his

assistant, Irma Grese, greeted Captain Derrick Sington at the entrance to the camp. Kramer said he wanted to collaborate with the British and expressed his desire for an orderly transition, even offering advice as to how to deal with the 'unpleasant situation'. He was arrested, put in leg-irons and was tried by a British military tribunal as a war criminal five months later.

The British already knew about the epidemics that were raging in the camps, so Brigadier Llewelyn Glyn-Hughes, a medical officer, was put in command of the relief operation. But even he was ill-prepared for the gruesome sight that greeted them. Glyn-Hughes said of the liberation:

> *The conditions in the camp were really indescribable. No description nor photograph could really bring home the horrors that were there outside the huts, and the frightful scenes inside were much worse. There were various sizes of piles of corpses lying all over the camp, some in between the huts. The compounds themselves had bodies lying about in them. The gutters were full and within the huts there were uncountable numbers of bodies, some even in the same bunks as the living. Near the crematorium were signs of filled-in mass graves, and outside to the left of the bottom compound was an open pit half-full of corpses. It had just begun to be filled. Some of the huts had bunks but not many, and they were filled absolutely to overflowing with prisoners in every state of emaciation and disease. There was not room for them to lie down at full length in each hut. In the most crowded there were anything from six hundred to a thousand people in accommodation which should only have taken a hundred.*

There were no bunks in a hut in the women's compound which now housed those suffering from typhus. The sick lay on the floor and were so weak they could hardly move. There was practically no bedding. Some patients had a thin mattress, but most had none. Others had draped themselves in blankets. Nearly a quarter of the people in Belsen died of typhus.

The wooden barracks were about 160 feet, each housing some seven thousand people. The beds were mere planks of wood. Poorly constructed, the huts had no windows or doors and effectively became wind tunnels in winter. The roofs leaked and the straw scattered on the floor was sodden. When the Nazis were in charge, inmates had been forced to stand outside for roll-call each day. This could take up to four hours, and in the depths of winter many fell down dead. The camp was so lice-ridden that the inmates' clothes appeared to move on their own. Victims scratched themselves on the struts that held the huts together and developed open sores and boils, which became infected.

One witness to the liberation was Iolo Lewis, a twenty-year-old British soldier from Wales. He recalled that when his comrades pushed sweets and cigarettes through the wire, the inmates fell on them with such ferocity that some were left dead on the ground, torn to pieces in the scramble. Lewis counted thirteen thousand unburied corpses and he said that the memory of what he saw there never left him.

On the day of the liberation, starving inmates plundered the kitchen and food stocks, leaving no food in the camp. Wehrmacht soldiers had to shoot into a ravening mob, killing many, and a number of the detested Kapos were lynched.

On 17 April, British medical units arrived and set up a hospital in the barracks of the Germany army training camp. The British then arrested the fifty SS men and thirty women who had stayed behind, and a Jewish Camp Committee was set up under the leadership of Josef Rosensaft.

The following day, the SS captives were forced at gunpoint to start loading the dead onto trucks while screaming mobs of inmates looked on. The corpses were then bulldozed into mass graves. The SS prisoners were not given any protective clothing and had to handle the bodies of those who had died from contagious diseases with their bare hands. Many later died of typhus. Meanwhile the conditions in the camp were being filmed for newsreels that would be shown around the world.

The evacuation of the camp began on 21 April. After being deloused, the inmates were moved into the barracks of the German army training centre next door. Later, the residents of Bergen were forced to leave their homes and Jewish inmates moved in. The Germans were ordered to leave all their china, linen and silverware for the former prisoners' use.

On 23 April, six detachments of the Red Cross arrived to help. Epidemics were still raging, with between four and five hundred prisoners dying each day. This began to abate after 28 April, when the SS guards had finished burying the dead. The following day they were taken to prison in Celle.

On 25 April, German civilians from the neighbouring towns of Bergen and Belsen were brought to the camp. Before they were given a tour of the grim sights, a British officer delivered a speech:

What you will see here is the final and utter condemnation of the Nazi party. It justifies every measure the United Nations will take to exterminate that party. What you will see here is such a disgrace to the German people that their names must be erased from the list of civilized nations...It is your lot to begin the hard task of restoring the name of the German people... But this cannot be done until you have reared a new generation amongst whom it is impossible to find people prepared to commit such crimes; until you have reared a new generation possessing the instinctive good will to prevent a repetition of such horrible cruelties. We will now begin our tour.

At the end of the month, ninety-seven medical students arrived in Bergen-Belsen to help with the sick prisoners, and on 4 May – the day the German army in that area surrendered – more British medical units arrived. But inmates continued to die, despite their best efforts. Nine thousand died in the first two weeks after the liberation; another four thousand died in May. Because of the danger of the epidemic spreading, their bodies were also thrown into mass graves, even when their identities were known.

By 19 May, all the former inmates had been evacuated. Two days later, the last hut burned to the ground. In July 1945, six thousand survivors were taken to Sweden to recover from their ordeal. Some stayed there for up to three years recovering from typhus.

The former inmates of Bergen-Belsen who wanted to return to their home countries were released from the camp, but had to find their way home by themselves. Those who wanted to go to Palestine had to stay in the Displaced Persons Camp at the German army training centre and await permission from the British, who controlled Palestine at that time. This was the largest DP camp in Europe and remained open until 1950.

The concentration camp at Dachau, twelve miles north of Munich, had to wait another two weeks before it was liberated by the American Seventh Army on 29 April 1945. Lieutenant-Colonel Walter Fellenz of 42nd Division recalled the scene:

Several hundred yards inside the main gate, we encountered the concentration enclosure itself. There before us, behind an electrically charged, barbed wire fence, stood a mass of cheering, half-mad men, women and children, waving and shouting with happiness – their liberators had come. The noise was beyond comprehension! Every individual who could utter a sound was cheering. Our hearts wept as we saw the tears of happiness fall from their cheeks.

Opened in 1933, just five weeks after Hitler came to power, Dachau had been a 'model camp' which was shown off to dignitaries, including some from America. It consisted of a main camp just outside the town and 123 sub-camps and factories around the town. These were liberated in the days that followed. What the US troops found was not the detention centre for communists and other political prisoners that it had been before the war, but a hellhole crammed with prisoners transported from other camps before they had been overrun. Conditions there had never been pleasant, but worsened considerably as Allied bombing destroyed supply lines for food and medicine.

Fifty-four deaths had been recorded at Dachau in January

1944, and 101 in February. But in January 1945 there were 2,888 deaths, and 3,977 deaths in February. Disposing of the dead became an impossible task. By the time the Seventh Army arrived, there was no coal left for the crematorium. Bodies had been left lying on the ground naked; their clothes had been stripped from them to give to the living.

On 26 April, three days before the Americans arrived, the last roll-call showed that there were 30,442 prisoners in the main camp and 37,223 in the subcamps. On Hitler's orders, the commandant of Dachau, Martin Gottfried Weiss, tried to evacuate the Dachau main camp that day – 1,759 Jewish prisoners were put on a train and 6,887 other prisoners, half of them Jews, began a forced march south to the mountains.

One of the prisoners who survived this march was Samuel Pisar, who was thirteen years old when the Bialystock ghetto in northeastern Poland was liquidated. His father was shot by the Gestapo. He was sent to the extermination camp at Majdanek, then Auschwitz where his mother and younger sister had already perished. He was given a job working near the crematoria at Birkenau within earshot of the cries of the dying. When Auschwitz was evacuated in January 1945, Pisar was one of the prisoners on the death march out of the camp. On the forced march out of Dachau, he managed to escape when American planes strafed the column. When he gave himself up to American soldiers, he had just turned sixteen.

Another survivor of the march out of Dachau was Jack Adler, who was just fifteen at the time. His twelve-year-old sister had been gassed at Auschwitz. In all, seventy-eight members of his extended family had perished in the Holocaust. Adler was saved from the gas chamber because he was selected for medical experiments, but he moved himself to another barrack where the inmates were slave labourers. He survived the march out of Auschwitz in January 1945 and was eventually brought to Dachau. When he was liberated from the march by American soldiers, he weighed only sixty-six pounds.

But while the SS were trying to evacuate Dachau, more prisoners were on their way, including between 1,100 and 2,500 survivors of the camp at Buchenwald. The emaciated bodies of the dead were still on the train when the Americans arrived, and more emaciated corpses were piled up inside the crematorium, outside the prison enclosure.

Lieutenant-Colonel Felix Sparks of the 45th Infantry Division later recalled:

During the early period of our entry into the camp, a number of I Company men, all battle-hardened veterans, became extremely distraught. Some cried, while others raged. Some thirty minutes passed before I could restore order and discipline. During that time, the over thirty thousand camp prisoners still alive began to grasp the significance of the events taking place. They streamed from their crowded barracks by the hundreds and were soon pressing at the confining barbed wire fence. They began to shout in unison, which soon became a chilling roar. At the same time, several bodies were being tossed about and torn apart by hundreds of hands. I was told later that those being killed at that time were 'informers'. After about ten minutes of screaming and shouting, the prisoners quieted down. At that point, a man came forward at the gate and identified himself as an American soldier. We immediately let him out. He turned out to be Major Rene Guiraud of our OSS [Office of Strategic Services, America's first intelligence agency, forerunner of the CIA]. *He informed me that he had been captured earlier while on an intelligence mission and sentenced to death, but the sentence was never carried out. I sent him back to regimental headquarters.*

Guiraud was one of eleven Americans who had been held at Dachau and was set up as head of the prisoners. He had to explain to them that they could not leave the camp until they had been deloused and given proper food and medical care.

Among the 2,539 Jewish prisoners liberated at Dachau was William Weiss, who had survived while his parents, grandparents, two sisters, ten aunts, ten uncles and forty cousins had all perished in the Holocaust. Weiss himself had narrowly escaped being sent to the death camp at Belzec, and had then escaped from the Janowska camp, near Lvov, the first night he was there. He survived a year in a Gestapo prison in Lvov before being sent to the death camp at Auschwitz in 1943. He then survived the fifty-mile death march out of Auschwitz in the dead of winter in January 1945, before ending up in Dachau.

Another Jewish survivor was Karel Reiner, the Czech composer and pianist. He had survived the Theresienstadt ghetto and Auschwitz before arriving at Dachau.

According to the official Seventh Army report, Poles were the largest ethnic group among the survivors. There were 9,082 Polish Catholics, including ninety-six women, in Dachau on liberation day. Many had been brought to Germany to work as slave labourers. One of them was John M. Komski, who had survived Auschwitz, Buchenwald, Gross- Rosen and a death march from the Hersbruck sub-camp of Nordhausen before arriving at Dachau on 26 April 1945. And fourteen-year-old Polish orphan Stephan Ross had survived ten different concentration camps before being liberated at Dachau.

Among the VIP prisoners newspaper reporters expected to find in Dachau was the Reverend Martin Niemöller, who had famously said:

> *First they came for the Communists, and I didn't speak up, because I wasn't a Communist. Then they came for the Jews, and I didn't speak up, because I wasn't a Jew. Then they came for the Catholics, and I didn't speak up, because I was a Protestant. Then they came for me, and by that time there was no one left to speak up for me.*

Niemöller had preached against the Nazi persecution of the Jews and defied the Nazis when Hitler banned Jewish converts becoming ministers in the Protestant Church. After being tried for treason, he was sent to Sachsenhausen concentration camp as an enemy of the state, then transferred to Dachau. However, he had been released along with a number of Catholic priests a few days before the camp was liberated.

According to the official report by the US Army, there were 31,432 survivors in the main camp on that day. But just as in Belsen, a typhus epidemic was raging. When the Americans arrived at the gate, nine hundred prisoners were already on their death beds. Eleven of the barracks had been converted into a hospital to house the 4,205 sick prisoners. Another 3,866 prisoners were bed-ridden. In the period after the camp was liberated, between one and two hundred inmates died every day, and American troops had to prevent the freed prisoners leaving the camp to stop the typhus epidemic from spreading throughout the country. In the following weeks, 2,422 died.

As the Americans examined the camp, they came across more grim evidence. Outside the prison compound, behind concrete ditches and electric barbed wire fences, they found a gas chamber area, hidden from the inmates by a line of poplar trees.

Lieutenant William Cowling wrote:

Several newspaper people arrived about that time and wanted to go through the camp so we took them through with a guide furnished by the prisoners. The first thing we came to were piles and piles of clothing, shoes, pants, shirts, coats, etc. Then we went into a room with a table with flowers on it and some soap and towels. Another door with the word 'showers' led off of this and upon going through this room it appeared to be a shower room but instead of water, gas came out and in two minutes the people were dead. Next we went next door to four large ovens where they cremated the dead. Then we were taken to piles of dead. There were from two to fifty people in a pile all naked, starved and dead. There must have been about a thousand dead in all.

The Americans also found laboratories where Nazi doctors had performed gruesome medical experiments on human guinea pigs. The perpetrators were tried at Nuremberg and seven were sentenced to death.

CHAPTER 13

From the Rhine to the Elbe

*By March 1945, the Western Allies were in possession
of most of the west bank of the Rhine, and had forced a
crossing at Remagen. The last great natural frontier was
exposed, and the way to Berlin now lay open.*

On 8 March 1945, nearly two months before the surrender
in Italy, Field Marshal Kesselring was relieved of his
command. The following afternoon he met Hitler, who told
him that the American First Army had crossed the Rhine at
Remagen. As a result, Field Marshal von Rundstedt was to be
sacked as commander-in-chief in the West and replaced by
Kesselring himself.

'Without attaching any blame to Rundstedt,' said Kesselring,
'Hitler justified his action with the argument that a younger
and more flexible leader, with greater experience of fighting the
Western powers, and still possessing the troops' full confidence,
could perhaps make himself master of the situation in the west.
He was aware of the inherent difficulties of assuming command
at such a juncture, but there was no alternative but for me to
make this sacrifice in spite of the poor state of my health. He
had full confidence in me and expected me to do all that was
humanly possible.'

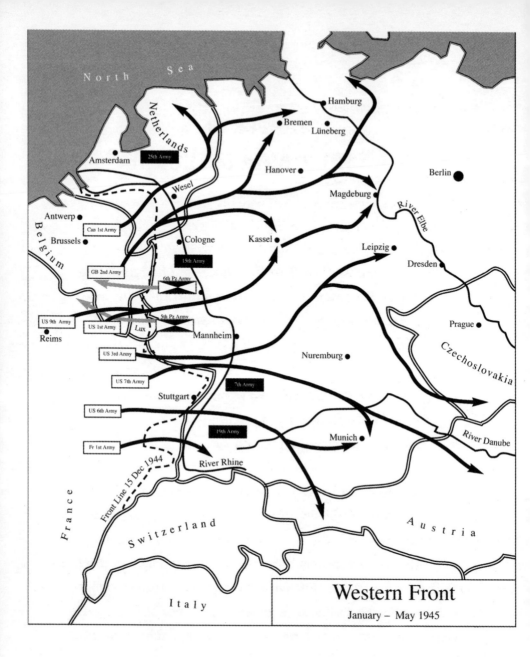

Western Front
January – May 1945

Labels on map: North Sea, Netherlands, Amsterdam, Antwerp, Brussels, Belgium, Reims, France, Switzerland, Italy, Wesel, Cologne, Kassel, Hanover, Bremen, Hamburg, Lüneberg, Magdeburg, Berlin, Leipzig, Dresden, Prague, Czechoslovakia, River Elbe, Mannheim, Lux, Nuremburg, Stuttgart, Munich, Austria, River Danube, River Rhine, Front Line 15 Dec 1944

Army labels: 25th Army, Can 1st Army, GB 2nd Army, 15th Army, 6th Pz Army, US 9th Army, 5th Pz Army, US 1st Army, US 3rd Army, US 7th Army, 7th Army, US 6th Army, 19th Army, Fr 1st Army

A FATAL OVERCONFIDENCE

Hitler and Kesselring spent several hours discussing the situation,
at first alone, then joined by the head of the army General Alfred
Jodl and head of the high command Field Marshal Wilhelm
Keitel. Hitler was optimistic. His main concern was the situation

224

on the eastern front. A collapse there would mean the end of the war, he thought. Immediately after the meeting, Kesselring noted: 'Our main military effort is directed to the east. Hitler envisages the decisive battle there with complete confidence. And he expects the enemy's main attack to be launched at Berlin.'

The German Ninth Army, under the command of General Theodore Busse, had already been pulled back to defend the city. Its defence took priority. The city had good anti-aircraft defences and artillery deployed in depth under the best artillery commanders available. There were good water barriers on both sides and behind the lines were the perimeter defences of Berlin itself. Hitler was sure that Berlin was untakeable and Field Marshal Ferdinand Schörner, who commanded Army Group Centre in Czechoslovakia, maintained that 'with reinforcements and sufficient supplies, he would repel all enemy attacks launched at him'.

On the western front, things were looking even better – in Hitler's eyes at least. Over months of heavy fighting, the British, Americans and French had sustained heavy losses that must, by now, be taking their toll. According to Hitler, 'the Allies could not dismiss the natural obstacles covering the German army's positions'. The Allied bridgehead at Remagen was seen as the danger point and it was urgent that it should be mopped up, but there too Hitler was confident.

Kesselring was ordered to delay the western Allies long enough for the Red Army formations on the eastern front to be broken up. After that, as many troops as he wanted would be transferred to the west. Although the Allies maintained superiority in the air – the cause of the German reverses of the last few months –

he was assured that this would soon be rectified. Grand–Admiral Dönitz's new submarines would turn the tide in the Battle of the Atlantic and the Third Reich would be saved.

That night Kesselring installed himself Rundstedt's old headquarters in Ziegenberg and was brief by Lieutenant-General Siegfried Westphal, his former chief of staff in Italy and a man he trusted implicitly. Westphal's report was not nearly as rosy as Hitler's. Under Kesselring's command were fifty-five battle-worn divisions, giving him an average of just sixty-three men for each mile of the front. Facing him were eighty-five full-strength Allied divisions, who enjoyed undisputed superiority in the air.

On 11 March, Kesselring met Field Marshal Walther Model, who had worked wonders on the eastern front but had failed to do the same as commander-in-chief in the west, and General Gustav-Adolf von Zangen, the commander of the Fifteenth Army, who had been ordered to wipe out the Remagen bridgehead. The three of them agreed that this could not be done unless von Zangen was given reinforcements and more ammunition. Otherwise the situation looked dire.

Kesselring made a lightning tour of the front. He found Army Group H in good spirits, particularly because the Americans had been slow to exploit their crossing of the Rhine at Remagen. But Army Group G had no mobile reserves and its situation looked perilous.

When Kesselring returned to his headquarters, he found that the Americans were mounting a series of operations that convinced him that they had abandoned their strategy of overrunning Germany from Italy through Austria.

'What clearly emerged was the rapid succession of operations,

US–Soviet Meeting *on the River Elbe, May 1945. The Nazi empire, which had once stretched from the west coast of France to the gates of Moscow, had now been reduced to a few square kilometres of central Berlin.*

as well as the competence of command and the almost reckless engagement of armoured units in terrain that was quite unsuited for the use of heavy tanks,' he said. 'On the basis of my experience in Italy in similar terrain, I was not expecting the American armoured forces to achieve rapid success in spite of the fact that the reduced strength of tired German troops gave undoubted advantage to the enemy operation.'

In the face of this onslaught, Kesselring asked for permission to pull back the First and Seventh Armies to the east bank of the Rhine. Typically, Hitler delayed giving the order until it was too late. Instead he promised reinforcements, but all he sent was a single division, and that not even combat-ready, coming as it did from garrison duties in Denmark. On top of that, the Americans mounted a surprise attack at Remagen while to the north intelligence indicated that Montgomery's 21st Army Group was preparing to cross the Rhine.

As the situation deteriorated, Kesselring was contacted by *Obergruppenführer* Karl Wolff of the Waffen SS, whom he had known as the commander of the rear echelons in Italy. For several weeks, Wolff had been negotiating terms for the surrender of German forces in Italy with the head of the US Secret Service in Berne, Allen Dulles, via Major Waibel of Swiss Army Intelligence. On 23 March, Wolff visited Kesselring's office in Ziegenberg and suggested that the armies in the west joined this bid for surrender. Kesselring refused. It was a question of loyalty, Wolff told Dulles: 'He was defending soil and was bound to continue even if he died himself in the fighting...he personally owed everything to the Führer, his rank, his appointment, his decorations.'

But there were practical considerations too. 'To this he added that he hardly knew the generals commanding the corps and divisions under him,' Wolff said. 'Moreover, he had a couple of well-armed SS divisions behind him that he was certain would take action against him if he undertook anything against the Führer's orders.'

Even so, Kesselring gave his blessing to the German surrender in Italy and told Wolff that he could convey that to Kesselring's successor there, General von Vietinghoff. But while Kesselring was prepared to fight on, he joined German Armaments Minister Albert Speer in doing his best to subvert the 'scorched earth' policy that Hitler had spelt out in his Führerbefehl (Führer's order) of 19 March:

THE DESTRUCTION OF GERMANY

The fight for the existence of our people obliges us to make total use, even within the Reich, of whatever means may weaken the fighting power of the enemy and prevent him from pursuing his advance [said Hitler]. *Any means capable, directly or indirectly, of inflicting lasting damage on the offensive strength of the enemy must be resorted to. It is erroneous to think that by leaving them intact or with only superficial damage we may more profitably resume exploitation of our communication and transportation systems and our industrial or productive installations when we reconquer our invaded territory. When the enemy comes to retreat, he will have no consideration for the population, and will leave only scorched earth behind him. For this reason I command ... that within the Reich the communications and military transport systems, and the industrial and productive installations, which the enemy may use immediately or within a limited period for the prosecution of the war must be destroyed.*

The order also contained a clause declaring invalid any other order that sought to nullify it. Hitler was ordering the destruction of Germany and was thereby unconsciously implementing the Morgenthau Plan, put forward by the US Secretary of the Treasury Henry Morgenthau Jr and supported by Churchill's scientific advisor Lord Cherwell, to reduce Germany to a pastoral state after the war.

Speer vehemently opposed Hitler's order. He wrote to Hitler, saying:

From what you have told me, the following emerges clearly and unequivocally, unless I have misunderstood you: if we are to lose the war, the German people are to be lost as well. This destiny is unavoidable. This being so, it is not necessary to secure the basic conditions for our people to ensure their own survival even in the most primitive form. Rather, on the contrary, we should ourselves destroy them. For they will have proved themselves the weaker, and the future will belong exclusively to the people of the east who will have shown themselves the stronger. Furthermore, only the unworthy will survive since the best and bravest have fallen.

Unable to convince Hitler of his folly, Speer did everything he could to oppose his scorched-earth policy. Hitler was aware of Speer's disloyalty, but gave him leeway because of his affection for the younger man's 'artistic' nature. Speer's conversion came too late for the Allies though. He had used slave labour on some of his projects and was given twenty years at Nuremberg.

Kesselring supported Speer and, as the army fell back, much was left intact. This was helped by the speed of the Allied advance after 31 March, and a shortage of explosives and transport.

CLINGING ON AT THE RHINE

In light of the Allied breakthrough in crossing the Rhine in several places, Kesselring considered his commanders' proposals that they withdraw from the Rhine. He said of them:

I finally refrained from doing so, because the only result would have been to retreat in disorder. Our troops were heavily laden, barely mobile, in large part battle-weary and encumbered by units in the rear that were still in a state of disorder. The enemy

*had all round superiority, especially in the air. If nothing occurred
to check or slow his advance, our retreating columns would be
overtaken and smashed. This type of combat would have become
an end in itself – no longer a means employed to an end – the
end being to gain time. Every day on the Rhine, on the contrary,
was a day gained, signifying a strengthening of the front, even
if it were only to enable points in the rear to be mopped up or
stray troops to be rounded up.*

Sappers from 21st Army Group had already opened seven forty-
ton bridges over the Rhine and the British Second Army and
the American Ninth Army came down both banks of the River
Lippe to overwhelm the German First Parachute Army, while
the Canadian II Corps wheeled left into Holland.

The remains of the First Parachute Army, the Fifteenth
Army and the Fifth Panzer Army – seven corps or nineteen
divisions in all – were now trapped in what Hitler fancifully
called 'the fortified region of the Ruhr', under the command
of General Model. General Omar Bradley formed a new
Fifteenth Army under Lieutenant-General Leonard T. Geow
with eighteen divisions taken from the First and Ninth Armies,
to reduce this force.

Beyond, there was now a 180-mile gap in the German line
between what remained of Army Groups G and H. In the Harz
mountains, there were the five divisions of the Eleventh Army
under General Wenck, and a Twelfth Army was being formed
on the right bank of the Elbe. But having stayed on the Rhine,
Kesselring was now in no position to fall back to defensive
positions along the rivers Wesser, Werra, Main, Altmuhl and

Lech, and General Bradley's Twelfth Army Group was now in a position to make a dash on Berlin.

Eisenhower decided against this. It would entail a risky lengthening of supply lines and there was still the Elbe to cross which was some 200 miles from the Rhine and some 125 miles short of Berlin. The priority was to make contact with the Red Army, cutting Germany in two and making it impossible for the enemy to regroup. Meanwhile, Montgomery's 21st Army Group was to head north-east towards Lübeck to cut off the German forces occupying Denmark and Norway.

A NATIONAL REDOUBT?

There were other dangers. Eisenhower wrote:

Equally important was the desirability of penetrating and destroying the so-called 'National Redoubt'. For many weeks we had been receiving reports that the Nazi intention, in extremity, was to withdraw the cream of the SS, Gestapo, and other organizations fanatically devoted to Hitler, into the mountains of southern Bavaria, western Austria, and northern Italy. There they expected to block the tortuous mountain passes and to hold out indefinitely against the Allies. Such a stronghold could always be reduced by eventual starvation if in no other way. But if the German was permitted to establish the redoubt he might possibly force us to engage in a long-drawn-out guerrilla type of warfare, or a costly siege. Thus he could keep alive his desperate hope that through disagreement among the Allies he might yet be able to secure terms more favourable than those of unconditional surrender. The evidence was clear that the Nazi intended to make the attempt.

On 11 March, the head of SHAEF intelligence, General Strong, described what they feared they would be up against in a memo. 'Here, defended both by nature and by the most efficient secret weapons yet invented, the powers that have hitherto guided Germany will survive to reorganize her resurrection,' he wrote.

> *Here armaments will be manufactured in bomb-proof factories, food and equipment will be stored in vast underground caverns and a specially selected corps of young men will be trained in guerrilla warfare, so that the whole underground army can be fitted and directed to liberate Germany from the occupying forces.*

So when the 12th Army Group reached the Elbe in the vicinity of Magdeburg, it was to turn south, make contact with the Soviets in Saxony and advance on Regenburg and Linz before the remnants of Army Group G could occupy the redoubt.

Eisenhower dutifully communicated his plan to Stalin, as he was obliged to do under the terms of the agreement reached at the conference between Roosevelt, Churchill and Stalin at Yalta in Febuary 1945. Stalin replied that Eisenhower's plan 'entirely coincides with the plan of the Soviet High Command... Berlin has lost its former strategic importance. The Soviet High Command therefore plans to allot secondary forces in the direction of Berlin.'

CRACKS IN THE COALITION

This was entirely disingenuous. At that very moment, the Soviets were sending five tank armies, along with 25,000 guns and 25,600 tons of shells against Berlin. Churchill saw through this cynical political manoeuvre. He believed that the agreements reached at Yalta, in Stalin's eyes, were worth no more than the pieces of paper they were written on. Already a pro-Soviet regime had been installed in Poland, despite assurances to the contrary. And the same thing was happening in Bulgaria and Rumania.

Churchill summed up his concerns:

First, that Soviet Russia has become a moral danger to the free world. Secondly, that a new front must be immediately created against her onward sweep. Thirdly, that this front in Europe should be as far east as possible. Fourthly, that Berlin was the prime and true objective of the Anglo-Saxon armies. Fifthly, that the liberation of Czechoslovakia and the entry into Prague of American troops was of high consequence. Sixthly, that Vienna, and indeed Austria, must be regulated by the Western Powers, at least upon an equality with the Russian Soviets. Seventhly, that Marshal Tito's aggressive pretensions against Italy must be curbed. Finally, and above all, that a settlement must be reached on all major issues between West and East before the armies of democracy melted, or the western Allies yielded any part of the German territories they had conquered, or, as it could soon be said, liberated from totalitarian tyranny.

To Churchill it seemed unthinkable that Britain and America should give up Berlin and, worse, that Eisenhower should signal his intention to Stalin. With the support of the British chiefs of staff and Montgomery, he tried to get Eisenhower to change his mind. When that failed he appealed over his head to Roosevelt, while the chief of the Imperial General Staff Field Marshal Alan Brooke did the same to his opposite number General George Marshall.

Churchill told Roosevelt:

The Russian armies will no doubt overrun Austria and enter Vienna. If they also take Berlin will not their impression that they have been the overwhelming contributor to our common victory be unduly imprinted in their minds, and may this not lead them into a mood which will raise grave and formidable difficulties in the future?'

Eisenhower made it clear that he was willing to change his plan if he was told to by Washington. He cabled Marshall: 'I am the first to admit that a war is waged in pursuance of political aims, and if the Combined Chiefs of Staff should decide that the Allied effort to take Berlin outweighs purely military considerations in this theatre, I should cheerfully readjust my plans and my thinking so as to carry out such an operation.'

But as far as Washington was concerned, the zones of occupation in Germany had already been fixed and there was little point in occupying territory that would later have to be given up. The US joint chiefs of staff backed Eisenhower. 'To deliberately turn away from the exploitation of the enemy's weakness does not appear sound,' Marshall concluded. 'The single objective should be a quick and complete victory.' And Eisenhower was given permission to 'continue communicating freely with the commander-in-chief of the Soviet Army' – Marshal Stalin himself.

INTO THE RUHR

On 12 April General Gerow took the coal basin of the Ruhr. Two days later the Ruhr pocket was split in two. Army

Group B surrendered, delivering 325,000 prisoners, including 29 generals, into Allied hands. Model could not be found. Fearing that he might be handed over to the Russians, Model committed suicide on 21 April.

As the American First, Third and Ninth Armies sped forward, the German army collapsed. Despite drumhead court martials and summary executions, German troops were surrendering at a rate of 50,000 a week by the middle of April. Their places were taken by *Volkssturm* – the German Home Guard made up of old men and young boys. Few had uniforms. When one of their battalion leaders was captured, he told his interrogators:

> *I had four hundred men in my battalion and we were ordered to go into the line in our civilian clothes. I told the local party leader that I could not accept the responsibility of leading men into battle without uniforms. Just before it was committed, the unit was given 180 Danish rifles, but there was no ammunition. We also had four machine guns and a hundred anti-tank bazookas. None of the men had received any training in firing a machine gun, and they were all afraid of handling the anti-tank weapon. Although my men were quite ready to help their country, they refused to go into battle without uniforms and without training. What can a Volkssturm man do with a rifle without ammunition? The men went home...the only thing they could do.*

When they did go into action, they were simply no match for well-trained and well-equipped Allied troops.

THE LAST ACT

Thanks to the *Autobahn* system Hitler had built, the invading armies sped through the German countryside, avoiding towns and other bottlenecks. Casualty rates plummeted. Between 22 March and 8 May, Patton's corps of twelve, then fourteen divisions, lost eleven thousand killed, wounded and missing, while fifteen thousand were evacuated due to accidental injury and illness. The American Ninth Army took Hanover on 10 April and reached the Elbe, eighty-five miles to the east, three days later. After taking Barby, upstream from Magdeburg, and establishing a bridgehead there, it turned south towards Dessau. The First Army pushed south into Saxony, covering nearly eighty miles in four days and cutting off the Eleventh Army in the Harz mountains. The Clausewitz Panzer Division was sent to rescue them. It hit the junction between British and Americans and penetrated nearly forty miles before being encircled and destroyed. The Eleventh Army was also annihilated.

Reaching the Elbe, the First Army established a bridgehead at Wittenberg while its right took Halle and Leipzig. On its way, it took the huge underground factories where the V-1 and V-2 missiles had been made. Then, on 26 April, to the south at Torgau, General Courtney Hodges met up with Soviet Fifth Guards Army under Colonel-General A.S. Zhadov.

Patton's Third Army broke the enemy's last serious resistance at Mülhausen and took its 400,000th prisoner on 7 April, then pushed south-east into Bavaria and the 'National Redoubt'. On the way, it captured the reserves of the Reichsbank, which contained gold bars worth five billion francs and three billion marks in cash.

While Kesselring fought on as head of the Southern Defence Zone between Main and the Swiss border, the American Seventh Army under General Patch took Mannheim and Heidelberg, then Munich where, it was thought, Hitler would take refuge once the National Redoubt had been established. His right wing met up with the French First Army in the area of Stuttgart, while his left stayed in touch with the American Third Army. On 25 April, Patch pushed across the Danube on an eighty-mile front and captured what was left of XIII Corps. Resistance in Bavaria then collapsed.

Patton pushed on into Austria, and on 2 May, his 13th Armoured Division under Major-General Millikin had just arrived at Braunau am Inn, Hitler's birthplace, as the dictator himself was committing suicide in the Chancellery in Berlin. Prague was Patton's next objective and he was already in Czechoslovakia on 6 May when he was ordered to halt.

Meanwhile, Montgomery had been racing for Lübeck. 'With the Rhine behind us, we drove hard for the Baltic,' he wrote. 'My object was to get there in time to be able to offer a firm front to the Russian endeavours to get up into Denmark, and thus control the entrance to the Baltic.'

Before him in Holland he found the German Twenty-Fifth Army and elements of the First Parachute Army. They were under the command of Field Marshal Busch who was head of the Northern Defence Zone which comprised the Netherlands, Norway, Denmark and north-west Germany. In quick succession, Münster, Bremen and Hamburg fell, though they still met fierce resistance. At Lingen, the 7th Parachute Division engaged in hand-to-hand fighting to crush a counter-attack by fanatical troops crying 'Heil Hitler', while it took three divisions to suppress the 2nd Kriegsmarine Division at Bremen.

Although delayed by the *Clausewitz* Panzer Division's counter-attack, VIII Corps on the right reached the Elbe opposite Lauenberg on 19 April. Eisenhower sent the US XVIII Airborne Corps, which included the British 6th Airborne Division, and under the cover of Gloster Meteors – the RAF's first jet fighters – they crossed the Elbe on 29–30 April. On 2 May, they took Lübeck, while the 6th Airborne Division entered Wismar, a small town twenty-eight miles to the east of Lübeck, just six hours before the Red Army arrived.

After taking Hamburg, General Ritchie crossed the Kiel Canal and stopped thirty-five miles outside Flensburg where Hitler's successor, Admiral Karl Dönitz, had set up his government in an attempt to bring a negotiated end to the war.

The Canadian First Army had been left to mop up in the Netherlands, with the help of the Dutch Resistance, the French 2nd and 3rd Parachute Regiments and the Polish I Armoured Corps. They faced desperate resistance from the German II Parachute Corps. When the Canadian I Corps reached the Zuiderzee, the Germans opened the sea-dykes. To spare the Dutch countryside the ravages of seawater, General Crerar agreed to a ceasefire with General von Blumentritt, stipulating in the negotiations that British and American planes be given free passage to deliver food and medical supplies to the Dutch populace.

On 3 May, the new head of the Kriegsmarine, Admiral von Friedeburg, and Field Marshal Busch's chief of staff General Kinzel presented themselves to Field Marshal Montgomery at his headquarters on Lüneburg Heath and offered the surrender of all the German forces in northern Germany, including those facing the Red Army. They were dismissed. Eisenhower maintained that, under the Yalta agreements, those forces facing the Russians must surrender to the Russians. The following day Friedeburg and Kinzel returned and, at 1820 hours, signed papers surrendering only the land and sea forces that faced the 21st Army Group in north-west Germany, the Netherlands, the Friesian Islands, Heligoland and Schleswig-Holstein. Even though Montgomery had abided by the Yalta agreements, the Red Army occupied the Danish island of Bornholme.

On 7 May 1945, the German delegation arrived at the school house in Rheims that SHAEF was using as its headquarters. Eisenhower's chief of staff Lieutentant-General Walter Bedell-Smith read out the document that would put an end to the European war. It confirmed the complete defeat of Germany's armed forces and ordered the simultaneous cessation of hostilities on all fronts at 2301 hours the following day, 8 May. It also settled the procedure for surrender according to the principles established on Lüneberg Heath. It was signed by Colonel-General Jodl for the German High Command, along with Major Oxenius for the Luftwaffe and Admiral Friedeburg for the Kriegsmarine.

For the Allies it was signed by Bedell-Smith and witnessed by Lieutenant-General Sir Frederick Morgan for Great Britain, General Sévez for France and Major-General Susloparov for the Soviet Union, along with Lieutenant-General Carl A. Spaatz for the US Army Air Force, Air Marshal Sir James Robb for the RAF and Vice-Admiral Sir Harold Burroughs for the Royal Navy. After five years and eight months, the war in Europe was over.

SECTION FOUR
THE EASTERN FRONT

Operation Barbarossa, the 1941 invasion of Russia, had carried Hitler's troops to the very gates of Moscow before stuttering to a halt in the depths of the Russian winter. By August 1942, a regrouped German Army had reached the River Volga and was besieging Stalingrad. Symbolic for both Hitler and Stalin, the battle for the city would see some of the most brutal fighting of the entire war, and would mark the moment when the Red Army began to take the initiative.

CHAPTER 14

Stalingrad

'The streets are no longer measured in metres, but in corpses. Stalingrad is no longer a town. By day it is an enormous cloud of burning, blinding smoke. At night it is a vast furnace lit by the reflection of the flames.'

GERMAN OFFICER, 24TH PANZER DIVISION, STALINGRAD, 1942

During the winter of 1941, despite the privations of his men on the Eastern Front, Hitler was not downhearted. Most of the Soviet Union's European territory was now in his hands and, by February 1942, the Soviet's winter counter–attack had petered out. Now Hitler began to make plans to crush the Red Army once and for all. The renewed campaign would attack Stalingrad (present-day Volgograd), a city that stretched some thirty miles along the Volga, 600 miles south-east of Moscow. It was a huge new industrial city and was paraded as one of the great achievements of the Soviet system. It also bore the name of the Soviet Union's leader, who had organized its defences against the White Russians in the civil war that followed the founding of the Soviet state. Stalin realized that the city must be held at all costs. If it fell, so would he.

For Hitler, too, Stalingrad was important. It was a symbol of Communism and had to be crushed. It was also an important

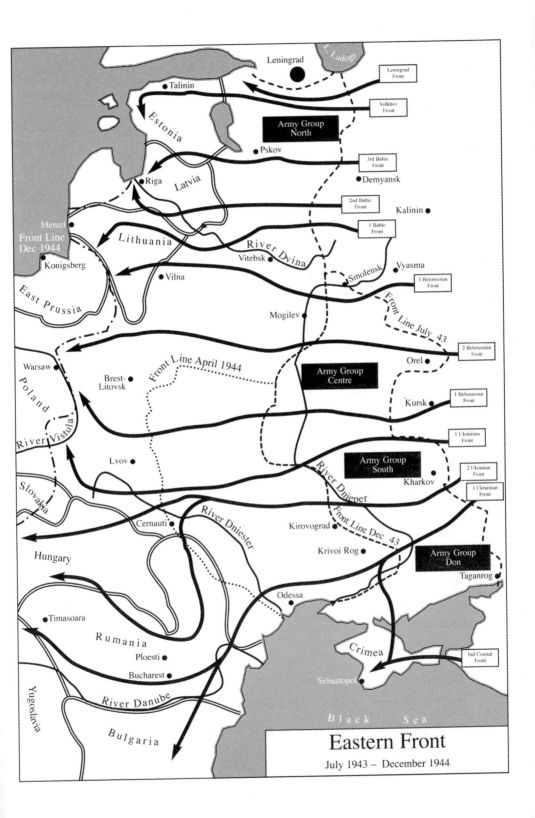

Eastern Front

July 1943 – December 1944

centre for mass production of armaments. Once it had been taken, his victorious army would head up the Volga to encircle Moscow, while a second army would move south-east to take the oilfields of the Caucasus and threaten Turkey and Persia.

Army Group Centre was split into two groups, under the overall control of Field Marshal von Bock. Army Group B, under General Freiherr von Weichs, was much the stronger of the two. It comprised Fourth Panzer Army under Hoth, Second Army, and the powerful Sixth Army, under General Friedrich Paulus, supported by other crack infantry and Panzer divisions. By comparison, Army Group A was practically a reserve force. It contained the crack First Panzer Army under Field Marshal Ewald von Kleist, which was going to take the oilfields of the Caucasus, and Seventeenth Infantry Army. But the numbers were made up with Italian, Rumanian and Hungarian troops. Altogether there were now twenty- five Panzer divisions compared with nineteen the year before. However, the war was very different now. The Wehrmacht no longer seemed to be invincible and Hitler was no longer infallible. German soldiers now feared being posted to the Eastern Front. The brutal treatment of the civilians there – including mass shooting, burnings, the summary execution of prisoners and the deliberate starvation of men, women and children – was sure to invite retribution.

In the spring of 1942, Stalin made a counter-attack in the Kerch Peninsula in the Crimea. This was crushed and the Germans took 100,000 prisoners. Two fresh Siberian divisions sent to relieve Leningrad were encircled. Then 600 Russian tanks, two-thirds of their force, punched through the Rumanian Sixth Army to take Kharkov. But then the trap closed. Von Kleist crushed the southern flank of the Soviet advance on 18 May, while Paulus swept down from the north the following day. The Soviets lost nearly a quarter of a million men, along with all their tanks. The stage was set for Hitler's summer offensive.

On 28 June, across a wide front stretching from Kursk to Rostov, the Panzers went roaring across the open steppes. The dust pall they kicked up could be seen for forty miles and it was soon joined by smoke from burning villages. There were no significant forces to oppose them as the reserves were still being held back for the defence of Moscow. The Red Army put up a fight at the industrial town of Voronezh. When von Bock attempted to crush them, rather than bypass them and continue the offensive, Hitler sacked him. Army Group A, led by von Kleist's Panzers, then crossed the River Don and headed southwards towards the oilfields, while Army Group B headed for Stalingrad.

While Army Group A progressed quickly and were almost in sight of the oil derricks of the Caucasian field by 9 August, Fourth and Sixth Armies, with 330,000 of Germany's finest soldiers, advanced more slowly over the 200 miles to Stalingrad and became strung out. As they massed to mount an assault, Stalin made the decision to commit the Moscow reserve to the defence of Stalingrad and the desperate race to get them there began. Between 25 and 29 August, Paulus's Sixth Army made a ferocious attempt to storm the city before reinforcements could arrive. Meeting stiff opposition, Paulus asked Hoth's Fourth Panzer Army for help. It attacked from the south, forcing the Soviet Sixty-fourth Army, which was defending the southern part of city, to extend its flank to meet the threat. The Soviet front was now eighty miles long, but only fifty miles wide. Paulus threw his entire Sixth Army, now supported by the IIII Army Corps, against it. On 22 August, German troops penetrated the northern suburbs, and on the following day they reached the Volga, within mortar range of a vital railway bridge. The Soviet Sixty-second Army in the northern sector was now outflanked. The Luftwaffe was then called in to deliver an all-out night bombardment. The idea was to demoralize the defenders and cause panic among the citizens. Much of the civilian population fled to the other side of the Volga and the authorities began evacuating the largest factories. When Stalin heard of this, he stopped the evacuations. The result was that the factories themselves became centres of resistance. Workers in the tractor factory continued producing new tanks and armoured cars until the Germans were on their doorstep. Then they would sling ammunition belts over their overalls, pick up grenades, rifles and anti-tank weapons, and take up their positions in the firing-points or bunkers with their comrades from the Red Army, while the remaining women, children and the elderly hid in cellars, sewers and caves in the cliffs above the Volga.

Despite fierce fighting following the terror-bombing, the German advance in the north of the city was halted. In the south, Hoth's Panzers pushed the Sixty-fourth Army back, but failed to penetrate the line. And once they entered the heart of the ruined city, their advance too ground to a halt.

INTO STALINGRAD

For Hitler, Stalingrad was going to be where the war was won or lost. He summoned his commanders to his new forward headquarters at Vinnitsa over 500 miles away in the Ukraine. The drive up the Volga was vital to the success of his Russian campaign, he told them. New Hungarian and Rumanian armies were brought in to protect the left flank along the Don and three new infantry divisions were sent to reinforce Sixth Army. Stalin, too, believed that the war would be won or lost at Stalingrad. He moved in a new team of commanders headed by Zhukov.

The Germans were the masters of the Blitzkrieg. They were not used to slow, grinding, man-to-man fighting through the rubble of a ruined city. The Russians, by contrast, quickly learned to adapt their tactics to the new situation, and every move the Germans made cost them dearly. After weeks of ceaseless fighting against crack German troops, the Red Army still held a nine-mile strip along the banks of the Volga. A series of gentle curves in the Volga and a number of small islands prevented German ground troops bombarding all the river crossings with artillery and mortar fire. Nor did the Luftwaffe bomb them or the Soviet artillery on the other bank. Instead, they continued to throw everything they had against the Soviet enclave on the west bank.

On 12 September, Hitler authorized a new offensive. The following day, Paulus sent in three Panzer divisions backed by eight divisions of infantry. Against them, the Soviets had forty tanks, all but nineteen immobile. The Sixty-second Army had been reduced to just three infantry divisions, the remnants of four others and two battle-damaged tank brigades. And there were no reserves as every man had already been thrown into the battle. However, the Soviet headquarters were on the spot. General Vasili Chuikov had made the dangerous crossing of the Volga and had set up his command post in a dug-out, by the river near Puskin

Street bridge. With their backs to the river, Chuikov inspired his men with the words, 'There is no land across the Volga'. For those who did not get the message, there were firing squads to deal with the deserters. Hundreds were shot.

The Germans flung themselves at the middle of the Russian line and, on the afternoon of 14 September, they broke through and seized Mamaye Hill. From the high ground there, they could concentrate artillery fire on the vital ferry link from Krasnaya Sloboda. The 76th Infantry Division overwhelmed the defenders at a ruined hospital in the middle of the Soviet line. Victory now seemed certain and many Germans got drunk on looted vodka. The only resistance now seem to be snipers.

Chuikov then threw his nineteen tanks in and the battle resumed. That night the fighting came within 200 yards of Chuikov's headquarters and staff officers joined in. But the Germans still pushed forward and the vital central landing stage came under machine-gun fire from close range. On the night of 14 September, Russian Guardsmen had to scramble ashore under fire. There was no possibility of them counter-attacking as a coherent division, and they were soon dispersed among the ruins in isolated pockets with no intercommunication.

The street fighting had also broken up the German formations. They now fought through the devastated streets in small battle groups comprising three or four Panzers and a company of German infantrymen, which had to laboriously clear each pocket individually. Russian riflemen and machine-gunners hid in ruined buildings and craters and behind mountains of rubble. They hid until the Panzers had gone by, then attacked the infantry. The Panzers then found themselves attacked by roving T-34s, or they ran into anti-tank guns or dug-in tanks. In the narrow streets, the Panzers were very vulnerable both to grenades dropped from directly above and to antitank guns of which the Russians had a plentiful supply, while their armourpiercing shells made a comparatively small hole in a building, most of which had been destroyed anyway. The battle hinged on house-to-house combat fought with bullet, grenade, bayonet and flame-thrower.

The Germans found that it took a whole day, and numerous casualties, to take 200 yards. Even then the Russians reappeared at night, knocking holes in attic walls so that they could reoccupy buildings over the heads of the Germans. Even so, victory seemed near. A German salient ran down the Tsarita tributary to the Volga itself. They had almost complete control of much of the city. And the landing stages and most of the river crossings were within range of their guns. The Russians' only lifeline lay to the north where the ferries were out of range.

But it did not seem to matter how much of the city the Germans occupied, the Russians would not give up. The remains of the 92nd Infantry Brigade formed isolated pockets of resistance across the south of the city. The grain elevators there, though bombed and blasted, still stood defiant. At all levels, from top to bottom, they were occupied by pockets of Guardsmen and Russian Marines who repelled wave after wave of attackers. Their stout resistance brought the German assault inexorably to a halt.

For the Germans, two months of fighting for a narrow strip of the ruined city of Stalingrad was a propaganda disaster. The German people were told that the Russians were throwing wave after wave of men into the battle and were exhausting their reserves. In fact, the opposite was true. During September and October, the Germans threw no fewer than nineteen newly formed armoured brigades and twenty-seven infantry divisions into the battle. In that same period, only five Soviet divisions crossed the Volga. Zhukov sent only the bare minimum needed to hold off the Germans, so that he could build up strength for a counter-attack.

Around this time a crucial change was made in the Red Army. Since the Red Army had been formed in the wake of the 1917 Revolution, its officers, many of whom came from the former Imperial Army, had been stripped of their badges of rank and their every move was watched over by political commissars attached to each unit. Now old-fashioned gold-braided epaulettes were distributed and old regimental traditions were revived. Political interference ceased, commissars were demoted, and soldiers were told that they were fighting for Mother Russia, not for the Communist party.

While Russian spirits received a boost, German morale sagged. Russian artillery fire grew teadily heavier. Meanwhile the nights began to draw in. The skie became grey, the weather chilly and the Germans began to fear that they would be spending another winter in Russia. Quickly Paulus planned a fourth all-out offensive. This time he was determined to score a great victory as he had heard that Hitler was considering promoting him to chief of the High Command and Hitler had also publicly promised that Stalingrad would fall 'very shortly'.

Forty thousand Russians now held a strip of the city barely ten miles long. At its widest it reached a mile and a quarter inland from the west bank of the Volga; at its narrowest, 500 yards. But the Russians defending it were hardened troops who knew every cellar, sewer, crater and ruin of this wasteland. They watched German advances through periscopes and cut them down with machine-gun fire. Snipers stalked the cratered streets, or lay camouflaged and silent for hours on end awaiting their prey. Against them were pitched veteran German troops, who were demoralized by the losses they had taken, or raw recruits, who could be in no way prepared for the horrors they were about to face.

On 4 October, the Germans were about to launch their offensive when the Russians counter-attacked in the area around the tractor factory. This threw the Germans off balance. Although little ground was lost, it cost them many casualties. The Luftwaffe sent in 800 dive-bombers and the German artillery pounded the city mercilessly. Occasionally a pet dog, escaping from a bombed building, would race through the inferno, leap into the river and swim to freedom on the other side. After a five-hour bombardment, which shattered glass deep below ground and killed sixty-one men in Chuikov's headquarters, the German attack eventually went ahead.

On 14 October, two new armoured divisions and five infantry divisions pushed forward on a front just three miles wide. They found themselves lured into special killing grounds the Russians had prepared, where houses and sometimes whole blocks or squares had been heavily mined. Combat became so close that the Germans would occupy one half of a shattered building, while the Russians occupied the other. When the Russians prepared a building as a stronghold they would destroy the stairs so that the

Germans would have to fight for each floor independently. And when it came down to hand-to-hand fighting, it was usually the Russians who came off best. If they lost a building, the survivors would be sent back with the first counter-attack to retake it. That day, 14 October, according to Chuikov, was 'the bloodiest and most ferocious day of the whole battle'.

By sheer weight of numbers, the Germans pushed forward towards the tractor factory. The Soviets reinforced it with 2,300 men. After an entire day, the Germans had taken just one block. But although they took enormous casualties the tractor factory eventually ended up in German hands and the Soviet forces were pushed back so close to the Volga that boats bringing supplies across the river came under heavy machine-gun fire.

Next door to the tractor factory, the ruined Red October factory looked as if it might fall too. But at the last moment a Siberian division was put in. Its men were told to fight to the death. They dug in among shattered concrete, twisted girders, heaps of coal and wrecked railway wagons. Behind them were the icy waters of the Volga – there was nowhere to retreat to.

Unable to shift the Siberians, the Germans bombarded them with mortars, artillery and dive-bombers. But the Siberians had dug a series of interconnecting trenches, dug-outs and strongpoints in the frozen ground around the factory. When the barrage was lifted and the German armour and infantry went in they found themselves under blistering attack. After forty-eight hours of continuous fighting, hardly a man was left of the leading Siberian regiment. But the German offensive had been halted.

For the next two weeks, the onslaught on the Red October

factory continued. The Germans made 117 separate attacks — twenty-three on a single day. But backed by artillery from across the river directed by observation posts hidden in the ruins, the Siberian division held out.

'Imagine Stalingrad,' wrote a German veteran, 'eighty days and nights of hand-to- hand fighting. The streets are no longer measured in metres, but in corpses. Stalingrad is no longer a town. By day it is an enormous cloud of burning, blinding smoke. It is a vast furnace lit by the reflection of the flames.'

Paulus's offensive was at a standstill. The defenders of the city were unyielding and he had no more men to throw against them. For the moment there was a stalemate, but winter was on its way. Then Sixth Army received reinforcements in the form of a number of battalions of Pioneers, front-line engineering and sapper troops. These would be used in the vanguard of a new offensive along a front just 400 yards wide. Instead of fighting from house to house, they would move through the sewers, cellars and tunnels under the city.

The offensive began on 11 November with a bombardment that turned what remained of the city into rubble. The first rush of fresh troops took the Germans through the last 300 yards under the city to the bank of the Volga. But when they reached it, the Russians emerged from their hiding places behind them, cutting them off. The German advance troops were trapped. But surrender was not an option. They were far past the point where prisoners were taken. The attack collapsed into sporadic pockets of desperate, hand-to-hand combat in hidden caverns under the rubble. On both sides men fought with unmitigated savagery. The troops were filthy, smelly, unshaven and red-eyed. They were high on vodka and benzedrene. No man could remain sane and sober in such conditions. After four days, only Russians were left. Then a terrible silence fell over Stalingrad – the silence of death.

TRAPPED

But at first light on 19 November, the air was full of sound again. Two hundred Russian guns opened fire to the north of the city. The next day, hundreds more opened up to the south. While the Germans had been exhausting their forces fighting inside the city, Zhukov had been busy building up a new army. He had massed 900 brand new T-34 tanks, 115 regiments of the dreaded Katyusha multi-rocket launchers, 230 artillery regiments and 500,000 infantrymen.

Two spearheads attacked the northern and southern tips of the German forces. The German flanks were turned fifty miles north and fifty miles south of Stalingrad and the Red Army rushed forward to encircle the German forces inside the city. This took the Germans completely by surprise. Paulus had imagined that the Russian reserves were drained and the German High Command was bracing itself for a new Russian winter offensive against Army Group Centre at Rzhev. The flanks of Paulus's army were held by Rumanian troops who were ill-equipped and had little stomach for fighting. As far as they were concerned, this was Germany's war.

The Germans never knew what had hit them. They found it impossible to judge the scale or direction of the offensive.

Opposite: Counter-attack Soviet troops launch an assault on the ever-diminishing German positions, Stalingrad, January 1943.

Paulus sent Panzers to the north, but they could not stem the tide there. Twenty miles to the rear of the main German forces besieging Stalingrad was the town of Kalach and its bridge across the Don, a vital link in Paulus's supply line. Demolition charges had already been placed so that the bridge could be blown if the Russians threatened to take it. But on 23 November the Russians took the Germans by surprise by turning up in a captured Panzer. They machine-gunned the guards and removed the demolition charges.

Meanwhile, the Russians' southern pincer had smashed through the German lines and turned northwards, and the two spearheads met at Kalach that evening. They had encircled 250,000 Germans and made the most decisive breakthrough on the Eastern Front. They had defeated an Italian army, a Hungarian army, and a Romanian army, and had taken 65,000 prisoners. Three days later, the Russians had thirty-four divisions across the Don and were breaking out to the north. Some armoured columns stayed behind to trouble Paulus's rear, while Russian infantry moved around the Germans and dug in. More than a thousand anti-tank guns were deployed to prevent a German breakout and the Germans menacing Stalingrad were bombarded by heavy artillery from the other side of the Volga.

Hitler told Paulus to hold his ground until 'Fortress Stalingrad' was relieved. Göring told Hitler that his Luftwaffe could fly in 500 tonnes of stores a day. Paulus was not wholly convinced and, knowing that winter was imminent, he prepared a force of 130 tanks and 57,000 men for a break-out. Hitler countermanded this. He had not given up on Stalingrad and ordered General Erich von Manstein, author of the attack through the Ardennes, to collect up the remaining Axis forces in the region as the new Army Group Don, and relieve Paulus.

Reinforcements were rushed to Manstein from Army Group Centre at Rzhev and Army Group A in the Caucasus. The attack began on 12 December and was led by LVII Panzer Corps, part of Hoth's Fourth Panzer Army and comprising 6th, 17th and 23rd Panzer Divisions. Following them was a convoy of trucks carrying 3,000 tonnes of supplies. They would make their attack from the south-west and punch their way into the city where Paulus was still holding his position. The ground was frozen, which made the going better for the Panzers, and the heavy snow made them difficult to spot. The Russians in Stalingrad were also having a hard time and ice floes coming down the Volga menaced their ferries.

But the Russians also knew how to turn the snow to their advantage. The winter sky denied the Germans air reconnaissance, and as Hoth made progress towards Stalingrad, he did not notice Russians hidden behind the snow in the gullies that criss-crossed the landscape. At dusk and dawn, T-34s would emerge and attack the infantry's trucks and the supply convoy following the Panzers. The German armour would then have to halt, turn around and deal with them. This slowed the German advance. On 17 December, Hoth reached the Aksai River, thirty-five miles from Stalingrad, where Zhukov had sent 130 tanks and two infantry divisions to meet him.

To the south, Manstein was also in trouble with his north-eastern flank crumbling along its entire 200-mile length. Manstein now realized that the only hope for the 250,000 Germans in Fortress Stalingrad was for Paulus and Hoth to attack at the same place on either side of the Russian line simultaneously. Paulus refused to try to break out, saying that Hitler had ordered him to stay where he was. There was to be no retreat from Stalingrad. Besides, his ill-fed troops were not physically strong enough to make the attack and they only had the fuel to go twenty miles, only just enough to reach the Russian lines. Göring was still promising that he would supply them and Hitler wanted Paulus's army in position for a new offensive the following spring.

On 19 December, Hoth crossed the Aksai and, two days later, Manstein talked to Hitler, telling him that it was vital for Sixth Army to attempt to break out to meet him. But Hitler backed Paulus. Manstein had no choice but to recall Hoth. He had lost 300 tanks and 16,000 men in the failed attempt to relieve Paulus. With Hoth pulling back, Army Group A also had to withdraw as it risked being cut off in the Caucasus.

The Sixth Army was now left to its fate. It was fanciful to believe that it could hold its position all winter. The infantry were running short of ammunition. The maximum allocation was thirty bullets a day. The Russians now had the 250,000 beleaguered Germans surrounded by 500,000 men and 2,000 guns. Meanwhile, the retreating German forces were being chased out of southern Russia by a new Soviet offensive.

In an effort to free up more manpower, the Soviets offered Paulus the chance to surrender on 8 January on the best possible terms. There would be food for the hungry, medical care for the wounded, guaranteed repatriation for everyone at the end of the war and the officers would even be allowed to keep their weapons. But Hitler had taken personal charge of Fortress Stalingrad from his bunker in Poland and refused these terms.

Instead he promoted Paulus to the rank of Field Marshal and told him to fight on.

It had been estimated that the remains of Sixth Army could be sustained on 550 tonnes of supplies a day – fifty less than Göring, at his most optimistic, had promised. The Luftwaffe had 225 Junkers Ju 52s available for the task. The nearest airfields were then an hour-and-a-half's flying time away and it was assumed that each plane could make one flight a day. In fact, there were rarely more than eighty Junkers serviceable on any one day. Two squadrons of converted Heinkel 111 bombers were brought in, but they could only carry one-and-a-half tons of supplies each. Then, as the Russians advanced, Sixth Army had to be supplied from airfields even further away. As the weather closed in, supply by air grew erratic. The Soviets massed anti-aircraft guns along the flight paths and Sixth Army could then only be resupplied at night. In all, 536 German transport planes were shot down and the average supply drop fell to sixty tons a night. The bread ration was cut to one slice a day and one kilogram of potatoes had to feed fifteen men. The horses of the Rumanian cavalry were eaten. Dogs, cats, crows, rats: anything the soldiers could find in the ruins was consumed. The only drinking water came from melted snow.

As the tightening Russian noose forced them to retreat, the Germans found that they were too weak to dig new defences. They slept with their heads on pillows of snow. Frostbite was endemic. Any wound almost inevitably meant death. Even if the wounded man's comrades were strong enough to carry him to the first aid post, there were few medical supplies left and little the doctors could do. Suicide was so common that Paulus had to issue a special order declaring it dishonourable. Even so, when a rumour circulated that the Russians were taking no prisoners, everyone kept one last bullet for themselves.

SURRENDER AT STALINGRAD

On 10 January, the Russians began their final attack. The perimeter shrank by the hour. By 24 January, the Germans were forced back behind the line the Russians had held on 13 September. The command structure collapsed. Medical posts and make-shift hospitals were full of wounded men begging their comrades to kill them. The airstrips – their only lines of supply – were taken and the remnants of Sixth Army were forced back into the ruined factories, the cellars and the sewers of the city.

Finally, on 30 January, Paulus's command post was overrun and he was captured. Two days later resistance was at an end. In all, 91,000 frozen and hungry men, including twenty-four generals, were captured. As they were marched away a Soviet colonel pointed at the rubble that was Stalingrad and shouted angrily at a group of German prisoners, 'That's how Berlin is going to look.' Two entire German armies had been wiped out including their reserves. Some 300,000 trained men had been lost. They were irreplaceable. The battle had been a bloodbath. In the last stages alone, 147,200 Germans and 46,700 Russians had been killed.

Stalingrad was the decisive battle on the Eastern Front. It humiliated what was once thought to be an invincible German army. On 5 February 1943, the Red Army newspaper Red Star wrote:

What was destroyed at Stalingrad was the flower of the German Wehrmacht. Hitler was particularly proud of the Sixth Army and its great striking power. Under Von Reichmann it was the first to invade Belgium. It entered Paris. It took part in the invasion of Yugoslavia and Greece. Before the war it had taken part in the occupation of Czechoslovakia. In 1942 it broke through from Kharkov to Stalingrad.

Now it was no more. This was a terrible blow to German morale. With the destruction of Sixth Army at Stalingrad, the German offensive in Russia was over. The tide had turned and the Red Army would eventually push the Wehrmacht all the way back to Berlin and beyond.

In captivity, the tide turned for Paulus too. Once one of Hitler's favourites, he agitated against the Führer among German prisoners of war. If they did not make peace, he warned, the whole of Germany would be turned into one 'gigantic Stalingrad'. He joined the Soviet-backed 'Free Germany Movement', broadcasting appeals to the Wehrmacht to give up the fight. After the war, he testified at the International Military Tribunal at Nuremberg. After his release in 1953, he settled in East Germany and died in Dresden in 1957.

CHAPTER 15

To the Vistula

The Battle of Stalingrad can truly be said to have been the turning point of the war on the Eastern Front. A Russian victory was never assured, however; even in retreat, when the German army turned and fought, it proved a dangerous beast indeed.

Following the Battle of Stalingrad, Germany was on the run in Russia. However, Field Marshal von Manstein, who had nearly managed the relief of Paulus's trapped Sixth Army at Stalingrad, had managed to get his Army Group Don, named after the Russian River Don, back to the River Donetz. Then, in February 1943, he retook Kharkov in the Ukraine, leaving the Soviet troops around the city of Kursk in a salient. This stretched 150 miles from north to south and protruded 100 miles into the German lines. It was a target that was simply too good to ignore. On 15 April 1943 Hitler ordered Operation *Zitadelle* (Citadel) to 'encircle the enemy forces situated in the region of Kursk and annihilate them by concentric attacks'. The German tank strategist General Heinz Guderian opposed this. He feared that they would lose more tanks than they would be able to replace. The new Panther tanks that the plan depended on were suffering teething troubles and he thought that they should be 'devoting our new tank production to the Western Front to have mobile reserves available for use against the Allied landings which could be expected with certainty to take place in 1944'.

THE BATTLE OF KURSK

General Walther Model, commander of the German Ninth Army on the Eastern Front, was also against the operation. It might have been successful in March, he said, but in May it was doomed to failure. He produced air reconnaissance photographs

Katyushas *Soviet multi-barrelled rocket-launcher, the Katyusha ('Little Katy') came to be feared on the Eastern Front by German troops.*

that showed that the Russians had prepared strong defences there in anticipation of a German pincer movement and withdrawn most of their mobile force from the salient. But Hitler ordered the assault to go ahead 'for political reasons'.

As it happened, the Panther tanks were not ready until the end of May and the operation was put back until 15 June. By that time the Wehrmacht had assembled an assault force of fifty divisions – 900,000 men. These would be led by seventeen armoured divisions, with 2,700 tanks and mobile assault guns.

The problem was that the Soviets knew exactly what the Germans were planning. Soviet spies had infiltrated the German High Command and Stalin heard of Operation *Zitadelle* forty-eight hours after Hitler had issued his orders. The Red Army had plenty of time to organize defences between sixteen and twenty-five miles deep in the salient. Their plan was to let the Germans exhaust themselves in their offensive, then smash them in a counter-offensive. Soviet intelligence was so comprehensive that Stalin knew not only how many divisions he faced, but also how they were equipped, the chain of command, the position of reinforcements and the supply columns, and the exact timing of D-Day and zero hour. This allowed Red Army engineers to lay 400,000 mines in fields that would channel the German armoured units into nests of anti-tank guns.

The Soviet defences were formidable. They had 6,000 anti-tank guns, 20,000 other artillery pieces, howitzers and mortars, and 920 rocket launchers. They outnumbered the Germans in the field, with seventy-five divisions and 3,600 tanks. In all, over two million men were involved, along with 6,000 tanks and 4,000 aircraft.

With the German offensive further delayed until 5 July, the Soviets had time to prepare their defences, which easily outstripped the German offensive capability. They also used their intelligence to bombard the German assembly points twenty minutes before zero hour. German Panzers were used to making lightning attacks, but by the evening of the first day they had advanced only six miles through the Soviet defences. One of the reasons was that the new tanks had been built with a cannon but no machine guns, making them useless against infantry.

The northern thrust of the pincer was halted on the second day just twelve miles from the start line. The southern arm manage to penetrate twenty miles. Eight days into the battle, the Germans had taken 24,000 prisoners and destroyed or captured a hundred tanks and 108 anti-tank guns. Even so, the gap between the two jaws of the pincers was still seventy-five miles.

On 12 July, a bitter engagement was fought near the village of Prokhorovka. It would be the largest tank battle in history, involving in the region of 6-6,500 tanks. The Red Army held. This was the turning point. The Soviets announced that the first phase of the battle was over and launched an offensive of their own against the Germans' Orel salient immediately to the north. The main thrust was led by the Eleventh Guards Army under Lieutenant-General I. K. Bagramyan with seventy regiments of infantry, 3,000 guns, 400 rocket-launchers and 250 tanks, which covered over fifteen miles in forty-eight hours. They faced the Second Panzer Army under Colonel-General Rudolf Schmidt, who had just twelve divisions forward and two in reserve, one of which was a Panzergrenadier. To the south, the Third and Sixty-Third Armies punched a hole through a seventy-five-mile stretch of front defended by just twenty-four battalions and infantry and armour poured through a breach between seven and ten miles wide.

Hitler now faced a dilemma. He had already lost 20,000 men. His offensive had stalled and he now had to withdraw some of his forces to defend Orel. Meanwhile British and American forces had landed on Sicily on 10 July, opening a second front. Troops would have to be sent to defend southern Italy. He decided to call a halt to *Zitadelle*.

The Soviets now had the initiative. On 15 July, they began a counter-attack with an artillery barrage that, they boasted, was 'ten times heavier than at Verdun'. The aim was to bombard the German minefields, blowing up as many mines as possible to reduce Russian casualties in their advance. Overhead there were huge air battles with heavy losses on both sides. But after three days, the Red Army broke through.

Behind the German lines, partisans began blowing up the railways to prevent supplies and reinforcements reaching the front. On the night of 20 July alone, 5,800 pieces of track were blown up. In all, between 21 July and 27 September there were 17,000 attacks on the railways by partisans. According to the official Soviet history, the partisans in Belorussia killed 500,000 Germans, including forty-seven generals. One of them was Hitler's High Commissioner for Russia, Wilhelm Kube, blown up by a bomb left under his bed by his Belorussian girlfriend. The Germans were forced to abandon the Orel salient, burning the crops behind them.

To the south, things were no better. On 17 July, between Belgorod and the Sea of Avov, Manstein's twenty-nine infantry divisions and thirteen armoured divisions faced 109 Soviet infantry divisions, nine infantry brigades, seven mechanized corps and seven cavalry corps, plus twenty independent tank brigades, sixteen tank regiments and eight anti-tank brigades. By 7 September, the Soviet numbers were increased to fifty-five infantry divisions, two tank corps, eight tank brigades and twelve tank regiments. The Germans were outnumbered seven to one, and the Soviets kept bringing up reinforcements. Hitler refused to allow the troops there to withdraw to new defensive positions. On 30 July, a Panzer group had a limited success, forcing the Red Army back over the River Mius, leaving behind 18,000 prisoners, 7,000 tanks and 200 guns. But on 3 August the Soviets pounded the gap between German armies to the north and south of Kursk and sent a huge mechanized force through the breach. On 4 August, Orel had to be evacuated. On the same day, Belgorod to the south fell.

German Panzer groups roamed the battlefield, fighting sporadic actions, but nothing could halt the Soviet onslaught. While the Germans lost men as they pulled back, the Red Army gained conscripts with every mile they took. Within four days, they had advanced seventy miles and on 23 August, Kharkov was in Russian hands. According to Josef Stalin's book *The Great Patriotic War of the Soviet Union*, addressing the crowds in Kharkov, General Vatutin's political aide Nikita Khrushchev cried out: 'Let us now get back to work! Let us remain firmly united! Everything for the front; all for victory! Let us further close our ranks under this banner which has brought us victory! Onwards to the West! Onwards for the Ukraine!'

The re-formed German Sixth Army and the First Panzer

Army defended a front of 1,300 miles with twenty-five divisions, including three Panzer divisions. Manstein's Panzer and Panzergrenadiers had just 220 assault guns and 257 tanks. These faced 1,300 Soviet tanks and sixty infantry divisions. There was nothing for it but to withdraw. The German army fought on for nearly two more years, but after Kursk there was nothing they could do to prevent the Red Army driving forward all the way to Berlin.

KURSK TO THE VISTULA

The Battle of Kursk effectively marked the end of the German offensive capability on the Eastern Front. Huge numbers of men were lost, along with their equipment. It was now doubtful whether the Panzers had enough tanks to hold the Eastern Front, let alone take on the British and Americans if they landed, as anticipated, in the west.

On 9 September, Hitler went to Zaporozh'ye on the Dniepr in the Ukraine to see the situation. After eight days' of discussion with Field Marshal von Manstein, the order was given for Army Group South to withdraw behind the deep valley of the Dniepr. Its right flank was against the right bank of the river, making it easy to defend.

Field Marshal von Kleist's Army Group A and the Seventeenth Army were now trapped in southern Russia, cut off by amphibious landings by the Black Sea Fleet at the port of Novorossiysk. The German Navy came to the rescue, and by 9 October it had ferried 202,477 troops, 54,664 horses, 1,200 guns and 15,000 vehicles across the Kerch Strait into the Crimea. However, the Soviets claimed to have sunk 70 barges in the strait, killing thousands.

It took Manstein ten days to pull his men back over six crossing points between Kiev in the north and Zaporazh'ye in the south. Behind them, they left fifteen miles of scorched earth. They also took with them all the men in the area, knowing that they would immediately be conscripted by the Red Army if they were left behind. Many of the women and children followed.

To the north, Field Marshal Gunther von Kluge's Army Group Centre was down to 191 assault guns and 108 tanks. For the one and only time, Stalin visited the front as preparations were being made for the advance on Smolensk on the borders of Belarus. The city was taken on 25 September, after the important communications centre of Bryansk on the Desna fell on the 19th.

Manstein's respite behind the Dniepr was short-lived. The Russians advanced, unhindered by the autumn rain or the destruction that the Germans had left behind them. As soon as they reached the river, they began to cross. By 1 October, General Ivan Konev had established a bridgehead ten miles deep and fifteen miles wide, putting the crossing point out of range of the German artillery.

To the south, the 4th Ukrainian Front pushed the German Sixth Army out of Melitopol and advanced unopposed to the mouth of the Dniepr. By the beginning of November they were outside Kherson and the Seventeenth Army was trapped in the Crimea. To its rear, the Russian Eighteenth Army was trying to force passage across the Kerch Strait.

Hitler refused to give Manstein permission to withdraw to the Dniepropetrovsk, and on 14 October Zaporazh'ye was taken by the Soviets in a night attack. However, a dash on Krivoy-Rog, eighty-five miles inland from the Dniepr, was thwarted by a counter-attack by the XL Panzer Corps, freshly arrived from Italy. Unfortunately for the Germans, their ammunition did not catch up with them and on 28 October they had to withdraw fifteen miles, leaving behind 10,000 dead, 5,000 prisoners, 378 guns and 357 tanks.

The Germans successfully withdrew from the Dniepropetrovsk salient, but Kiev was under threat from a bridgehead established by the 1st Ukrainian Front to the north. It contained two thousand guns, more then five hundred per mile. These could now operate without camouflage as there was no threat from the Luftwaffe. On the night of 5 November, 1,500 tanks and thirty infantry divisions attacked. Before dawn, the capital of the Ukraine had been liberated.

By 12 November the bridgehead upriver of Kiev was 143 miles wide and 75 miles deep. There was little opposition. Eleven German infantry divisions had the strength of one regiment and the 20th Panzergrenadier Division was on its way to being wiped out. However, with the Soviet forces spread out across such a wide area, and columns advancing to the north-west and south-west, the opportunity for a German counter-attack presented itself. The first plan was to attack Kiev, but with the alternate freezing and thawing that was a characteristic of the Ukrainian weather in November, this was considered too risky. Instead, Manstein chose the more modest objective of Zhitomir, eighty miles short of the capital.

Under low cloud that hampered the Red Air Force, the Fourth Panzer Army attacked from the south and cut the Kiev–Zhitomir road, taking the Soviet Third Guards Tank Army by surprise. It managed to extricate itself, but at a cost of 3,000 killed, and the loss of 153 tanks and seventy guns. This success was followed by an all-out German counter-offensive. On 1 December, the LVII Panzer Corps retook Korosten. A few days later, the Fourth Panzer Army retook Teterev, Malin and Radomyshl. Together they tried to encircle three tank corps and twelve infantry divisions, but the Germans could not close the jaws of the pincers fast enough. However, by 23 December they were back within twenty-five miles of Kiev. Twenty thousand Russians had been killed and around 500 taken prisoner. Six hundred tanks, 300 guns and 1,200 antitank weapons had been captured or destroyed. But this effort had weakened the German centre. On 10 December, Konev took the important railway junction of Znamenka, and on the 14th, after stiff resistance, Cherkassy on the Dniepr.

To the north, things were little better. On 6 October the Kalinin Front, soon to be renamed the 1st Baltic Front, attacked the Third Panzer Army at the point where Army Group Centre met Army Group North. The Second and Third Shock Armies broke through and attempted to open the way to the Baltic coast. However, the German Fourth Army made a determined stand. The Soviet West Front under General Sokolovsky made repeated attempts to force its way through the narrow strip of land between Orsha on the Dniepr and Vitebsk on the Dvina. But General Heinrici concentrated the fire of seventy German batteries under a unified command on the narrow front and massacred the oncoming forces.

However, the 2nd Baltic Front reached the Dniepr at Zhlobin and the Belorussian Front moved fifty-six miles beyond, making contact on the left with the 1st Ukrainian Front. The Red Army was inexorably pushing the Germans back along a 1,250-mile front.

GERMAN REORGANIZATION

The mood among the Germans was gloomy. Some 104,000 men had been lost since July – Stalin claimed it was 2.6 million. But Manstein still believed that the Wehrmacht could force a stalemate in the East, if reforms were made in the high command. Hitler's chief of staff Colonel-General Heinz Guderian agreed.

I went to see Jodl, to whom I submitted proposals for a reorganization of the Supreme Command, [said Guderian.] The Chief of the Armed Forces General Staff would control the actual conduct of operations, while Hitler would be limited to his proper field of activity, supreme control of the political situation and of the highest war strategy. After I had expounded my ideas at length and in detail Jodl replied laconically: 'Do you know of a better supreme commander than Adolf Hitler?' In view of his attitude I put my papers back in my briefcase and left the room.

The Soviet winter offensive began on 24 December when the 1st Ukrainian Front attacked on an eighteen-mile front down both sides of the Kiev-Zhitomir road. The XXIV Panzer Corps put up stubborn resistance but, despite being reinforced by the XLVIII Panzer Corps, it broke after forty-eight hours. The Third Guards Tank Army poured through the breach and took Zhitomir on 31 December. By 3 January 1944, it had advanced eight-five miles, taking Novograd-Volinsky. To the right, the

Conqueror of Berlin Field Marshal Georgy Zhukov, commander of 1st Ukrainian Front which captured Berlin, May 1945, with his staff officers.

Soviet Thirteenth and Sixtieth Armies had retaken Korosten and were now nearly at the pre-war Polish border.

With the Fourth Panzer Army in tatters and the 1st Ukrainian Front moving south-west, Manstein asked for reinforcements. Without them, he would have to pull out of the loop of the Dniepr and evacuate the Crimea to shorten his line. He even went to Rastenburg to asked Hitler personally. Hitler rejected his proposals. Manstein was not to pull out of the Dniepr loop because manganese was needed from the mines at Nikopol. Furthermore, pulling out of the Crimea risked the capitulation of Germany's ally Bulgaria and Turkey entering the war on the side of the Allies. Nor could he have any reinforcements as these would have to be taken from Army Group North, forcing Field Marshal von Klücher to abandon his position in the Gulf of Finland and giving Soviet submarines free rein in the Baltic when iron ore was needed from Sweden.

Hitler gave express orders that the First Panzer Army be kept on the Dniepr. This left no defence against the 1st Ukrainian Front, which swept towards Ternopil, further lengthening the German line. Exploiting his bridgehead at Cherkassy, Konev and his 2nd Ukrainian Front moved south, taking Kirovograd on 10 January. A dangerous salient formed a hundred miles wide and ninety miles deep. But the Russians were slow to exploit it because an unusually early spring melted the snow in early January. The thaw and rains caused the rivers to overflow their banks and mired the advancing forces in thick, sticky mud.

MASSACRE AT ZVENIGORODKA

Now under the command of Marshal Zhukov, the 1st and 2nd Ukrainian Fronts met up in the region of Zvenigorodka, encircling the German Eighth Army, XLII Corps of the First Panzer Army, four infantry divisions, the 5th SS Pangergrenadier Division and the *SS-Freiwilligen-Sturmbrigade Wallonie*, recruited from the French-speaking provinces of Belgium. The 3rd Ukrainian Division was also on its way to help obliterate this enemy enclave.

General W. Stemmermann took command of the encircled German forces and the pocket was supplied by air. Stemmermann then received orders to break out to the south, but this was impossible if he was to maintain his position on the Dniepr as Hitler had ordered. As the airlift faltered, Stemmermann had no choice but to try and break out to the west. He mustered his forces on the night of 16 February and charged. They were met by Soviet tanks, artillery and aircraft. General von Vormann wrote:

Until now our forces had dragged all their heavy equipment across gullies filled with thick, impacted snow. But then enemy shelling proved our undoing. Artillery and assault guns were abandoned after they had exhausted their ammunition. And then the wounded moving with the troops met their fate... Veritable hordes of hundreds of soldiers from every type of unit headed westwards under the nearest available officer. The enemy infantry were swept out of the way by our advancing bayonets; even tanks turned in their tracks. But all the same the Russian fire struck with impunity at the masses, moving forward with their heads down, unevenly and unprotected. Our losses multiplied.

Major Kampov was with a column of Soviet tanks and cavalry that caught up with the fleeing Germans at about six o'clock in the morning.

The Germans ran in all directions, [Kampov said]. And for the next four hours our tanks raced up and down the plain crushing them by the hundred. Our cavalry, competing with the tanks, chased them through the ravines where it was hard for the tanks to pursue them. Most of the time the tanks were not using their guns lest they hit their own cavalry. Hundreds and hundreds of cavalry were hacking at them with their sabres, and massacring Fritzes as no one had ever been massacred by cavalry before. There was no time to take prisoners. It was the kind of carnage that nothing could stop until it was all over. In a small area over twenty thousand Germans were killed.

Fleeing men reached the Gniloy-Tikich, a stream that had thawed a few days before. Now it was eight yards wide and deep enough to drown in. Léon Degrelle of the SS Sturmbrigade Wallonie reported:

> *The artillery teams that had escaped destruction plunged first into the waves and ice floes. The banks of the river were steep, the horses turned back and were drowned. Men then threw themselves in to swim across the river. But they had hardly got to the other side when they were turned into blocks of ice, and their clothes froze to their bodies. They tried to throw their equipment over the river. But often their uniforms fell into the current. Soon hundreds of soldiers, completely naked and red as lobsters, were thronging the other bank. Many soldiers did not know how to swim. Maddened by the approach of the Russian armour which was coming down the slope and firing at them, they threw themselves pell-mell into the icy water. Some escaped drowning by clinging to trees that had been hastily felled…but hundreds drowned. Under the fire of tanks thousands upon thousands of soldiers, half-clothed, streaming with icy water or naked as the day they were born, ran through the snow towards the distant cottages of Lysyanka.*

III Panzer Corps retrieved only 30,000 mostly unarmed survivors from Lysyanka. General Stemmermann was not among them. He had been killed by shrapnel. As a result of this action, Konev was made Marshal of the Soviet Union.

UKRAINE LIBERATED

To the south the 3rd and 4th Ukrainian Fronts encircled Nikopol, which fell on 22 February. The German Sixth Army retreated, but it was exhausted. Some Panzer divisions had as few as five serviceable tanks. However, during the fighting in January and February, Manstein reckoned that the Red Army had had 25,353 men taken prisoner, and lost 3,928 tanks and 3,536 guns. But, he concluded, this only showed the enormous resources the Soviets now had at their command, and the drop in the ratio of prisoners to equipment meant that they were no longer simply throwing infantrymen at a better-equipped enemy.

Zhukov now took command of the 1st Belorussian Front with its sixty divisions and at least 1,000 tanks. On 4 March 1944, he went on the attack on a front 120 miles wide. In two days, he was approaching Volochisk on the L'vov–Odessa railway which was Manstein's last supply route east of the Carpathians. Army Group South now risked being cut off from the rest of the German army. To prevent this, Manstein rushed every available man to the defence of Ternopil. This could only be achieved by slipping columns through the 1st Ukrainian Front without engaging them. At Ternopil, the Germans held up the Russians for a month.

While Zhukov attacked to the north, Konev advanced in the south. Again Manstein begged Hitler to send reinforcements or allow him to withdraw. After hours of discussion, Hitler sent the Waffen-SS II Panzer Corps, which was stationed at Alençon in France in anticipation of an invasion across the Channel, and allowed the First Panzer Army, which was already encircled, to fight its way out to the west. Nevertheless, on 30 March both Manstein and Kleist were sacked. General Walther Model took command of the renamed Army Group North Ukraine, while General Schörner took over the new Army Group South Ukraine.

Nothing could check Zhukov's advance and he soon reached the foothills of the Carpathians. Reinforced with two Panzer divisions, Model managed to extricate the First Panzer Army. Schörner did less well. By the end of April, Army Group South Ukraine had been pushed out of the Ukraine completely, though to his credit Schörner had managed to save the Sixth and Eighth Armies in the process.

Odessa was evacuated on 9 April, abandoning the Seventeenth Army on the Crimean peninsula. The Soviet's Independent Coastal Army had already established a bridgehead at Kerch on the eastern tip of the Crimea with twelve divisions in it. The 4th Ukrainian Front now sent eighteen infantry divisions and four armoured corps from the north. The offensive began on 8 April under a Soviet air umbrella. By mid-day on the 9th, the Rumanian 10th Division had collapsed, and two days later, Soviet tanks took Dzhanskoy, an important railway junction on the way to Sebastopol.

The Independent Coastal Army broke out of its bridgehead on 11 April and by the 16th had joined up with the 4th Ukrainian Front on the south coast at Yalta.

The Germans could not resist these advances. The five divisions of the Seventeenth Army were now down to a third of their strength. Schörner and the commander of the Seventeenth, General Jaenecke, both flew to Bechtesgaden to see Hitler and beg him to evacuate their troops. Hitler refused and Jaenecke was replaced by General Allmendinger on 27 April.

After forty-eight hours of artillery bombardment, the Russians attacked in the Crimea again on 7 May. On 9 May, Hitler finally authorized the evacuation. But it was too late. That night two small ships got through and took off around a thousand men. Then the Soviets started firing Katyusha rockets and there was a massacre. When tanks rolled in on the morning of 12 May, the Germans surrendered in large numbers. There were thousands of wounded who were evacuated to the tip of the promontory. Some 750 SS men refused to give up and continued firing. A few dozen survivors tried to escape on rafts or small boats. They were machine-gunned in the water by Soviet aircraft.

RETREAT IN THE NORTH

Over a thousand miles to the north, the German army was also on the retreat. At the beginning of the year, General von Klücher had been holding a five-hundred- mile front with forty divisions of infantry. They were dangerously exposed. Klücher asked permission to withdraw to prepared positions along the 'Panther' line abutting Lake Peipus, effectively shortening the front by 160 miles. Aware that Russia and Finland were already extending peace feelers in Stockholm, Hitler refused.

On 14 January, the Leningrad Front's forty-two infantry divisions and nine tank corps attacked the left wing of the German Eighteenth Army while the eighteen infantry divisions and fifteen tank divisions of the Volkhov Front attacked the right. The German left held out for nearly a week, but when the three divisions there collapsed the Russians broke through. By 26 January they had captured a huge amount of weapons, including eighty-five guns of larger than ten-inch calibre. On the right, the Volkhov Front recaptured Novgorod and re-established the rail link with Moscow. Finally, on 27 January, the siege of Leningrad was lifted after nine hundred days.

Klücher was replaced by Model who was given two extra divisions. The Baltic Front then attacked the German Sixteenth Army and Model was given permission to withdraw to the

Westward Soviet T-34 tanks roll toward the Russo-Polish border, 1943.

'Panther' line. After he successfully withdrew to the line that ran from the shores of Lake Peipus to Narva on the Baltic, Model was called to replace Manstein at Army Group South and was replaced at Army Group North by Colonel-General G. von Lindemann.

Contrary to Hitler's fears, the German withdrawal did not lead to Finland's capitulation. Peace talks were broken off when the Soviet Union demanded that all German troops on Finnish soil be interned within thirty days and the Finns pay $600 million in reparations in five annual instalments. Meanwhile Hungary, Germany's reluctant ally in the 'crusade against Bolshevism', tried to withdraw from the war and Hitler invaded with eleven divisions.

SUMMER OFFENSIVE

But there would be no stopping the Russians. As the Soviets prepared for their summer offensive of 1944, Stalin had at his disposal 500 infantry and 40 artillery divisions, 300 armoured or mechanized brigades with 9,000 tanks and 16,600 aircraft.

The first blow would fall on Finland, who had six divisions strung out along three lines of fortifications. Stalin sent against them twenty infantry divisions, four armoured brigades, five or six tank regiments, four regiments of assault guns, 450 armoured vehicles and 1,000 planes.

The assault began on 9 June with an artillery barrage along a ten-mile front with 250 guns per mile. It was in the coastal sector so that the Red Navy's Baltic Fleet could join in the bombardment. The following day, the Red Army sent in three divisions of infantry for every one Finnish regiment defending.

They broke through and advanced six miles, taking much of the Finnish artillery. The following day, the Finnish 1st Armoured Division staged a counterattack to no avail.

The Russians then delayed for five or six days while the Finns withdrew. When the jaws of the Soviet pincers closed in early July, there was nothing there. The Finns then withdrew to their last line of defence, but continued fighting furiously. Few prisoners were taken. Moscow had other objectives in mind, and wiping out the Finnish Army was more trouble than it was worth. On 4 September 1944, Helsinki and Moscow signed a peace treaty and Finland changed sides. The Finnish Army then fought one last campaign to drive their former German allies out of Lapland.

By 22 June, the Soviet Union had already turned its attention to the German forces on its western borders. The Red Army attacked down the north bank of the Pripet river with 166 infantry divisions; 5,200 tanks and self-propelled guns; 31,000 artillery pieces and mortars; and 6,000 aircraft. This was the largest concentration of fighting power yet seen on the Eastern Front. Twenty-five thousand two-ton lorries were needed to carry ammunition and supplies alone. The objective was nothing less than the destruction of Army Group Centre, which now comprised just thirty-seven divisions.

In the initial thrust of Operation *Bagration*, the 166 Soviet infantry divisions fell on a mere twenty-eight German divisions along a 435-mile front. The Soviet divisions were up to strength with 10,000 men apiece. The German divisions were very much under-strength and, in some places, they could only muster 150 men per mile. As far as tanks went, the Germans were outnumbered by more than ten to one. Army Group Centre could not even take advantage of the Panzers' famed manoeuvrability: in a *Führebefehl* of 8 March 1944, Hitler had ordered the construction of a series of fixed positions. These fortified areas were designed to 'prevent the enemy from seizing centres of decisive strategic importance. [The troops] are to allow themselves to be encircled so as to engage as many of the enemy as possible.' They were to hold out to the last man and only the Führer could order a withdrawal.

There were nine of these strongpoints, manned by men taken from the field. Panzer commander General Georg-Hans Reinhardt objected to this, pointing out that this left gaps in the line that the Soviets could easily breach. He was told that the five divisions shut away in the fortified area at Vitebsk in Belarus could engage between thirty and forty enemy divisions that would otherwise be free to attack to the west and south. Holding Vitebsk was considered 'a matter of prestige,' Hitler said. 'Vitebsk is the only place on the Eastern Front whose loss would resound throughout the world.'

Besides, Hitler was not expecting an attack in Belarus at all. As soon as the ground was hard enough, he thought Stalin would attack again in the Ukraine. When Hitler was told of a major military build-up north of the Pripet river, he dismissed it as a clumsy decoy. Even when the Third Panzer Army in the area of Vitebsk and the Ninth Army between the Dniepr and the Berezina were on the brink of collapse, he refused to send reinforcements, claiming the attack was a diversion. This was not just because of Hitler's pigheadedness. Little information was coming in from the front. Two nights before the attack, 240,000 partisans in the forests of Belorussia had cut the communication lines of Army Group Centre in more than ten thousand places, even as far west as Minsk.

Within forty-eight hours of the start of the attack, the Third Panzer Army had been overpowered and Vitebsk was surrounded. At 1520 hours on 24 June permission was sought for LIII Corps there to break out. At 1528, Hitler refused. At 1830, he relented, but insisted that one division be left behind to garrison Vitebsk. But, by then, it was too late. LIII Corps was intercepted and destroyed. When its commander General Gollwitzer surrendered on 27 June he had just two hundred men with him, 180 of whom were wounded. There was now a twenty-eight-mile gap in the line, with nothing to fill it but three worn-out divisions and seventy guns.

To the south, XXXV Corps, defending the fortified area at Bobruysk, suffered the same fate as LIII Corps, while to the north, the 1st Baltic Front ignored the fortified areas, advanced between them, defeated XLI Panzer Corps and cut off the retreating XXXV Corps.

On 28 June, Hitler finally conceded that the attack in Belarus was more than just a diversion. Once again, he sacked the commander of the army group there, General Busch, and installed Field Marshal Model. But there was little Model could do. On 29 June, 16,000 Germans surrounded in the pockets surrendered. Eighteen thousand of their comrades were already dead. By then, the 1st Belorussian Front were eight miles from Minsk. The fortified areas at Orsha and Mogilev were overrun, and the entire Fourth Army was in retreat through forests and marshlands crawling with partisans.

Model was sent three divisions from Army Group North and ten, including four Panzer divisions, from Army Group North Ukraine. But these were simply swallowed up in a breach in the line now 185 miles wide. Minsk was taken. Some 285,000 Germans were killed or captured, and 215 tanks and 1,300 guns were lost. It was a greater disaster than Stalingrad, especially as the Third Reich was now fighting in Normandy.

To celebrate, Stalin had 57,600 prisoners of war marched through Moscow with their generals at their head. According to the Moscow correspondent of the *Sunday Times* Alexander Werth:

Youngsters booed and whistled, and even threw things at the Germans, only to be immediately restrained by the adults; men looked on grimly and in silence; but many women, especially elderly women, were full of commiseration (some even had tears in their eyes) as they looked at these bedraggled 'Fritzes'. I remember one old women murmuring 'just like our poor boys... tozhe pognali ne voinu (also driven into war)'.

The 1st Baltic Front poured through the gap that had been created between Army Group Centre and Army Group North. They headed into Lithuania, capturing Vilnius on 13 July. As there was nothing to stop them swinging north through Riga in Latvia and attacking Army Group North from the rear, Lindemann asked for permission to withdraw. He was replaced by General Friessner, who also requested permission to retreat. He was summoned to Rastenburg, where he pointed out to Hitler that his 700,000 men were beleaguered and outnumbered eight to one.

'I am not trying to hang onto my job,' Friessner told the Führer. 'You can relieve me of it. You can even have me shot if you want. But to ask me, in full knowledge of the facts and against the dictates of my conscience, to lead the men entrusted to me to certain destruction – that you can never do.'

With tears in his eyes, Hitler seized Friessner's hand and promised him every support. But still he refused to let Army Group North withdraw. Instead Friessner was to swap commands with General Schörner in Army Group South Ukraine.

The 3rd Baltic Front to Army Group North's rear then went on the offensive and on 25 July the Leningrad Front attacked. Schörner was besieged by eighty divisions. To the south the Russians reached Praga, a suburb on the Vistula opposite Warsaw on 31 July. On 1 August, they reached Kalvariya, just fifteen miles from the frontier of East Prussia and the Gulf of Riga, just west of the port. The Sixteenth and Eighteenth Armies were now cut off in Estonia and northern Latvia. That autumn the remaining twenty-six divisions were compressed into a small pocket around Memel on the Kurland peninsula in Latvia, where they would remain besieged until the end of the war.

While Army Group Centre was being crushed and Army Group North surrounded, Army Group North Ukraine was attacked by Konev. For the assault he had seven armies at his disposal, along with 16,213 guns and rocket launchers, 3,240 aircraft, 1,573 tanks and 463 assault guns. Army Group North Ukraine had just forty-three divisions and were outnumbered by more than two to one in tanks, and five to one in the air.

The attack came on 13 July. The following day, the 8th Panzer Division was caught on the move by the Red Air Force and destroyed. With it, said Major-General von Mellenthin, 'all hope of counter-attack disappeared'. Within twenty-four hours Konev had broken though. Pincers closed around General Haffe's XIII Corps. Several thousand men escaped in hand-to-hand fighting, but on 23 July, Haffe surrendered, along with 17,000 of his men. Another 30,000 lay dead on the battlefield.

Model tried to hold a defensive line on the Bug, but with the army crumbling around him he finally got permission to fall back to the Vistula.

When the Red Army reached Praga, it had stopped. The Soviets then encouraged the underground in the city – the Home Army of around fifty thousand – to revolt. This army, loyal to the Polish government-in-exile in London, seized on this chance as the best way of stopping a Communist-led takeover in Poland. The Home Army attacked the German garrison on 1 August and within three days had taken over most of the city. But the Germans sent reinforcements. For the next sixty-three days Warsaw was pounded by bombs and shells.

The Red Army did nothing and Stalin refused the western Allies permission to use Soviet airfields to fly in supplies to the beleaguered Poles. Without ammunition and food, the Home Army was forced to surrender on 2 October, as Stalin had anticipated. Warsaw's population was deported and the city destroyed. When the Soviets finally forced the Germans out of Poland, the way was open for them to install their own pro-Soviet regime on 1 January 1945.

'Such was their liberation of Poland,' said Churchill, 'where they now rule. But this cannot be the end of the story.'

Communist rule in Poland was only relinquished in 1989.

CLEARING THE BALKANS

After Germany's defeat at Stalingrad, her staunch ally Rumania grew restive. Rumanian diplomats attempted to reestablish contact with Britain and the US. However, as Rumanian troops were fighting alongside the Germans in the Soviet Union, the western Allies refused to respond until Bucharest had agreed conditions for a ceasefire with Moscow.

RUMANIA

On 2 April 1944, Soviet Foreign Minister Vyacheslav Molotov issued a statement saying: 'The Soviet Union in no way seeks to acquire any part of Rumanian territory or to change the present social order. Russian troops have entered Rumania solely as the result of military necessity.'

Molotov was referring to the 3rd Ukrainian Front, by this time pursuing Army Group South Ukraine into the Carpathians.

Molotov's statement opened the way for clandestine peace talks. The leader of the National Peasants' Party, Julius Maniu, who was in league with King Michael, told the Allies he was willing to enter negotiations on that basis. He also agreed to pay substantial reparations to Moscow. On the other hand, there was an understanding that Transylvania, which had been transferred to Hungary in the Vienna agreement of 30 August 1940, would be returned.

Rumania's Fascist dictator General Ion Antonescu knew what was going on behind his back, but he did not try to stop it. However, Rumania's officer corps had sworn allegiance to the king, not to Antonescu and in Army Group South Ukraine Friessner began to distrust the Third and Fourth Rumanian Armies under his command. He began to intermingle German and Rumanian units at all levels so that the Germans could keep an eye on them.

Army Group South Ukraine was now facing over ninety divisions with overwhelming superiority in artillery and control of the skies. By 20 August the 2nd Ukrainian Front was at the gates of Iasi, capital of Moldavia. The Rumanian divisions collapsed and, without waiting for Hitler's authorization, Friessner had no alternative but to make a 'fighting withdrawal'.

On 22 August, King Michael summoned Antonescu and his foreign minister to the palace and ordered them to conclude an armistice with the Allies. When they demurred, he had them arrested and at 2200 hours Bucharest Radio broadcast an order to all Rumanian forces to cease fire. Friessner immediately contacted Generals Dumitrescu and Steflea, commanders of the Third and Fourth Rumanian Armies. Refusing to break their oath of loyalty to their king, they laid down their arms: Germany had lost another ally.

Hitler then ordered the Luftwaffe to bomb Bucharest. Rumania's new prime minister, General Sanatescu, seized the opportunity to declare war on Germany. Rumanian troops occupied the crossings of the Danube, Prut and Siretul rivers and opened them to the Russians.

Friessner's Sixth Army was then encircled. Fourteen divisions were wiped out. Only two divisional commanders escaped, and all four corps commanders were captured. IV Corps of the Eighth Army retreated along the Prut, but was trapped by the

2nd Ukrainian Front and forced to surrender. In the space of a fortnight, General Friessner had lost sixteen of the twenty-four divisions under his command.

On 6 September, Rumania declared war on Hungary and the formal armistice agreement with the Allies, signed on 12 September, required it to put at least twelve divisions under the command of the Soviet High Command.

BULGARIA

The capitulation of Rumania put Bulgaria in an awkward position. In December 1941, King Boris had declared war on Britain and the US, but not on the Soviet Union: Russia was a traditional ally. But King Boris had died mysteriously in August 1943, after visiting Hitler. His son, Simon II, was only a child and a three man regency council took control. They began peace negotiations with London and Washington. Seeing Bulgaria as part of the Soviet sphere of influence, Stalin responded by declaring war on Bulgaria on 5 September. Bulgaria responded by declaring war on Germany. Peace negotiations were then transferred to Moscow, where an armistice was signed on 28 October.

Meanwhile the 3rd Ukrainian Front had entered Bulgaria. A Communist government took over in Sofia. The three regents were put in front of a firing squad – naked, as the authorities did not want to damage their clothes. However, Simon II survived. He lived in exile in Madrid for fifty years, then returned to Bulgaria and was elected prime minister as Simon Saxe-Coburg-Gotha in 2001.

RETREAT FROM GREECE

The day after the Rumanian ceasefire Army Group E in Salonika received orders to evacuate the Aegean and Ionian islands and the south of mainland Greece. But when Bulgaria declared war on Germany, it was ordered to make contact with the Second Panzer Army to form a continuous line of defence from the Carpathians to the Adriatic. As it was, the Germans no longer had the air transport to evacuate all of the islands and Rhodes, Crete, Leros, Kos and Milos remained in German hands until the end of the war.

The forces withdrawing from the Peloponnese were harassed by royalist guerrillas and the British 2 Airborne Brigade which had liberated Patras on 4 October. Control of Athens was relinquished to its mayor the same day. However, the Germans eased their way out of Greece by agreeing to give the Communist-backed Greek Peoples' Liberation Army a large cache of arms.

The Russians reached the Danube on 1 October while the Bulgarian Fifth Army took Nis on the 14th, hindering any counter-attack from the German troops in Yugoslavia. Then they marched on Belgrade which, with Tito's guerrillas, they took on 20 October.

Army Group E now had to take the coast road to withdraw. Harassed by partisans it managed to fall back on Sarajevo before the Russians could cut off its retreat. Behind the German lines the guerrillas liberated Kotor, Dubrovnik and Split – which had been given the Italian names Cattaro, Ragusa and Spalato – and took the Italian town Zara, slavicizing its name as Zadar.

A few days after liberating Patras, British airborne troops took the airfields at Elevsis and Megara, and on 14 October a mixed British and Greek fleet dropped anchor in Piraeus and landed III Corps. Its aim was to prevent Greece going Communist. The result was a civil war that lasted until 1948, and only ended then because Tito fell out with Moscow and stopped giving the Greek Communists his backing.

Bitter fighting broke out in Rumania and the Germans fell back into Hungary. The Soviet armour sped ahead of the infantry, but on the almost treeless Great Hungarian Plain Friessner's Army Group South – as the Army Group South Ukraine had now been renamed – reverted to the tactics they had perfected in North Africa. The Panzers raced across the open country, attacking the flanks and rear of the Soviets, who kept to the roads. On 10 October, using these tactics, III Panzer Corps managed to trap the Sixth Guards Tank Army in the outskirts of Debrecen and brought the Soviet Twenty-Seventh Army to a halt. The German High Command claimed to have killed 12,000 Russians and taken 6,662 prisoners, capturing or destroying around 1,000 tanks and over 900 assault guns. But the German Sixth Army also suffered considerable losses and its six Panzer divisions now had just sixty-seven tanks and fifty-seven assault guns.

Friessner had prevented the Russians cutting off the retreat of the German Eighth Army, but had checked them only temporarily. On 20 October Debrecen fell to the 2nd Ukrainian Front, while the 4th Ukrainian Front moved into Czechoslovakia. And behind the lines in Slovakia, partisans began stopping trains and killing any German soldiers they found on board.

HUNGARY

Although the Germans had occupied Hungary on 27 March 1944, they had kept Admiral Miklos Horthy on as regent, even though he opposed the deportation of the Jews. Secretly Horthy contacted London and Washington who insisted that he negotiate an armistice with Moscow. On 11 October, Hungary agreed to an immediate cessation of hostilities. Horthy also demanded that the British and Americans share in the occupation of Hungary. It was not to be.

On 15 October, Budapest Radio announced the armistice and condemned Hitler and his policies. The broadcast concluded: 'Today for anyone who can see plainly, Germany has lost the war. All governments responsible for the fate of their countries must draw their conclusions from this fact, for, as was said once by the great German statesman Bismarck: 'No nation is forced by its obligations to sacrifice itself on the altar of alliance'.

Hungarian Nazis responded by kidnapping Horthy. He was taken to Germany and imprisoned in Weilheim Castle near Munich. His replacement was the fanatical Fascist Major Ference Szalasi, leader of the 'Arrow Cross', Hungary's Fascist party. But Szalasi could not stop the army chief of staff General Voros, the commander of the First Army General Miklos and the commander of the Second Army General Veress, surrendering to the Russians. Veress even turned up at the headquarters of the 2nd Ukrainian Front in a car recently given to him by General Guderian.

The Hungarian Third Army fought on. But when the Soviets attacked Baja on the Danube, it broke, leaving the road to Budapest open to three Soviet tank corps. The Germans counter-attacked, hitting the Soviets on the flanks. But the capitulation of the Hungarians in the centre and the collapse of the German Sixth Army allowed the Soviets to establish several bridgeheads on the west bank of the Tisza river.

By this time, German infantry battalions had shrunk to around two hundred men and there was a shortage of tanks. Factories rushing out new vehicles cut down the test and inspection procedures at the end of the assembly line, and tanks reaching the front frequently broke down. Divisions only had five or six tanks available daily. Three new Panzer divisions, along with a battalion of Panther tanks, were to be sent to Hungary, but in the meantime Friessner pulled back from the Tisza and dug in along the heights of the Matra mountains.

Then the 3rd Ukrainian Front arrived in Hungary at Mohacs. It had driven 125 miles up the Danube from Belgrade, brushing aside the weakened defences of the Second Panzer Army along the way. The 2nd Ukrainian Front then broke through the German Sixth Army on the Matra mountains and took Pliev. From there it could shell the barges that supplied Budapest, which Hitler now proclaimed to be a 'fortress'. It was garrisoned by the SS IX Mountain Corps under General Pfeffer-Wildenbruch.

On 14 December the Sixth Guards Tank Army took Ypolisag, outflanking the right of the Eighth Army and trapping it against the Carpathians. Hitler ordered Friessner to mount a counterattack against the Sixth Guards Tank Army using the 3rd and 6th Panzer Divisions which were stationed on the isthmus between Lake Velencei and Lake Balaton. Friessner pointed out that weeks of sleet and rain had left the ground impassable. Rather than wait for the frost, Friessner was ordered to attack with his infantry, leaving the Panzers behind. Friessner protested that this would deprive him of his striking power. He was told to obey orders or resign.

Two days later, the 3rd Ukrainian Front's infantry attacked and inflicted a crushing defeat. The Kremlin claimed that the Germans had lost twelve thousand dead and that 5,468 prisoners had been taken, and 311 tanks and 248 guns had been captured or destroyed.

Friessner wanted to counter-attack using the SS IX Mountain Corps, but this would have meant evacuating Budapest. As it was, the corps was no longer under his control. Then on the night of 22 December, Friessner was relieved of his command and replaced by General Wöhler.

Two SS cavalry divisions, the *Feldherrnhalle Panzergrenadier Division* and the 13th Panzer Division, were now cut off. Without telling the High Command, Hitler tried to relieve them by taking two divisions of the IV SS Panzer Corps – the 3rd *Totenhopf* ('Death's Head') Panzer Division and the 5th Wiking Panzer Division – from Army Group Centre where they were vital to the defence of East Prussia. Guderian tried to get them recalled.

'All my protests were useless,' he said. 'Hitler thought it was more important to free the city of Budapest than to defend Eastern Germany.'

But then, Guderian was born in East Prussia. Guderian also warned Hitler that the Soviets were building up for an attack in the Bulgarian sector. But Hitler merely replied: 'My dear general, I do not believe in this Russian attack. It is all a gigantic bluff. The figures produced by your 'Foreign Armies East' section are far too exaggerated. You worry too much. I am firmly convinced that nothing will happen in the East.'

CHAPTER 16

From the Vistula to Berlin

The Russian people had suffered agonies under three years of German occupation. As 1944 drew to a close, the Red Army stood on the border of Germany itself, poised to wreak a terrible revenge.

The Soviets made their first attempt to invade East Prussia on 16 October 1944. East Prussia was part of Germany on the Baltic, bordering Lithuania to the east, Poland to the south and separated from the rest of Germany after the First World War by the Polish Corridor and the free port of Danzig, now Gdansk in Poland. After the Second World War it was divided between Russia and Poland.

The attack on East Prussia was made by the 3rd Belorussian Front under Colonel-General Chernyakhovsky. His forty divisions, backed by aircraft and armour, covered a front of just ninety miles. They faced the fifteen divisions of the German Fourth Army which was stretched out over 220 miles. However, the defending commander, General Friedrich Hossbach, had the advantage of permanent fortifications. The attack also lacked the element of surprise. The build-up had been well signalled in advance and followed the same route used by the Russian army in 1914. Hossbach managed to pull five or six divisions from less

Charge *Advancing Russian troops charge down a Polish street during the push to the Elbe, 1944.*

threatened sections of the front and plug the gaps. And when he was sent more armour he managed to counter–attack.

While trying to cross the River Angerapp on 21 and 22 October, the Eleventh Guards Army was attacked from both north and south. They were thrown back to the right bank of the Rominte, leaving some 1,000 tanks and over 300 guns. They also left evidence of atrocities in some 300 villages. Even though the Germans had done the same, and worse, in Russia, Hitler's propaganda minister Joseph Goebbels made great play of this. As a result, some three months later, six million Germans fled before the Russian invasion in temperatures of twenty degrees below zero.

As Germany's main effort was now in the west, Guderian was ordered to stabilize the Eastern Front. The autumn promised to be mild and the frosts delayed, so it seemed likely that a Russian winter offensive might be put off until the New Year. Guderian planned the construction of strongpoints along the front and, by mid-December, had pulled all the Panzer and Panzergrenadier divisions out of the line to form a mobile reserve. But twelve under-strength divisions was not an adequate reserve to hold a front 725 miles long.

Guderian's plan was to establish a major line of defence, well camouflaged, twelve miles behind the line they were holding. As soon as the Russian artillery started the barrage that heralded an attack, everyone, save a rearguard, would pull back. The barrage would then be wasted as it would fall on positions already evacuated. The well-prepared assault would be fruitless, and the Russians would simply run up against another line of defence where they would have to begin their preparations all over again. When Guderian submitted this plan to Hitler, he lost this temper. He refused to accept the loss of twelve miles without a fight and ordered that the second line be prepared just one or two miles behind the front. This, Guderian said, was First World War thinking.

The fortifications themselves were well prepared, but the Ardennes offensive had left the 'Great Defensive Line' poorly defended. Worse, Hitler ordered the reserves to be held near the front. This meant that when the great Russian tidal wave came, it simply swamped both the defensive lines and the reserves. Hitler blamed the men who had built the fortifications, and claimed that he had always favoured a twelve-mile gap between the defensive lines rather than a one- or two-mile gap.

'Who was the halfwit who gave such idiotic orders?' he asked.

Guderian pointed out that it was he himself who had made the decision. Hitler called for the minutes of the autumn planning meetings to be brought. But he broke off reading them after a couple of sentences. As the Red Army advanced relentlessly on Germany, the atmosphere in Hitler's headquarters became increasingly unworldly. Hitler insisted that he was the only one there with real front-line experience – though he had not visited the front line once during the war. His ego was inflated, fed by the flattery of party officials, particularly Göring and von Ribbentrop, and he resolutely refused to learn from others.

'There is not need for you to try to teach me,' he told Guderian. 'I've been commanding the Wehrmacht in the field for five years now and in that time I have had more practical experience than any of the gentlemen of the General Staff could ever hope for. I've studied Clausewitz and Moltke and read all the Schlieffen papers. I'm more in the picture than you are.'

But all that experience could not stop the Russians. By 5 December they had reached the outskirts of Budapest, and by Christmas Eve they had encircled the city.

When it became clear on 23 December that the Ardennes offensive was a failure, Guderian begged for the attack to be called off and for the remaining forces to be switched to the Eastern Front. He reckoned that the Russian winter offensive would start on 12 January and he calculated that the Russians had a superiority of seven to one in tanks, eleven to one in infantry and twenty to one in guns. That gave them an overall superiority of fifteen to one on the ground and twenty to one in the air. Guderian reckoned that German soldiers could still triumph with odds of five to one against them. But against these odds, victory was impossible.

Guderian believed that the only hope was to build up a large Panzer army in the area around Lodz and, when the Russians broke through, fight a war of movement, a Panzer war – 'for this was a type of battle in which the German commander and soldiers, despite the long war and their consequent exhaustion, were still superior to the enemy,' he said.

On 24 December, Guderian visited Hitler's headquarters for a conference. When he presented his report about the situation on the Eastern Front, Hitler refused to believe his figures on the estimated strength of the enemy and said that he doubted that the Russians would attack at all. Hitler was by this time in a state of utter delusion, ordering the formation of Panzer brigades consisting of just two battalions – the strength of a regiment – and anti-tank brigades of just one battalion.

Jodl opposed Guderian's request for forces to be switched to the east. He wanted more attacks in the west, believing that the British and Americans could be halted if they went on the offensive in Alsace. Guderian pointed out that the production from the factories in the Ruhr had been halted by enemy bombing. If they lost the industrial area of Upper Silesia to the Russians, they would no longer have the weapons-making capacity to continue the war. But his request to have forces switched to the Eastern Front was denied and Hitler ordered a further weakening of the Polish Front by ordering General Reinhardt's reserves to go to Budapest to lift the siege. As a result, two of the fourteen and a half Panzer and Panzergrenadier divisions assembled to take on the Russian winter offensive were sent to a secondary front.

On New Year's Eve, Guderian went once again to Hitler's headquarters to ask for reinforcements in the east. This time he had a preliminary meeting with von Rundstedt, who informed him that there were three divisions on the Western Front and one division in Italy that he could have. They were already near railway stations, ready to be transferred. But when Guderian got to see Hitler, Jodl opposed the movement of forces to the Eastern Front once more, saying that there were no units available. Guderian contradicted him and when Jodl asked where he had got the information from, Guderian replied that it was from von Rundstedt, Commander-in-Chief of the Western Front. Jodl could say no more and Hitler approved the transfer of the four divisions. However, instead of sending them to Poland were they were needed, he sent them to Hungary.

At a meeting on 9 January, Guderian again begged Hitler to strengthen his mobile reserve, but when he showed Hitler the enemy dispositions and strengths, Hitler claimed that they were completely idiotic and ordered the man who prepared them locked up in a lunatic asylum. Guderian pointed out that they had been prepared by one of his very best officers and he would not have presented them if he had not agreed with them.

'So you had better have me certified as well,' he said.

Again Hitler refused Guderian's request for a strengthening of his Panzer reserve.

'The Eastern Front has never possessed such a strong reserve as it does now,' said Hitler. 'It is all your doing and I thank you for it.'

Guderian replied: 'The Eastern Front is a house of cards. If the front is broken at one point, the rest will collapse. Twelve and a half divisions is far too small a reserve for such an extended front.'

As Guderian left, Hitler said: 'The Eastern Front must help itself and make do with what it has got.'

This sent a chill though Guderian. When the Russians broke through it would be his homeland of East Prussia that would be lost.

INTO EAST PRUSSIA

On 12 January, huge numbers of men and tanks began pouring over the Vistula into the Russian bridgeheads. The following day the Russian Third and Fourth Guards Tank Armies broke though south of Warsaw. Over the next few days, the Russians went on the offensive down the entire line and the front began to disintegrate.

Guderian kept Hitler informed of the worsening situation by phone and by 15 January Hitler began interfering. Over Guderian's head, he ordered the transfer of the *Gross-Deutschland* Panzergrenadier Corps from East Prussia to the area around Kielce. Guderian protested that it was too late to stop the Russian breakthrough at Kielce and weakened the defences in East Prussia at the very time they were coming under attack.

On 16 January, Hitler returned to the partly bombed Chancellery in Berlin to be nearer to the Eastern Front. He now decided that, as the Allied advance in the west was currently stalled in Alsace, the Western Front should go on the defensive to release troops to fight in the east. He also decided that they must hit the southern flank of the Russian spearhead and Hitler ordered Guderian to send the Sixth Panzer Army to Hungary. It was necessary, Hitler said, to keep possession of the oilfields in Hungary, otherwise there would be no fuel for the Panzers.

With the Red Army advancing rapidly across Poland, the Nazi extermination camp of Auschwitz-Birkenau near Oswiecim in Galicia was abandoned. Established in April 1940, it became the biggest of the death camps and it is thought that between 1 and 2.5 million people died there, most of them deliberately gassed. On 17 January 1945, inmates were transported to other concentration camps including Dachau and Mauthausen. The Nazis also began a death march out of the camp ahead of the Soviet advance. When the Red Army arrived at Auschwitz on 27 January, there were 7,650 inmates left in the camp.

General Nehring's XXIV Panzer Corps was stemming the Russian attack around Kielce, but the XLVI Panzer Corps had to pull out of the Warsaw area when it risked being encircled. It was supposed to go south to stop a Russian breakthrough that would cut East and West Prussia off from the rest of Germany. But the Russians threw it back onto the north bank of the Vistula and began their dash on the German border unhindered.

The German garrison in Warsaw now risked being cut off. Guderian told Hitler that they should be withdrawn, but Hitler, predictably, insisted that Warsaw be held at all costs. However, the garrison commandant had little artillery and only four infantry battalions with limited combat experience. It would have been impossible for them to hold the city and the commandant withdrew his garrison despite Hitler's orders to the contrary. Hitler was furious and spent the next few days investigating the loss of Warsaw rather than devoting himself to more pressing matters. When Hitler ordered the arrest of members of the General Staff, Guderian said that he alone was responsible for the loss of Warsaw, so it was he who should be arrested, not his staff. Nevertheless Hitler had three of Guderian's staff arrested at gunpoint. Guderian again insisted that he was the one whose conduct should be investigated, so he submitted to lengthy interrogations at a time when he should have been concentrating all his efforts on the battle for the Eastern Front. Two of his staff were then released, but instead of returning to their staff duties, they were sent to command regiments on the Eastern Front. Three days later one of them was killed. The third member of Guderian's staff was sent to a concentration camp, which he later swapped for an American prisoner of war camp.

On 18 January, the Germans in Hungary attacked in an attempt to lift the siege of Budapest. They fought their way through to the banks of the Danube. But that same day the Russians entered the city, so the effort had been wasted. Nevertheless, Hitler sent the Sixth Panzer Army to Hungary in an attempt to hold the Russians in check there.

On 20 January, the Russians set foot on German soil. Guderian's wife, who had been under constant surveillance by the local Nazi party, was allowed to leave and flee to the safety of Guderian's headquarters half an hour before the first shell landed in Deipenhof.

The Russian onslaught could not be resisted. Hitler began to accuse his Panzer commanders of treason. Guderian tried to calm him, but Reinhardt and Hossbach were relieved of their commands.

The Russians had now mastered the art of Panzer warfare. They advanced rapidly, bypassing strongpoints and outflanking fortified lines – though most of the fortifications in the east had been stripped to build the Atlantic Wall. Germany's only hope now was that the Western Allies might realize what the rapid Russian advance might mean for the future of Europe, and sign an armistice. Guderian proposed to the German Foreign Minister von Ribbentrop that he open negotiations for an armistice on at least one front – preferably the Western. Von Ribbentrop told Guderian that he was a loyal follower of Hitler and he knew that the Führer did not want to make peace.

'How would you feel if in three or four weeks the Russians were at the gates of Berlin?' asked Guderian.

'Do you believe that that is possible?' asked a shocked von Ribbentrop.

When Hitler heard of this, Guderian too was accused of treason – though he was not arrested. Hitler had few enough capable officers left.

HIMMLER'S ARMY

Guderian proposed a plan that would give them some breathing space. They should form a new army group specifically to hold the centre of the line. Guderian suggested that its commanding officer should be Field Marshal Freiherr von Weichs, a commander in the Balkans. Hitler approved Guderian's plan for the creation of a new army group, but gave its command to Himmler. Guderian was appalled. Himmler was not a military man. He was a politician, the head of the SS and architect of the 'final solution' to exterminate Europe's Jews. He was also Chief of Police, Minister of the Interior and Commander-in-Chief of the Training Army. Any one of these positions was a full-time job. But Hitler was insistent. Guderian tried to persuade

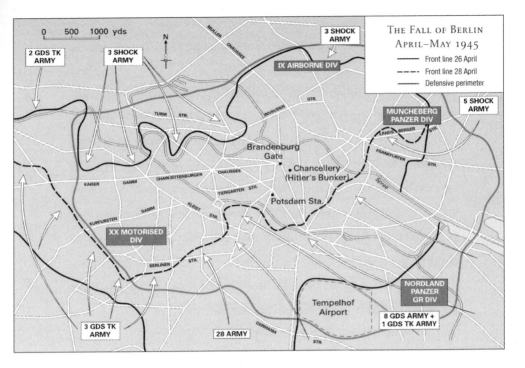

him at least to give Himmler von Weichs' experienced staff. But Hitler, who was now wary of all his generals, allowed Himmler to choose his own staff. Himmler surrounded himself with other SS leaders who were largely incapable, in Guderian's opinion, of doing the jobs they had been given.

SS Brigade Leader Lammerding was Himmler's chief of staff. Previously the commander of a Panzer division, Lammerding had no idea of the duties of a staff officer. Adding to the air of unreality, the new army group was to be called Army Group Vistula, though the Russians had crossed the Vistula months before.

Hitler set up new 'tank-destroyer' divisions. These consisted of men issued with Panzerfaust and bicycles. Somehow they were expected to stop the huge armies of T-34s that were now driving westwards. By this time sixteen-year-old boys were being conscripted into the army.

By 28 January, Upper Silesia was in Russian hands. Speer wrote to Hitler saying: 'The war is lost.' Hitler now cut

Speer completely and refused to see anyone alone in private, because they always told him something he did not want to hear. Hitler began demoting officers on a whim and brave soldiers, denounced by party members, found themselves in concentration camps without even the most summary investigation. Guderian found that more and more of his day was spent listening to lengthy monologues by Hitler as he tried to find someone to blame for the deteriorating military situation. Hitler often became so enraged that the veins on his forehead stood out, his eyes bulged and members of staff feared that he might have a heart attack.

THE NOOSE TIGHTENS

On 30 January, the Russians attacked the Second Panzer Army in Hungary and broke through. Guderian proposed evacuating the Balkans, Norway and what remained of Prussia, and bringing back all the Panzers into Germany for one last battle. Instead Hitler ordered an attack.

On 15 February the Third Panzer Army under General Rauss went on the offensive. In overall command of the offensive was General Wenck. But on the night of the 17th, after a long briefing by Hitler, Wenck noticed that his driver was tired and took the wheel himself. Wenck then fell asleep while driving and crashed into the parapet of a bridge on the Berlin–Stettin highway. He was badly injured and, with Wenck in hospital, the offensive bogged down and never regained its momentum.

In March, Rauss was summoned to the Chancellery and asked to explain himself. Hitler did not give him a chance to speak. After he had dismissed Rauss, Hitler insisted he be relieved of his command. When Guderian protested that he was one of his most able Panzer commanders, Hitler replied that he could not be trusted because was a Berliner or an East Prussian. It was pointed out that Rauss was an Austrian, like Hitler himself. Even so, he was relieved of his post and replaced by General Manteuffel.

Himmler's Army Group Vistula did little to halt the Russian advance and he was eventually replaced by a veteran military man, Colonel-General Gotthard Heinrici, then commanding the First Panzer Army in the Carpathians. At Heinrici's disposal were the Third Panzer Army under General von Manteuffel, which occupied the northern part of the front; General Theodor Busse's Ninth Army, which held the centre, and Field Marshal Ferdinand Schörner's depleted army group, which held the south. Heinrici could also call on another thirty divisions in the vicinity of Berlin.

Guderian continued to come up with strategies for how the Russians' advance could at least be slowed. But after one final falling out with Hitler, he was ordered to take six-weeks' convalescent leave for the sake of his health. He left Berlin on 28 March and intended to go to a hunting lodge near Oberhof in the Thuringan Mountains, but the rapid advance of the Americans made this impossible. Instead he decided to go to the Ehenhausen sanatorium near Munich for treatment of his heart condition.

Warned that he might invite the attentions of the Gestapo, Guderian arranged to have himself guarded by two members of the Field Police.

ENDGAME IN BERLIN

Although Stalin had told Eisenhower that he did not intend to attack Berlin until May, this was entirely disingenuous. Konev and Zhukov were clear that Stalin wanted to capture Berlin in time for the annual Soviet May Day parades, even though their armies were exhausted after weeks of heavy fighting. Konev's 1st Ukranian Front – or Army Group – was on the eastern bank of the River Neisse, some seventy-five miles south-east of Berlin. He proposed starting his offensive with a two-and-a-half hour artillery bombardment with 7,500 guns. At dawn, he would lay smoke and force a river crossing with two tank armies and five field armies, over 500,000 men in all. The tanks on his right flank would smash through the German defences, then swing north-westwards and make a dash on Berlin. Unfortunately this plan relied on two promised extra armies, which could not be relied on to arrive in time. Zhukov's 1st Belorussian Front was on the River Oder, fifty miles east of Berlin, with a bridgehead on the western side of the river at Küstrin. He proposed a predawn bombardment with ten thousand guns. He would then turn 140 anti-aircraft searchlights on the German defenders, blinding them while he attacked. Two tank armies and four field armies would stream out of the Küstrin bridgehead, with two more armies on each flank. With complete air superiority and 750,000 men as his disposal, Zhukov was confident of a quick victory.

Stalin gave Zhukov the green light as he was closer to Berlin and better prepared. But, still encouraging the rivalry between the two field marshals, he also let Konev know that he was free to make a dash on Berlin if he thought he could beat Zhukov to it. The starting date for the offensive was 16 April. The two field marshals had just thirteen days to prepare.

On 15 April, the Americans entered the race when Lieutenant-General William Simpson's Ninth Army crossed the Elbe. Between him and Berlin stood the remnants of the German Twelfth Army under General Walther Wenck. There would be little that it could do to prevent Simpson making a dash for the capital. But Eisenhower ordered Simpson to halt on the Elbe until the link-up with the Red Army had been made at Dresden. The following morning at 0400, three red flares lit up the skies over the Küstrin bridgehead. It was followed by the biggest artillery barrage ever mounted on the eastern front. Mortars, tanks, self-propelled guns, light and heavy artillery – along with four hundred Katyushas – all pounded the German positions. Entire villages were blasted into rubble. Trees, steel girders and blocks of concrete were hurled into the air. Forests caught fire. Men, deafened by the guns and blinded by the searchlighes, shook uncontrollably. Then, after thirty-five minutes of pounding, the Soviets attacked.

In his fortified bunker under the Reichschancellery, Hitler still believed that he could win the war. He predicted that the Russians would suffer their greatest defeat at the gates of Berlin. His maps told him so. They were still covered in little flags representing SS and Army units. Unfortunately, most of these little flags were just...little flags. The units they represented had long since ceased to exist or were so chronically understrength that they were next to useless. Anyone who pointed this out to Hitler was dismissed.

Heinrici was now in charge of the defence of the city. He was an expert in defensive warfare. On the eve of the Soviet attack, he had pulled his front-line troops back so that Zhukov's massive bombardment fell on empty positions. The Ninth Army had dug in on the Seelow heights, blocking the main Küstrin–Berlin road. Zhukov's men attacking down the road suffered terrible casualties. They eventually overwhelmed the Seelow line with sheer weight of numbers, but then they came up against more German defences, reinforced by General Karl Weidling's 56th Panzer, and were halted. Stalin was furious. He ordered Konev, who was making good progress to the south, to turn his forces on Berlin. And on 20 April, Marshal Konstantin Rokossovsky's 2nd Belorussian Front made a separate attack on von Manteuffel's Third Panzer Army.

Busse's Ninth Army began to disintegrate and Zhukov got close enough to Berlin to start bombarding the city with long-range artillery. Konev's forces were also approaching from the south and the German capital was caught in a pincer movement. To ensure that the Americans would not come and snatch their prize at the last moment, both Zhukov and Konev sent forces on to meet up with Simpson on the Elbe. They made contact at Torgau on 25 April to find Simpson sitting on the Elbe, facing no one. Two days earlier, Wenck had been ordered back for the defence of Berlin. But on 28 April, he had reached the suburb of Potsdam, where he met fierce Soviet resistance. Wenck extricated his force and linked up with remnants of the Ninth Army in the forests south of Berlin. Together, the battered remnants of the two armies struggled westwards in the hope of surrendering to the Americans, all the while shelled and harassed by the advancing Russians. Hitler cursed Wenck's treachery.

What propaganda minister Joseph Goebbels now called

'Fortress Berlin' was defended by ninety-thousand ill-equipped boys from the Hitler Youth, and elderly men from the *Volkssturm*. The two million Berliners still trying to go about their business in the ruined city joked: 'It will take the Russians exactly two hours and fifteen minutes to capture Berlin – two hours laughing their heads off and fifteen minutes to break down the barricades.'

To the end Hitler maintained that a relief column of Tiger IIs was on its way, and SS-*Obersturmfuhrer* Babick, battle commandant of the Reichstag, was at his map day and night planning for the arrival of these King Tigers.

Gerhard Zilch, an NCO with the 3rd Heavy Flak Battery, recalled:

Babick was still bubbling over with confidence. He thought he was safe in his shelter. SS sentries were posted outside. Others guarded the corridors of the Reichstag and the King Tigers, our finest weapon, were apparently just around the corner. He had divided his men into groups of five to ten. One group was commanded by SS-Unterstürmfuhrer Undermann – or something like that, I did not quite catch his name. He was posted to Ministry of the Interior – 'Himmler's House' – south of the Moltke Bridge, with the bridge itself in his line of fire. Then an SS subaltern, about nineteen years old, came to Babick and reported that Undermann and his men had come across some alcohol and that they had got roaring drunk. He had brought Undermann with him and he was waiting outside. Babick roared: 'Have him shot on the spot.' The subaltern clicked his heels and marched out. Moments later, there was a burst of machine-gun fire. The boy returned and reported that the order had been carried out. Babick put him in charge of Undermann's unit.

Among the Ruins *Soviet artillery and tank soldiers on Berlin's Kurfürstendamm, once the city's most fashionable boulevard. The Kaiser Wilhelm II church can be seen in the background.*

Himmler, Göring and other top Nazis left the city. Hitler refused to go, pretending, for a while, that the situation could be reversed. He issued a barrage of orders to his non-existent armies. Then, as the Soviets drew the noose tighter and fifteen thousand Russians guns pounded the city, Hitler dropped all pretence of running things and announced that he would commit suicide before the Russians arrived. Meanwhile, the forty or fifty people left in the cellar of the Reichstag began looking for places to hide.

As Soviet troops entered the city, Hitler sacked Göring as his designated successor, for trying to take over while Hitler was still alive, and also Himmler for trying to put out peace feelers to the

British and Americans. Grand Admiral Karl Dönitz was named as Hitler's new successor.

Even though the situation was now hopeless, fanatical Nazis continued their resistance in hand–to–hand fighting. While a corps of Konev's tank troops entered the city from the south and Zhukov's Second Guards Tank Army entered from the north, taking Charlottenburg, detachments of the Hitler Youth held the Pichelsdorf Bridge over the Havel and the bridge to Spandau. Elsewhere the last few Tiger tanks of the SS *Hermann von Salza* battalion took on the Third Shock Army and the Eighth Guards Army in the Tiergarten.

Then news came that Mussolini was dead. The following day, 29 April, Hitler married his mistress Eva Braun. The next day, he dictated his will and his final political testament. That afternoon, in their private quarters, Hitler and his wife of one day committed suicide. Their bodies were burnt in a shallow trench in the Chancellery Gardens.

Both Zhukov's and Konev's troops were now in the city. But Konev was ordered to halt so that Zhukov's men would have the honour of raising the Red Flag on the Reichstag. Zhukov's resulting popularity was seen as a threat by Stalin who banished him to obscurity in 1946.

There were still pockets of resistance, and those remaining in Hitler's bunker tried to negotiate surrender terms. The Soviets would accept nothing but unconditional surrender and unleashed a new hurricane of fire. Goebbels and his wife killed their six children, then committed suicide. Hitler's closest adviser Martin Bormann tried to escape the city, and he is thought to have been killed. If so, he was the only one of the top Nazis to have died in the fighting. The rest committed suicide. There were persistent rumours in the 1960s that Bormann had escaped to South America and was living in Paraguay. However, forensic experts established 'with near certainty' that one of two bodies unearthed during construction work in Berlin in 1972 was Bormann.

General Weidling eventually agreed to unconditional surrender in Berlin on 2 May. Later that day, the Reichstag was taken. Soviet reports say that a howitzer was rolled into Wilhelmplatz to blow off the doors and hand-to-hand fighting continued inside, though this seems unlikely. Major Anna Nikulina, from the political department of the IX Rifle Corps of the Fifth Shock Army, placed a red banner on the roof.

The surrender of the German forces in north-western Europe was signed at Montgomery's headquarters on Lüneburg Heath on 4 May. Another surrender document, covering all the German forces, was signed with more ceremony at Eisenhower's headquarters at Rheims. And at 0028 on 8 May 1945, the war in Europe was officially over.

That day, Eisenhower's deputy, Air Chief Marshal Sir Arthur Tedder, and Lieutenant-General Carl A. Spaatz of the USAAF flew to Berlin to witness the signing of another surrender document at the headquarters of the 1st Belorussian Front in front of Marshal Zhukov and General de Lattre de Tassigny. It was signed by Field Marshal Keitel, Admiral Friedeburg and Colonel-General Stumpff for the Luftwaffe. Most of the fighting ended that day, but due to difficulties in communication some resistance continued until 10 May.

While the various signings of the surrender were going on,

hundreds of thousands of Wehrmacht soldiers managed to get past Bradley and Montgomery's advance guards and surrender to the Western Allies, and the Kriegsmarine used its last hours of freedom to evacuate as many troops as possible from the Baltic. Colonel-General C. Hilpert, in charge of the beleaguered soldiers of what was now known as Army Group Kurland, surrendered just under 200,000 men to the Russians – all that was left of his two armies – five corps or sixteen divisions – and General Noak surrendered the three divisions of XX Corps on the Hela peninsula at the mouth of the Vistula. The fourteen divisions of the German Twentieth Army occupying Norway – 400,000 Germans and 100,000 former Soviets – surrendered in Oslo to General Sir Alfred Thorne. The garrisons left behind on the Channel Island, Dunkirk Lorient, San Nazaire and La Rochelle also laid down their arms.

It is not known how many people perished in the Battle of Berlin. Estimates put the number of German dead as high as 200,000 and the Russian at 150,000. The Soviet troops then went on an orgy of drinking, looting and raping. It is thought that as many as 100,000 women suffered rape – often public and multiple – during that period in Berlin. An estimated two million women were raped in the whole of eastern Germany. The Russians sometimes shot their victims afterwards. Other women committed suicide. It is estimated that ten thousand died.

It had been agreed at the Yalta conference in the Crimea in February 1945 that Berlin would be divided between the four powers – Britain, France, the US and the USSR. By the time the Four Power Control Commission arrived to take control the orgy was over. On 4 June, Marshal Zhukov, Field Marshal Montgomery, General Eisenhower and General de Lattre de Tassigny met in Berlin to approve agreements on the occupation, administration and disarmament of Germany. It was also agreed that the principal Nazi war leaders should stand trial before an international court of military justice (see Section Eight).

The leaders of the victorious Allies met in the Berlin suburb of Potsdam in July 1945. They put out peace feelers to Japan, but received no reply. Preparations were then made to drop the atomic bomb on Japan, ending the war in the Far East (see Section Seven).

Almost immediately, the Cold War started. The part of the city in the hands of the Western powers became West Berlin, an enclave of democracy and free-market capitalism deep inside the region dominated by the Soviet Union, which extended a hundred miles to the west of the capital. This was a bone of contention for the next fifty-five years, until the reunification of Germany in 1990.

SECTION FIVE

BURMA & CHINA

After the fall of Singapore in February 1942, the British Army made the longest retreat of its history, 1,000 miles to the Indian border. Here, it was resupplied and reorganized under General William Slim. After withstanding prolonged Japanese assaults, the Fourteenth Army would sweep down through Burma and into Rangoon in a triumphal homecoming.

CHAPTER 17

The Pacific Theatre to 1944

*The Japanese advance across Southeast Asia was as
swift as it was unexpected. By the end of 1942, vast
swathes of territory had come under Japanese sway.
Their victory was not quite complete, however.*

The attack on the US Pacific Fleet in Pearl Harbor on
7 December 1941 was not the beginning of the war as far
as the Japanese were concerned. For Japan, the Second World
War was an extension of the war against China which began in
1937. When the Japanese broadened the war on 7 December,
Pearl Harbor was not the only target. Addressing a joint session
of Congress on 8 December, President Roosevelt read out a
roll call of infamy:

> *Yesterday the Japanese government also launched an attack
> against Malaya. Last night Japanese forces attacked Hong
> Kong. Last night Japanese forces attacked Guam. Last night
> Japanese forces attacked the Philippine Islands. Last night the
> Japanese attacked Wake Island. This morning the Japanese
> attacked Midway Island…I ask that Congress declare that
> since the unprovoked and dastardly attack by Japan on*

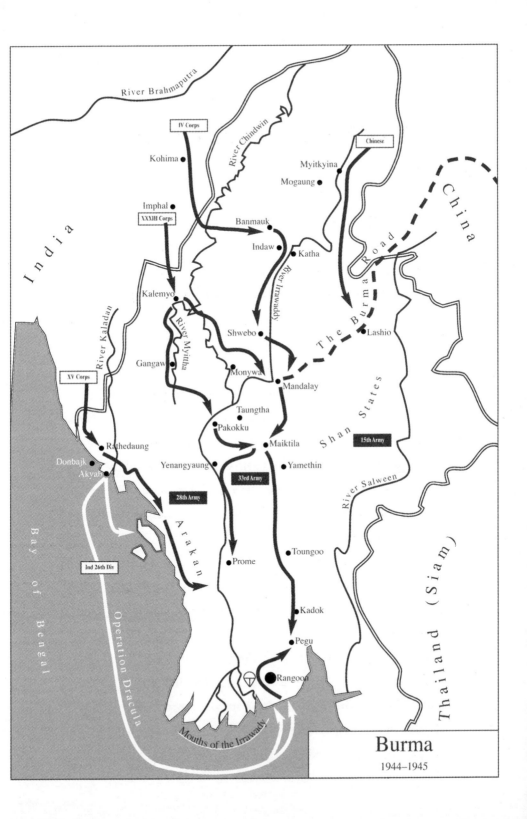

Burma

1944–1945

Sunday, December 7th, a state of war has existed between the United States and the Japanese Empire.

These attacks were a prelude to the 'Southern Operation'. Eleven infantry divisions and seven tank divisions, supported by 795 planes and the rest of the Japanese navy, were to undertake two massive assaults to drive white colonialists out of Asia and set up a Japanese 'Coprosperity Zone' – in other words, an overseas empire. Japanese forces would send one thrust from Formosa, now Taiwan, to take the Philippines. Another thrust would start from French Indochina and the island of Hainan in the Gulf of Tonkin and sweep through Malaya. The two thrusts would converge in the Dutch East Indies and, after 150 days, occupy Java. Along the way they would take Guam, Wake Island, the Gilbert Islands, New Guinea, Hong Kong and Burma.

The Japanese moved with lightning speed, attacking Clark and Iba airfields in the Philippines on 8 December. They took Manila unopposed on 2 January 1942, though American forces hung on in the Bataan peninsula until 9 April.

British air bases in Hong Kong were also bombed on 8 December and the colony capitulated on 25 December. Bangkok was occupied on 9 December and southern Burma fell on the 16th.

There were landings in southern Malaya on 8 December. On 10 December, Britain's two most powerful warships east of Suez – the ultra-modern 35,000-ton battleship Prince of Wales and the 32,000-ton battle cruiser Repulse – steaming to the defence of Singapore had been sunk in the Gulf of Siam. By the end of January, two Japanese divisions occupied all of Malaya, except Singapore Island. This was thought to be impregnable because of its strong seaward defences. But the Japanese made their way down the Malay peninsula and attacked from the landward side. On 15 February the 90,000-strong British, Indian and Australian garrison at Singapore surrendered.

The attack on Pearl Harbor that had brought America into the Second World War had gained Britain another valuable new ally in the Far East. After four years of fighting China formally declared war on Japan. It also declared war on Germany and Italy. In March 1942, two Chinese armies under the command of the US General Joseph W. Stilwell moved into Burma to support British and Indian forces, but the Japanese counterattacked and took a huge swathe of China, including the airfields where the American planes that had staged a dramatic bombing raid on Tokyo in April 1942 had landed. With the Japanese now in control of the whole of Burma, British rule in India was under threat.

With the Battle of Midway in June 1942, the Americans checked the Japanese advance in the Pacific and in autumn the Japanese were thrown into retreat. In Burma, though, there was little that could be done to dislodge them. A counter-attack by the Fourteenth Army in December 1942 in the Arakan area of western Burma met with stiff resistance.

Brigadier-General Charles Orde Wingate formed a group of irregulars into a 'long-range penetration group' to cause disruption behind enemy lines. His men were British, Gurkhas and Burmese and took as their badge the mythical chinthé – the half lion, half griffin figure seen guarding Burmese pagodas

– giving them their name, Chindits. Far from their bases, they would communicate by radio and were supplied by air – all of which were innovative at that time.

In February 1943, the Chindits crossed the Chindwin river in eight columns and for six weeks they struck against the Japanese rear. Some had difficulty extricating themselves and Wingate returned to India in May 1943, having lost a thousand men, a third of his original force. Because of the harsh treatment the Japanese meted out to their prisoners, those too badly injured to make the journey back to India were shot. Weakened by malaria and exhaustion, the Fourteenth Army also pulled back.

In August 1943, General William Slim took command of the Fourteenth Army and completely reorganized it. Stilwell now came under Slim's control and Wingate trained some American troops along Chindit lines. They became known as 'Merrill's Marauders'. During the dry season of 1943–44 they made a number of forays into Burma, along with Stilwell's Chinese forces.

Under Slim's command, the Fourteenth Army attacked again south-eastwards towards Arakan. As the Japanese usually got the better of them when the British were advancing by outflanking them, Slim came up with a new tactic. When the Japanese attacked, the British would not fall back. Instead, they would let themselves be encircled in strong defensive positions, where they would be supplied by air. The Japanese would then find themselves crushed between the defenders and the forces sent in to relieve them, while their supply lines would be harassed by the Chindits. Using these tactics, Slim halted the Japanese advance at Chittagong (now in Bangladesh) and Imphal in India. Now Slim planned the reconquest of Burma. For eighteen months he had been building up troops, supplies, transport and ammunition at Imphal and Dimapur for just this occasion; now, the time was right.

CHAPTER 18

Defeating Operation U-Go

While the British began laying plans to retake Burma, the Japanese had been doing some planning of their own. India had always been a target of Japan's expansion during the Second World War.

The Japanese High Command had, however, long considered that moving troops overland across the terrain of Upper Burma made a successful invasion of India almost impossible. The increasing activity behind their lines of the Chindits, Merrill's Marauders and Chinese Army detachments was not making the logistics of such an invasion seem any more appealing.

By 1944, however, the Japanese had suffered repeated defeats at the hands of the Americans in the Pacific, both on land and at sea, and knew that the nation desperately needed a victory to boost morale.

The High Command decided on a 'March on Delhi'. As well as dealing a crippling blow to the British Empire by installing an Indian nationalist government under Subhas Chandra Bose, head of the 7,000-man Japanese-backed Indian National Army, they would knock out American air bases which were supporting nationalist forces in China also fighting the Japanese.

OPERATION U-GO

In early 1944, the Japanese Fifteenth Army under the command of General Renya Mutagachi – 'the victor of Singapore' – received orders to put a stop to the British preparations in Assam and march on northern India. The Japanese offensive was known as 'U-Go'. It involved three Japanese divisions, the 15th, 31st and 33rd, assigned to the destruction of the Anglo-Indian forces at Imphal and Kohima. The latter was a town in the Naga Hills in north-east India that lay on the only road from the British railhead at Dimapur, thirty miles to the north-east, to the supply depot in Imphal, sixty miles to the south.

Another offensive to the south, on the coast at Arakan, was known as 'Ha-Go' and was aimed at drawing off British reserves. Here Slim's new tactic showed its true worth. The penetration force under Major-General T. Sakurai depended for its provisions on captured British supplies.

THE ADMIN BOX

But the British stood firm in the supply depot called the Adminstration Area – or Admin Box – at Sinzewa. This time there would be no retreat. The defenders of the encirled position were for the most part a motley crew of administration and headquarters, reinforced, however, by elements of 25th Dragoon Guards, equipped with Lee tanks, and three companies of the 2nd Battalion West Yorkshire Regiment. For nineteen days the Admin Box defenders held out against increasingly desperate Japanese attacks, until the 7th Division could move up to relieve them, cutting Sakurai's lines of communication. Sakurai's code books, radio frequencies and call signs were captured, robbing him of command on the battlefield. On 24 February 1944, 'Ha-Go' was called off, and this time it was the Japanese who retreated, leaving 5,000 dead behind them.

Churchill seized on the victory, sending the following congratulatory telegram to Admiral Lord Louis Mountbatten, appointed supreme commander of the newly created South East Asia Command in October 1943:

> *'I sent you today my public congratulations on the Arakan fighting. I am so glad this measure of success has attended it. It is a sign of the new spirit in your forces and will, I trust, urge everyone to keep closer to the enemy. . .'*

Just how close to the enemy it was possible to get would shortly be demonstrated by the troops at the British outposts of Kohima and Imphal.

HOLDING THE LINE AT KOHIMA

The Japanese plan was for the 31st Division to split into three columns that would cut the Kohima-Imphal Road and envelop the hill station from three different angles. Meanwhile, the 15th and 33rd Divisions would surround Imphal to the south. By 22 March, elements of the British IV Corps – 17th, 20th and 23rd Indian Divisions – based in and around Imphal, were engaging the first of the Japanese troops. Then, on the 24th came the news that Wingate had been killed in a plane crash while visiting his troops in northern Assam.

General Slim knew that a major Japanese offensive was under way, but British intelligence had assumed that no more than a few battalions would be able to cross the system of parallel ridges, some as high as 7,000 feet, between the Chindwin River and Kohima. However, with the Kohima-Imphal road cut and the town surrounded, it became clear that an entire Japanese division was bearing down on Kohima.

The only troops stationed in the Kohima area were a few units of Assam Rifles and the 1st Assam Regiment, who had been stationed east of Kohima and had pulled back after heavy fighting. Slim sent the 5th, then the 7th, Indian Divisions, who had seen action in Arakan, by air to reinforce both Imphal and Kohima.

The battle-hardened 161st Indian Brigade of the 5th Indian Division was flown to Dimapur in late March. From there it moved down the road towards Kohima. By early April, it was setting up defensive positions in and around the hill station. They dug in with a series of trenches along Kohima Ridge. The bitterest fighting would take place on Garrison Hill, and a long wooded spur on a high ridge to the west. It was so small that only one battalion of the 4th Royal West Kent Regiment could be deployed there. The rest of the 161st Indian Brigade and its artillery were placed two miles west of Kohima, in Jotsoma. Units from Jotsoma were sent forward to reinforce the 4th Royal West Kents during the fighting.

By 5 April, the defenders were in position. That evening, more than 12,000 men of the Japanese 31st Division attacked. Realising they were vastly outnumbered, the 4th Royal West Kents had to shorten their defences. After the first assault, they withdrew from the more isolated positions, giving the Japanese significant inroads into the ridge and handing over positions they had been preparing for their own defence. However, on 7 April, reinforcements in the form of the 4th Rajput Regiment arrived from Jotsoma, boosting morale.

On 8 April, the Japanese launched a series of attacks into the north-east defences. By 9 April, the British had been forced back. There was hand-to-hand combat in the garden of the district commissioner's bungalow and around the tennis court. By then, the Japanese had cut the between the road between Jotsoma and Dimapur and the tracks between Jotsoma and Kohima. The defenders of Kohima could expect no more reinforcements and, on 10 and 11 April, they were again forced to shorten their lines.

The defenders of Kohima halted the Japanese advance and forced the 31st Division into a battle of attrition. This was very much to the advantage of the British, who were supplied by air daily. The Japanese had not carried supplies with them, thinking that they would take what they needed from the British. They were soon reduced to eating bamboo shoots, grubs and whatever they could find in the jungle. The siege lasted thirteen days and the supreme Allied commander in Southeast Asia, Earl Mountbatten, described it as 'probably one of the greatest battles in history. . .the British–Indian Thermopylae' and praised the 'naked heroism' of the defenders.

On 13 April, the Japanese launched another assault against the British positions on the ridge. The troops defending around the district commissioner's bungalow came under increasingly heavy artillery and mortar fire. And they had to repel frequent infantry assaults and bayonet charges with grenades being tossed across the tennis court. These attacks were eventually beaten off by fire from the artillery on Jotsoma ridge, which found itself under attack. But, again, the British and Indian troops were able to fight off the Japanese.

The turning point of the siege came on 14 April. While the Japanese kept up their artillery bombardment of Kohima and Jotsoma, there were no infantry attacks. The Japanese now realized that their position was impossible. Seeing his men starving, the commander of the 31st Division, General Sato, asked to be allowed to withdraw but General Mutaguchi, commanding the action from a pleasant hill station some three hundred miles behind the lines, told him that the throne of the Emperor depended on his staying put. Although other commanders were replaced, Sato remained and was warned that he would be court-marshalled if he retreated.

Meanwhile the 2nd British Division had arrived at Dimapur and was coming down the road to Kohima, destroying Japanese roadblocks on its way. When news of this reached Kohima on the 15th, morale soared.

The Japanese launched one last desperate attack on the evening of 16 April. In heavy fighting, positions changed hands more than once, but heavy casualties forced the British to withdraw to the Garrison Hill. This tiny enclave was assaulted from the north, south and east. The position seemed hopeless but, on the morning of 18 April, British artillery opened up from the west against the Japanese positions. The 2nd British Division had arrived with tanks from XXXIII Corps. But it was only when a tank was manhandled onto the tennis court that the Japanese were forced from their positions and the siege was lifted. The defenders had suffered over six hundred casualties. The last Japanese were only driven out of the Kohima area on

13 May. None were captured and the surrounding jungle reeked of unburied corpses.

IN THE VALLEY AT IMPHAL

While Kohima was being attacked, Imphal valley was completely surrounded by the Japanese army, who put heavy artillery on the hilltops. However, they had no air support, as all Japanese aircraft were needed in Arakan where British forces were counter-attacking. The attack on Imphal was headed by Netaji – 'Respected Leader' – Subash Chadra Bose and the Indian National Army, but they did not receive the help they expected from the local people. However, two Japanese soldiers disguised themselves as local workers, stole an aircraft from the airstrip at Palel and dropped leaflets saying that Bose had come to liberate India from the British and allying him with the pacifist independence leader Mahatma Gandhi. It made little difference, but on 14 April 1944 the Indian tricolour was hoisted for the first time at Moirang, thirty miles south of Imphal on the Tiddim road.

Imphal itself was besieged by the Japanese 15th Division, which had surrounded the town, dug in on the peaks to the north and cut the Kohima road. However, unlike Kohima, Imphal had an airstrip. Captain P. A. Toole of 305 Field Park Company in the Indian Army landed there in a Dakota in early April 1944. He recorded that when he arrived there was a blazing plane at the end of the runway and gunfire at the distance.

'I had been through the Blitz but this was real war and not like the movies,' he said.

He was lucky. Many planes were lost. Although there were no Japanese aircraft in the skies, landing at Imphal was tricky as

The Rangoon Road *Troops of 11th East African Division on the road to Kalewa, Burma, during the Chindwin River crossing.*

planes were subjected to continuous ground firing from the hill tops. By then, the Japanese had caught on to the trick of having a Royal Air Force fighter circle the valley several times in order to confuse the Japanese artillery, while the cargo planes put down on the airstrip below. Even so, the air campaign was successful. Dakotas flew in food and other supplies, including forty-three million cigarettes and 12,000 sacks of mail, to maintain morale. The RAF also evacuated 13,000 casualties. Out in the jungle, the Japanese received nothing from the outside. Behind Japanese lines, the Chindits had destroyed the railways in Burma and prevented three hundred trucks getting through.

On 22 June 1944, the Fourteenth Army joined the column advancing down the road from Kohima and made contact with IV Corps holding Imphal. To the east, Ukhrul, a Japanese stronghold between Imphal and the Chindwin, was cleared by mid-July with heavy Japanese casualties. At Bishenpur to the south the Japanese 33rd Division held out against the 17th (Black Cat) Division, but they were eventually routed when British artillery bombarded their positions so heavily that not a single leaf was left on the trees.

By early August 1944, Myitkyina, two hundred miles to the east in Burma, was captured. This left the Japanese positions around Imphal stranded. The monsoon was at its peak. The Japanese soldiers suffered from the heat, mosquitoes, malaria, hunger, homesickness and a shortage of ammunition. Subash Chandra Bose's dream of liberating India had failed. He flew back to Singapore and was never heard of again. Meanwhile the sick and malnourished Japanese soldiers retreated through the hills and plains of Manipur. Despite the monsoon, the British started an advance that would be the beginning of the reconquest of Burma. The Japanese Fifteenth Army was finished. Some fifty thousand bodies were counted on the battlefield. How many more were left unburied in the jungle is not known.

CHAPTER 19

The Reconquest of Burma

The British victories at Kohima and Imphal had shown that the Japanese army, despite its undoubted skills at jungle warfare, could be taken on and defeated. Putting this experience to use, the British army was soon poised to attempt the recapture of Burma.

When Slim crossed the Chindwin river in December 1944 with 260,000 men, he faced a Fifteenth Army of just 21,400 men. Stillwell had another 140,000 troops. He faced two other armies and the 49th Division fresh from Korea, but all Japanese units were under-strength and some artillery regiments had less than half their full complement of guns. The Allies also had forty-eight fighter and bomber squadrons – giving them a total of 4,464 RAF and 186 USAAF aircraft. The Japanese had just sixty-six aircraft, reduced to fifty by 1 April 1945.

With such overwhelming odds in the Allies' favour, the reconquest of Burma was not going to be about tactics, but about supply. The Allied armies would have to take airfields and ports. Air Command had at their disposal four troop-carrier squadrons and sixteen transport squadrons, upped to nineteen in March and twenty in May. But even this was insufficient for such a large army, and shortages of transport aircraft slowed the advance.

A new command was set up to coordinate Allied forces in Burma. This was the Allied Land Forces South-East Asia, under the command of Lieutenant-General Sir Oliver Leese. Leese was experienced in seaborne operations and also took over direct control of XV Corps which was employed in combined operations with the navy along the coast. Slim was also relieved of responsibility for communications back to India to allow him to concentrate on the tactics of the land battle.

CROSSING THE IRRAWADDY

Slim's plan was to crush what was left of the Fifteenth Army between Mandalay and Meiktila, eighty miles to the south. Several crossings were made over the Irrawaddy to hold the Fifteenth Army in place, while the 7th Division under Lieutenant-General Frank Messervy made its crossing ninety miles to the south. By 20 February the 17th Division and 255th Tank Brigade were across the Irrawaddy, and the following day, they began their dash across the eighty miles of sandy scrub to Meiktila.

By the end of the month, the entire Fourteenth Army was across the Irrawaddy. On 2 March the 17th Division under Major-General D.T. Cowan took the airfield outside Meiktila and overran the town itself the following day. Slim and Messervy flew in in time to see the Japanese counter-attack being broken up by British tanks. Two men in the commander's party were wounded by shellfire as Slim, Messervy and Cowan observed the action from a hilltop.

While Cowan and a brigade of reinforcements withstood a series of counter- attacks, Slim ordered Lieutenant-General

M.G.N. Stopford to take Mandalay. Although Stopford's men faced stiff resistance, Slim realized that Mandalay was not held in strength and ordered a column to move south. Caught between this column and Meiktila, the Japanese Fifteenth Army was destroyed by heavy bombers. Mandalay fell on 20 February.

Meanwhile Stilwell had attacked across the Salween river, and cleared much of north-east Burma before fighting his way through to China, taking Kunming on 4 February. The Chinese Nationalist leader Chiang Kai-shek then detached his forces to push the Japanese out of a huge area of eastern China that they had recently taken. The Allies supported this move as the airfields there could be used to bomb enemy shipping in the South China Sea and Japan itself. However, Stilwell remained active in the area with his 'Mars' force, the successor to Merrill's Marauders. On 6 March, his Chinese 36th Division took Lashio, and by 24 March the Burma Road from Lashio to Mandalay was in Allied hands. After that the 'Mars' force went China to train the Chinese army, ending the American involvement in Burma.

XXXVII Corps, which had captured Mandalay, lost 1,472 killed, 4,933 wounded and 120 missing. IV Corps had lost 835 killed, 3,174 wounded and 90 missing since crossing the Irrawaddy. The high number of wounded was due to the fact that in the Indian Army anyone wounded, no matter how slightly, was entitled to a pension, while in British units there was no point in recording minor injures. IV Corps had also lost twenty-six tanks, with another forty-four damaged. Air support had flown 4,360 sorties – 2,085 were against Japanese positions or their communications – and 1,560 tons of bombs were dropped.

Once the Fourteenth Army had crossed the Irrawaddy, the

supply lines from Assam grew too long and unwieldy, and it became necessary to capture ports and airfields along the coast of Arakan. The build-up of Allied navies in the Indian Ocean had forced the Japanese out of the Bay of Bengal, permitting amphibious assaults on the coast. The 81st West African Division forced the Japanese out of the port of Akyab, where XV Corps landed unopposed on 2 January.

From there, XV Corps moved down the coast to make landings on the Myebon peninsula and on Chebuda and Ramree Islands, taking the port of Kyaukpyu. Akyab and Kyaukpyu, along with Chittagong, had to supply the 971,828 men of the British fighting force in Burma. Store houses and all-weather airfields had to be built. For the Fourteenth Army alone, a build-up of 42,000 tons of supplies was required. Some 1,500 tons per day had to be brought in by ship.

BREAKING THE 54TH

Inland, the Japanese 54th Division under Lieutenant-General S. Miyazaki held the An and Taungup passes. XV Corps sought to disrupt them by breaking their line of communication at Kangaw. The battle for Kangaw was the bloodiest of the Burma campaign. On 21 January an amphibious force of fifty vessels arrived at the mouth of the Diangbon Chaung, two miles south-west of Kangaw. The Royal Navy and Royal Indian Navy bombarded the beaches, while bombers of No. 224 Group laid a smokescreen. Then No. 1 Commando went ashore and pushed on to Hill 170. No. 5 Commando had landed by nightfall and the following day 42 Royal Marine and 44 Royal Marine Commandos landed.

The Japanese counter-attacked and rebuffed all attempts to enter the village of Kangaw. On 24 and 25 January they bombarded the beaches. But on 26 January the 51st Brigade got ashore, along with a troop of medium tanks, followed by the 53rd Brigade.

The 54th Division was one of the few Japanese divisions that had not suffered a defeat. General Miyazaki sent Major-General T. Koba and his 'Matsui' Detachment, comprising three infantry battalions and an artillery battalion, to repel the invaders. Koba arrived at Kangaw on 31 January and immediately started an assault on Hill 170, which was held by 1 and 42 Royal Marine Commandos, supported by three tanks. Battle raged for thirty-six hours. Eventually, Koba sent in parties of engineers armed with pole charges. These destroyed two tanks and damaged the third at a cost to the Japanese of seventy men. But by this time the 74th Brigade were moving in from the Myebon peninsula to relieve that landing force. Over three hundred Japanese were killed, while the British lost sixty-six killed, fifteen missing and 259 wounded.

With Ramree Island occupied, Miyazaki feared that the British might make an attack at the rear, and he pulled the 'Matsui' Detachment back to the An Pass, continuing to block XV Corps passage into the Irrawaddy valley – had that been their intention. For the British, though, the landings had achieved their objectives and had the additional benefit of keeping most of the 54th and 55th Divisions occupied while the Fourteenth Army made its advance on Meiktila and Mandalay.

The campaign in Arakan then came to a halt as all available air transport was needed elsewhere. During the fighting there,

XV Corps had lost 1,138 killed and 3,951 wounded and missing. Luckily, none of the seaborne landings had been seriously opposed. Nevertheless the Royal Navy had fired off 23,000 rounds varying from four-inch to fifteen-inch in calibre. In all, 54,000 men, 800 animals, 11,000 vehicles and 14,000 tons of stores were landed.

The 25th and 26th Indian Divisions were taken back to India, along with the British 26th Division which was readied for the attack on Rangoon. The Commandos were also withdrawn in preparation for landings in Malaya.

THE RECAPTURE OF RANGOON

The assault on Rangoon began on 27 April with an airborne attack on Elephant Point, overlooking the mouth of the Irrawaddy. To guard the rear and intercept fleeing Japanese, a Royal Navy task force of two battleships, four cruisers and six destroyers sailed for the Andaman and Nicobar Islands. They bombarded the airfields and shipping there, simultaneously with airstrikes on 30 April. The task force then attacked Victoria Point and Mergui near the Malay border before renewing the bombardment on the Andamans and Nicobars.

A second force sailed into the Gulf of Martaban. It intercepted small ships carrying a thousand men from Rangoon to Moulmein on the night of 29 April. Ten were sunk and the survivors rescued.

At 0545 on 1 May, thirty-eight Dakotas dropped the 50th Gurkha Parachute Brigade on Elephant Point. They quickly defeated the thirty-seven Japanese they found there. Five Gurkhas were injured in the drop and they suffered another thirty-two casualties when some Liberators, aiming at another target, dropped a stick of bombs on them.

Flying over Rangoon, Wing Commander A.E. Saunders of the RAF's 110 Squadron saw the words 'EXTRACT DIGIT' and 'JAPS GONE' painted on the roof of the Rangoon jail. Seeing no sign of the enemy, he landed at Mingaladon Airfield, though he damaged his Mosquito in the bomb craters there. Contacting prisoners of war in the jail he was told that the Japanese had evacuated Rangoon on 29 April. Then he went to the docks, commandeered a boat and sailed down the river to report that the Japanese had gone. The 26th Division then came up the river on landing craft and occupied the city.

Meanwhile the Fourteenth Army had been moving southwards through Burma, with XXXIII Corps advancing down the Irrawaddy valley and IV Corps taking the main road through Pergu. The Karens in the hills had remained loyal and some 3,000 were recruited to defend IV Corps' eastern flank.

XXXIII Corps entered Prome (Pye), 150 miles north of Rangoon on 3 May, while IV Corps were held up at Pegu, forty-five miles north-east of Rangoon, on 2 May by unseasonal rain and the 1,700 men of an improvised brigade made up of training unit personnel.

Engineers cleared 500 mines and threw a bridge across the Pegu River and at 0630 on 4 May IV Corps continued its advance. The 1/7th Gurkhas crossed the blown-up bridge at Hlegu on 6 May and met a column of the Lincolnshire Regiment from the 26th Division advancing northwards from Rangoon.

By this time a patrol from XV Corps advancing from Taungup

on the coast had made contact with XXXIII Corps, so all three corps in Burma were now in contact.

The remnants of the Japanese 54th and 55th Divisions managed to cross the Irrawaddy and join up with the Twenty-Eighth Army under General Sakurai, who had 30,000 men in the jungle-covered hills between the Irrawaddy valley and the valley of the Sittang. Sakurai's aim was to join the rest of the Burma Area Army that was regrouping east of the Sittang. However, the Sittang was flooded fifty miles upstream from the Gulf of Martaban so the Twenty-Eighth Army had to try and exfiltrate in small dispersal groups north of Shwegyin.

These small groups were hunted down by Indian battalions in tanks and armoured cars. The strength of the Twenty-Eighth was reported as 27,764 on 28 June 1945. On 22 September, 7,949 were on duty, 1,919 in hospital and 3,822 listed as missing. In that period, IV Corps in the Sittang valley reported only 435 killed, 1,452 wounded and 42 missing.

By that time though, the war had ended. The atomic bombs dropped on Hiroshima and Nagasaki in August 1945 made any further action against the Japanese in Southeast Asia unnecessary: the 'forgotten Fourteenth', had, however, proved their mettle time and time again.

THE PACIFIC FRONT

The Japanese surprise attack on Pearl Harbor
on 7 December, 1941, was swiftly followed
by assaults on Malaya, Hong Kong, and the
Philippines. The Japanese strategy was to try and
achieve its territorial gains before the USA could
fully mobilize its armed forces. It was a strategy
doomed to failure from the beginning.

CHAPTER 20

Fighting Back

In the months following Pearl Harbor, nothing could stop the Japanese advance. They overran the Philippines, the East Indies, Guam and Wake Island. By mid-April of 1942, they held most of the South Pacific, and showed little sign of slowing their advance.

The next objective for the Japanese was to take Tulagi to the north of Guadalcanal in the British Solomon Islands and Port Moresby on New Guinea. They would cut then the supply route between America and Australia, in preparation for the invasion of Australia itself. An invasion force assembled at Truk in the Carolines. On 30 April, it sailed for Rabaul in northern New Britain, where Vice-Admiral Shigeyoshi Inouye was mustering a separate naval force as part of his intricate plan. The Japanese now occupied much of the area and Inouye's ships would be supported by 140 land-based aircraft.

Australia was a British dominion whose soldiers were fighting fiercely in North Africa. It was also a long-time ally of America, and the Commander in Chief of the US Pacific Fleet, Admiral Chester Nimitz, rallied to its defence. He sent Task Force 17, under the command of Rear Admiral Frank J. Fletcher, to the Coral Sea. His flagship was the *Yorktown*, which

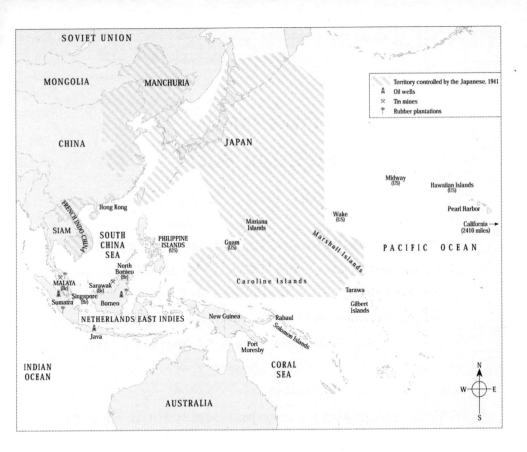

had been transferred back from the Atlantic after the attack on Pearl Harbor. It was accompanied by the *Lexington*, a converted cruiser, under Rear Admiral Aubrey W. Fitch. These two carriers were escorted by seven cruisers and a screen of destroyers. They carried three types of plane. They had thirty-six Douglas TBD-1 Devastators, which were the first all-metal monoplanes to be carried by the US Navy. Designed in 1934, they were slow and had a poor rate of climb and a limited range, and carried a torpedo which tended towards the unreliable. The bomber force comprised seventy-two Douglas SBD-2 Dauntless dive-bombers which were already considered obsolete. Fighter support was provided by thirty-six Grumman F4F-3 Wildcats.

Fletcher's ships would meet Rear Admiral Takagi's main strike force which comprised two of the aircraft carriers that had attacked Pearl Harbor, the *Shokaku* and the *Zuikaku*, two cruisers and a screen of destroyers. They carried forty-two Mitsubishi A6M5 Zero fighters, forty-two Aichi D3A Val divebombers and forty-one Nakajima B5N torpedo planes. Although the Japanese planes were superior to anything the Americans had at this point in the war, Fletcher had more dive-bombers. The American carriers also had radar and the *Yorktown's* planes carried IFF (Identification, Friend or Foe) equipment. The Japanese possessed neither of these innovations.

Takagi's strike force set off from the Carolines and swung to the east to stay out of the range of US reconnaissance planes for as long as possible. On 3 May, a small force landed on Tulagi, and by 1100 the island was in Japanese hands. It was here that Fletcher decided to strike back. At 0630 on 4 May twenty-eight Dauntless dive-bombers and twelve Devastators took off from the *Yorktown*. At 0815 they were over the island. The first two strikes sunk a destroyer, three minesweepers and a patrol boat. A third sank four landing barges and five Kawanishi H6K Mavis flying-boats. Returning to the *Yorktown* at 1632, they had lost one Devastator, downed over the target, and two Wildcats which had strayed off course on their return to the carrier and crash-landed on Guadalcanal. Their pilots were recovered later.

Meanwhile Takagi's strike force had headed west towards the Coral Sea but, due to bad weather, US reconnaissance planes could not find it. A Japanese flying-boat spotted the US fleet, but was shot down by Wildcats.

THE BATTLE OF THE CORAL SEA

The New Guinea invasion force set off from Rabaul with six Japanese army transports, five navy transports and a destroyer escort, under the command of Rear Admiral Kajioka in his flagship Yubari. It rendezvoused with a support group under Rear Admiral Marushige off the island of Bougainville and headed south towards the Jomard Passage, which would take it into the Coral Sea.

The fleets then began to sight each other. The *Yorktown* and the *Lexington* were spotted by a Japanese flying-boat, though the report did not reach Takagi until 18 hours later. Meanwhile the Shoho, which was supporting the invasion force, was spotted by USAAF B-17Es on 6 May. However, they did not spot Takagi's strike force due to the bad weather. That evening the two fleets were within seventy miles of each other, though they did not know it. Later they both changed course and the gap widened again.

There was another Allied force in the area. Under the command of Rear Admiral Crace of the Royal Navy, it comprised two Australian cruisers, one American cruiser and a destroyer escort. On 7 May, Fletcher told Crace to close the southern end of the Jomard Passage, while Fletcher himself closed in from the south-east.

At 0815, US reconnaissance planes reported seeing 'two carriers and four heavy cruisers' approaching the Louisiade Archipelago, north of the Jomard Passage. Fletcher thought that this was the main force and, between 0926 and 1030, ninety-three planes were sent off to attack it, leaving only forty-seven with the fleet. When the spotter plane returned, it became clear that there had been an error in encoding. It had only seen two heavy cruisers and two destroyers. But soon after 1100, Lieutenant-Commander Hamilton, leading *Lexington's* squadrons, spotted the *Shoho* and her escort of four cruisers and a destroyer off Misima Island in the Louisiades. Despite its powerful escort, the first wave of American planes blew five aircraft over the side of the *Shoho*. Successive waves hit the carrier with six torpedoes and thirteen bombs, leaving her listing and on fire. She sank at 1135 with 600 of her 800 hands. Six American planes had been lost.

The invasion force now had no air cover and halted north of the Louisiades until the Jomard Passage was cleared. That afternoon, Crace's fleet was attacked by waves of land-based torpedo bombers, but they failed to sink any of the Allied ships. Meanwhile reconnaissance planes from Takagi's strike force had mistakenly reported that they had located Fletcher's carriers. They launched over sixty sorties and sank the USS *Sims*, a destroyer, and the oil tanker USS *Neosho*. At 1630, fifteen torpedo planes and twelve dive-bombers were launched with instructions to seek out Fletcher's force and destroy it. But the weather closed in and, without radar, the Japanese planes had little chance of finding the American fleet. However, the American fleet picked up the bomber force on radar and the *Lexington* sent up its Wildcats. They shot down nine bombers, losing two fighters in the process.

The Japanese torpedo squadron did not find the fleet either and gave up the search. They dumped their torpedoes in the sea and headed back to their carriers. But they had been closer to the American fleet than they had realized. At 1900, three of the Japanese planes spotted an Aldis lamp sending out morse code from the *Yorktown,* but got clean away. At 1720, another Japanese plane was not so lucky and was shot down. A further eleven planes failed to find their carriers and crashed into the sea in the darkness. And, of the original twenty-seven, only six planes returned safely to their carriers.

Unable to clear Crace's force from the Jomard Passage, the invasion force withdrew, leaving Fletcher and Takagi to fight it out in the Battle of the Coral Sea – the first sea battle in history in which the opposing ships neither saw nor engaged each other. That night, the two fleets deliberately sailed away from one another, neither willing to risk a night engagement. Next morning, while the skies over Takagi's fleet remained overcast, Fletcher's fleet was bathed in sunshine. At around 0600 both sent out reconnaissance planes. Even though the weather gave the Japanese the advantage, at 0815 one of the *Lexington's* Dauntlesses dived through the clouds and saw ships. As it went in for a closer look, the plane was rocked by a shell exploding near its left wing-tip and it quickly climbed back into the clouds. The Japanese fleet was 175 miles north-east of the American position. Its position was radioed back. At 0850, twenty-four dive-bombers and two fighters took off from the rolling deck of the *Yorktown*. They were followed by nine torpedo planes escorted by four fighters. Ten minutes later, the *Lexington* started sending a flight consisting of twenty-two dive-bombers, eleven torpedo planes and nine fighters. By 0925 all the planes were away.

The Japanese had also spotted the American fleet and, while the American planes headed for the Japanese fleet, fifty-one bombers and eighteen fighters were going the other way. At 1030, the American dive-bombers saw the *Zuikaku* and the *Shokaku* eight miles ahead and pulled up to hide in the clouds until the slower torpedo planes caught up. Then, as the *Shokaku* appeared from under the cloud cover, they attacked. Seeing them coming, the Japanese sent up fighters, which downed three of the Dauntlesses. This disrupted the American attack, and only two of their bombs hit the ship. One damaged the flight deck enough to prevent any more fighters taking off. The other started a fire in a machine shop. But the *Shokaku* was still able to steer and weaved violently, and all the torpedoes either missed or in some cases, failed to go off.

The *Lexington's* dive-bombers failed to find the carriers. They ran low on fuel and had to return to the 'Lady Lex'. But the torpedo planes and their fighter escort continued the search and spotted the enemy fifteen miles out. They were immediately attacked by Japanese Zeros which drove off the Wildcats. The lowflying Devastators managed to release their torpedoes but, again, none of them hit. However, by this time, the *Shokaku* was on fire and out of action. One hundred and eight of its crew had been killed, but it had not been hit below the waterline. It limped back to Truk, while most of its planes transferred to the *Zuikaku*, which had briefly emerged from the murk only to disappear again.

The American fleet had no such protection. Above it the skies were clear and it had little fighter cover. The Wildcats were low on fuel, and even though the bandits had been spotted on radar sixty-eight miles out, they were badly positioned for a fight. Only three Wildcats spotted the Japanese planes as they started their attack at 1055, and those were at 10,000 feet and did not have the fuel to climb to meet the Vals, which began their dive from 18,000 feet. Twelve other Dauntlesses, having been trained to expect a low-level attack, patrolled at 2,000 feet three miles outside the destroyer screen. The Japanese Kate torpedo planes and their fighter escort flew over them at 6,000 feet, only to descend to their release height inside the ring of destroyers. Nevertheless the Dauntlesses reacted quickly and managed to down two Kates before they could release their torpedoes. They also managed to shoot down two Zeros, a Val and two more Kates for the loss of four Dauntlesses.

The *Yorktown* managed to dodge the eight torpedoes launched at her port quarter, and everything the divebombers threw at her. But, five minutes later, when a second wave of Japanese planes arrived, an 800-pound bomb went through her flight deck and exploded three decks down, killing sixty-six American sailors. Black smoke streamed from the gaping hole in her deck. She was on fire but still afloat.

The Japanese pilots then turned their attention to the *Lexington*. They attacked both bows, dropping their torpedoes at between 50 and 200 feet, 1,000 yards out. Two hit and all three boiler rooms were flooded. Two dive-bombers also scored hits and the *Lexington* was listing badly when they turned for home. Although both American carriers had been hit, the returning planes could still land on them.

But the jubilant Japanese pilots returning to the *Shokaku* found they had to ditch in the sea. This left the Japanese fleet with only nine planes, while the Americans still had twelve fighters and thirty-seven attack aircraft. At that point in the battle, the Japanese had lost eighty planes and some 900 men; the Americans sixty-six planes and 543 men. But worse was to come. Fuel was escaping and vapour built up inside the damaged

Lexington. At 1247, a spark from a generator ignited it and the ship was rocked by a massive explosion. A second internal explosion tore through her again at 1445. The fires on board got out of control and, at 1710, the crew abandoned ship. At 1956, a destroyer put her out of her misery with five torpedoes and the *Lexington* went to her watery grave.

THE BATTLE OF MIDWAY

The outcome of the Battle of the Coral Sea had been indecisive. The Japanese were forced to cancel their sea-borne invasion of Port Moresby, but it did not ruin their appetite for a fight. Yamamoto went back on the offensive. He planned to take Midway Island, 1,300 miles north-west of Oahu. From there he would be able to mount further attacks on Pearl Harbor, denying America a navy base west of San Francisco. This was a response to the 'Doolittle' raid, in which Lieutenant-Colonel Jimmy Doolittle led a force of sixteen B-25s from the USS *Hornet* on a bombing raid on Tokyo on 18 April 1942. In fact, the *Hornet* could not get close enough to Japan for Doolittle's planes to land back on the carrier, and they had to fly on to airstrips in China. But Yamamoto wanted to push the Japanese naval perimeter back so that no American aircraft carrier could get in range of the imperial capital again.

As the US now employed enough code breakers to read all the Japanese code 'Purple' intercepts they collected, Admiral Nimitz knew what to expect. He understood that Yamamoto's plan was to stage a diversionary attack on the Aleutians, the chain of islands belonging to the US that run out into the Pacific from the coast of Alaska. They would invade and occupy two of the inhabited islands – Attu and Kiska – and intern the people there. Such a humiliation would force America to react. To make sure that America sent sufficient of its strength northwards, Yamamoto would also have to commit capital ships, including the aircraft carrier *Junyo* and the light carrier *Rjujo* which would have been useful at Midway. Thanks to the code-breakers, the US did not respond to this attack.

Admiral Nagumo, the victor of Pearl Harbor, would lead the attack on Midway with four of the carriers that had been there that day – the *Akagi, Kaga, Hiryu* and the *Soryu* – while the light carrier *Zuiho* would be part of a central covering force, that could help out either in the Aleutians or at Midway. They would face the *Enterprise* and the *Hornet*, along with the rapidly refitted *Yorktown* which was ready to put to sea again after only three days in the all-important navy yard at Pearl. Its fighter complement had been increased from eighteen to twenty-seven as it was carrying the new F4F-4 Wildcats, which had folding wings allowing the carrier to accommodate the extra planes, and six machine guns instead of four. Her pilots were the survivors from the *Yorktown* and the *Lexington*, who now had combat experience.

On 30 May, Admiral Fletcher sailed north-westwards to meet up with the two cruisers and five destroyers surviving from Task Force 17. They then joined up with Task Force 16, under Admiral Raymond Spruance on board the Enterprise. On Midway, the USAAF stationed four squadrons of Flying Fortresses and some B-26 Marauders, while the Marine Corps had nineteen Dauntless dive-bombers, seven F4F-3 Wildcats, seventeen Vought SB2U-3 Vindicators (or 'Wind Indicators' as the Marines called them), twenty-one obsolete Brewster F2A-3 Buffaloes and six new Grumman TBF-1 Avenger three-man torpedo bombers.

Yamamoto himself led the main Japanese force from the battleship *Yamoto* and sent Nagumo's carrier strike force towards Midway from the north-west, while the minesweepers, transports and supply ships of the invasion force approached from further to the south. The invasion fleet was spotted by a US Catalina reconnaissance flying-boat 700 miles west of Midway on 3 June. At 1230, nine Flying Fortresses took off. Four hours later they found the invasion force 570 miles to the west. Short of fuel, they dropped their bombs amid heavy anti-aircraft fire, but hit nothing. However, at dawn the following morning, four Catalinas from Midway torpedoed a tanker.

At 0415 hours, fifteen Flying Fortresses were on their way to bomb the invasion fleet again, when they got word that another fleet – complete with carriers – was approaching Midway and was then only 145 miles away. Fifteen minutes later, ten Dauntless scouts were airborne, searching for the carriers to the north of the island. At the same time, thirty-six Val dive-bombers, thirty-six Kate torpedo-bombers carrying 1,770-pound bombs, and thirty-six Zeros took off from Nagumo's carriers. They headed for Midway, intending to soften up its defences for the invasion scheduled for two days later. Once the strike force was airborne, more Kates were hoisted up to the flight deck, armed with torpedoes to attack shipping. At the same time, spotter planes were despatched to hunt for the US fleet. Here America got lucky. One of the two float-planes launched from the cruiser *Tone* was delayed for half an hour, when the catapult malfunctioned.

It was headed for the search sector where the fleet was located.

At 0534 a Navy flying-boat reported to Midway that there was a Japanese carrier fleet 250 miles away to the east. The *Yorktown* also picked up the message and Fletcher told Spruance to take

Battle of Midway *US and Japanese carrier aircraft engage in dogfights while the fleets below exchange heavier gunfire at Midway.*

the *Enterprise* and the *Hornet* to attack the Japanese carriers. Radar operators on Midway spotted 108 Japanese planes heading for the island at 0553. They warned the flying-boats and Flying Fortresses to stay away while the seven Wildcats and twenty-one Buffaloes of the island's defence force went to take on the attackers. They managed to shoot down four Japanese bombers and damage several others before they were overwhelmed by the nimble Zeros. In the ensuing dogfights, three Wildcats and thirteen Buffaloes were shot down. Seven more were damaged beyond repair. Of the twenty-eight US planes, only five survived intact – and one of those had not even been involved in the engagement as it had engine trouble and had to turn back. They had managed to down just two Zeros. A further three Japanese planes were downed by ack-ack fire over Midway.

While this disastrous dogfight had been going on, six Grumman Avengers and four Marauders headed off to attack the Japanese fleet. As they attacked at low-level, seventeen Zeros pounced on them from 3,000 feet. The unprotected bombers were easy prey and turned back. Two of the B-26s made it back to Midway, where they crash-landed. The Avengers managed to loose their torpedoes, but furious fire from the Zeros and the fleet shot down five of them. Only one Avenger, badly damaged and with a wounded radio operator and a dead gunner on board, made it back to Midway.

This attack convinced Admiral Nagumo and the strike force commander Lieutenant Joichi Tomonaga that a second wave of bombers needed to be sent against Midway, so the Kates were lowered from the flight deck to be rearmed with bombs. This was a time-consuming process. At 0728, the *Tone's* second float-plane had finally located the 'ten enemy surface ships' around 240 miles from Midway. Nagumo waited, weighing up the information. Then, at 0813, he ordered that the Kates' torpedoes be replaced. Then a report came, saying that the ships were only cruisers and destroyers – not carriers – and posed no imminent threat as they were well out of range, so arming the Kates with bombs could resume.

It was then that Midway's bomber force – fifteen USAAF Flying Fortresses and sixteen Marine Corps Dauntless dive-bombers – arrived. The Flying Fortresses dropped their bombs from 20,000 feet, but when the pluming sea subsided, the Japanese carriers were still intact. As the Flying Fortresses turned for home, Nagumo could see that the pilots of his eighteen airborne Zeros were wary of these heavily armed bombers. They needed reinforcing. He ordered the thirty-six Zeros intending to escort the Kates to take off in time to intercept the Dauntlesses as they came in. The Zeros fell on the American dive-bombers, whose inexperienced pilots were bringing them in too low. The Dauntlesses being land-based, their pilots had not been trained to attack shipping, and posed no threat to the Japanese fleet. Only a handful got close enough to release their bombs. Just eight of the sixteen made it back to Midway and they were riddled with shrapnel and bullet holes.

Then Nagumo got the bad news. The *Tone's* float-plane now reported that the ten American ships they were shadowing were a vanguard for the carrier force which was following in the rear. They were streaming south-east and were now just 200 miles away – well within range, and carrier aircrew were trained to attack enemy ships. Nagumo's second-wave attack aircraft were still below decks being rearmed. His fighters were getting low on fuel and ammunition, and his first wave force was expected back any minute. Rather than muster what planes he had that were ready to go, Nagumo decide to retire to the north until his fighters were refuelled and his first wave recovered. Then he would send a properly armed force into the attack.

Admiral Spruance coolly assessed the situation and realized that he had the upper hand. If he bided his time, he could attack the Japanese carriers when they were at their most vulnerable – when their decks were full of returning aircraft. His timing was immaculate and, within a few minutes of the last Japanese plane arriving back from Midway putting down, Nagumo's destroyer screen reported American planes approaching.

The timing may have been immaculate, but the tactics were not. Broken cloud along the route had scattered the American formations. Nagumo's change of course meant that the Japanese carriers were not where they were thought to be. Some planes grew short of fuel as they searched for the fleet, and had to return. Others lost their fighter escort and ten Wildcats ditched in the sea. But, piecemeal, the US squadrons found their target.

The first into the attack were fifteen obsolete Devastators. They came skimming in at 300 feet but, unescorted, they were no match for the fifty Zeros that attacked them. Fourteen were blown out of the skies before they got near enough to release their torpedoes. But the last one, piloted by Ensign George H. Gay, who was wounded in the leg and arm and carried a dead gunner, pressed on. He managed to loose his torpedo before he skimmed over the deck of the carrier and crashed in the sea. The torpedo missed its mark, but Gay managed to get out of his plane before it sank and he kept himself afloat with his rubber seat cushion which had floated clear. When night fell and he was no longer in danger of being strafed by Zeros, he inflated his dinghy. The next day he was picked up by a US Navy Catalina.

The Japanese sailors were still cheering, when fourteen more Devastators from the *Enterprise* arrived and began attacking the *Kaga* from the starboard. At the same time, twelve more Devastators from the *Yorktown* turned up and attacked the *Soryu*. They were accompanied by seventeen Dauntlesses and six Wildcats. These drew some of the Zeros away from the Devastators. Even so, eleven of the *Enterprise's* torpedo planes were downed.

With the support of the six Wildcats, the *Yorktown's* Devastators were within three miles of their target before they were attacked. Almost immediately one Wildcat was downed and two others so badly damaged that they had to break off. The remaining three could do little to help the torpedo planes other than try to draw some of the Zeros off. And they too were soon forced to break off and return to the *Yorktown*.

As well as being attacked by the Zeros, the cumbersome Devastators drew withering fire from the Japanese ships. Some of them managed to release their torpedoes before they were blasted from the skies. Again not one of the torpedoes hit their targets, but two passed within fifty feet of the *Kaga*.

However, these three suicidal attacks had served to keep the Zeros at low altitudes and some were landing to refuel when the Dauntlesses came in. They saw below them an unforgettable sight – four Japanese carriers completely unprotected. Three dive-bombers from the *Yorktown* peeled off and attacked. One bomb hit the *Akagi* amidships, ripping through the hangar deck and exploding among the stored torpedoes, carelessly stowed bombs and refuelling tanks, setting off secondary explosions. A second set the planes on the flight deck ablaze. The stern was shattered, the rudder useless and, as the huge ship lurched drunkenly around, Nagumo's officers begged a stunned admiral to abandon the blazing hulk.

Then a squadron of Dauntlesses from the *Enterprise* turned up and directed their attentions to the unprotected *Kaga*. The carrier took four direct hits. Three bombs hit the planes that were being prepared for take-off, setting them ablaze. The fourth hit a petrol tank on deck. Burning gasoline engulfed the bridge, killing the captain and the staff officers and putting the ship out of action.

The *Yorktown's* dive-bombers regrouped and attacked the *Soryu*. In minutes, she was a raging inferno. All three carriers stayed afloat while they burnt. But they had to be abandoned and were later sunk by Japanese or American torpedoes. However, the *Hiryu* had escaped and its air group, now augmented by twenty-three Zeros seeking refuge from their blazing carriers, still posed a threat, and Yamamoto had not yet abandoned his plan to invade Midway. Thinking there was only one American carrier in the area, he steamed on towards the island. The rest of the task force was to join up with his battleships and bombard the island's defences before the Japanese invasion force, standing by 500 miles away, went ashore.

In the attack on the *Akagi*, *Kaga* and *Soryu*, seven Dauntlesses had been lost, while eight Zeros had been shot down. However, eleven more Dauntlesses had been ditched when they ran out of fuel on the way back to their ships. Fletcher knew that his fleet was still in danger. He ordered the remaining Dauntlesses aloft to search for the *Hiryu*, while twelve Wildcats flew a defensive patrol around the *Yorktown*. What Fletcher did not know was that a reconnaissance plane from the *Soryu* had already spotted the *Yorktown,* and eighteen Vals and six Zeros from the *Hiryu* were on their way. At midday, they were picked by the *Yorktown's* radar about forty-six miles out. The Wildcats intercepted them 15 miles out and shot down four Zeros and seven Vals. The surviving bombers broke away and attacked the *Yorktown.* Six more were shot down – two by anti-aircraft fire from the American cruisers. However, before it broke up, one of them managed to lob a bomb through the *Yorktown's* flight deck, causing a fire in the hangar below. A second bomb knocked out the engine room; while a third caused a fire that threatened the forward ammunition stores and petrol tanks. Despite severe loss of life, the crew managed to get the fires under control.

While the *Yorktown's* Wildcats were refuelled and rearmed on the *Enterprise,* engineers on board the *Yorktown* managed to get her underway again and Captain Elliot Buckmaster ran up a huge new Stars and Stripes. As it fluttered defiantly above the wrecked ship, a second wave of Japanese planes came screaming low over the horizon. This time there were ten Kate torpedo planes, escorted by six Zeros. The Wildcats managed to down three Zeros, at a cost of four F4Fs. Five Kates were also downed in the curtain of fire put up by the cruisers. But four torpedoes were launched within a range of 500 yards. Two hit the *Yorktown* below the waterline. They knocked out all power, lights and communications, and the great ship listed to port. Fearing a further wave, Buckmaster gave the order to abandon ship at 1500.

Revenge was not long in coming. An American scout-plane had already spotted the *Hiryu*. Fourteen Dauntlesses from the *Enterprise*, along with ten transferred from the *Yorktown*, set off to attack the remaining Japanese carrier. They were followed by sixteen more dive-bombers from the *Hornet*. As they neared the *Hiryu*, they were intercepted by thirteen Zeros who shot down three Dauntlesses as they dived. Nevertheless, four bombs pierced the *Hiryu's* flight deck, causing uncontrollable fires. When the planes from the *Hornet* arrived, they turned their attention to a battleship and a cruiser in the carrier's escort. Some Flying Fortresses en route from Hawaii to Midway also joined in, to little effect. Some of the Zeros attacked the B17s, but the fighters were soon out of fuel and ditched in the sea. That night, more bombers set out from Midway to try and discover what had happened to the *Hiryu*, but could not find it and flew back to their base guided by the fires still burning on Midway.

The loss of the *Hiryu* still did not put paid to Yamamoto's plan to invade Midway. However, he knew his invasion force would be vulnerable to the land-bombers. To have any chance of carrying off the invasion, they would have to attack that night. But then came the news that two of the cruisers he had designated to bombard the island could not make it before nightfall. Then he learned that there were other American carriers in the area and bowed to the inevitable. At 0255 on 5 June, he issued an order, saying, 'The occupation of Midway is cancelled.'

His admirals were mortified. Some would rather lose the entire fleet than lose face.

'How can we apologise to His Majesty for this defeat?' asked one.

'Leave that to me,' said Yamamoto. 'I am the only one who must apologise to His Majesty.'

The *Hiryu* was finally abandoned and sunk by Japanese torpedoes. But the defenders of Midway did not know this and went on searching. Yamamoto had already turned for home and was out of range, but a dozen dive-bombers put the *Mikuma* and the *Mogami*, two heavy cruisers, out of action. The *Mikuma* was badly damaged, not by a bomb, but by the Dauntless of Captain Richard E. Fleming hitting the rear gun turret. Gasoline from the aircraft seeped into the engine room and ignited, killing the entire engine room crew.

The last victim of the Battle of Midway was the *Yorktown*. Now unable to sail under her own steam, she was being towed back to Pearl Harbor by a minesweeper when, soon after dawn on 6 June, a Japanese submarine torpedoed her again and sunk one of her destroyer escorts, the *Hannan*. The *Yorktown* stayed afloat until the early hours of 7 June, when she suddenly rolled over and plunged to the bottom of the Pacific.

The Battle of Midway was the decisive battle in the Pacific war. America had had its revenge on the carriers whose planes had attacked Pearl Harbor. The Japanese Imperial Navy which, before Midway, had matched the strength of the US Navy was now a shadow of its former self. Although Japanese pilots had beaten their American adversaries, who had lost eighty-five out of 195 aircraft, in the air, most of their elite fliers were dead. But crucially the Japanese shipyards could not hope to replace the carriers they had lost. The US was already turning out new carriers in large numbers and its aircraft factories were producing more powerful planes to put on them. With Midway, the Japanese expansion across the Pacific had reached its height. But as the Japanese Imperial Navy turned for home, they left hundreds of small islands occupied by Japanese troops, which it would take a bloody campaign of island-hopping to clear.

A STRATEGY EVOLVES

During the expansion of their 'Co-Prosperity Sphere', the Japanese had occupied much of south-east Asia and numerous Pacific islands. While the British fought their way back across south-east Asia, the Americans turned their attention to the Pacific islands. The strategy was to hop island by island across the Pacific, until they were within striking distance of Japan itself. As they were pushed back closer and closer to their homeland, however, the Japanese put up an increasingly fanatical defence of their island conquests.

The defeat of the Japanese at the Battle of Midway called for an immediate American initiative. The plan was to start from the south, where their own men could be supplied easily from Australia and New Zealand. There would be two thrusts, one up through Port Moresby to clear northern New Guinea; the other would come though the Solomon Islands. Both would have as their objective the capture of Rabaul on the northern tip of New Britain, which was, by then, the principal Japanese naval base in the south-western Pacific.

The Japanese had landed on New Guinea at Salamaua, 200 miles due north from Port Moresby on the other side of the island. They were kept at bay by a successful guerrilla campaign in the mountains. The main invasion force heading for Port Moresby itself was turned back in the Battle of the Coral Sea. This allowed the Allies to reinforce the island with the Australian 6th and 7th Divisions who had returned from Europe. By June 1942, the Allies had 369,000 Australian and 38,000 US troops on the island, under overall command of General Douglas MacArthur.

There were two areas considered crucial by both sides. One was Buna, which lay on the north side of the island at the head of the Kokoda Trail, a track just wide enough for men to travel single file across the mountains to Port Moresby. The other was Milne Bay, which lay at the extreme eastern end of the island. Two Australian Brigades, under Brigadier Porter, were on their way down the Kokoda trails when, on the night of 21 July, 1,800 Japanese landed at Sanananda, just north of Buna. They met at Wairope on 23 July, where the Australians held them for four days, before falling back on Kokoda. The Japanese were soon reinforced in overwhelming number and forced the Australians back. But the Australians conducted a valiant rearguard action, inflicting heavy casualties on the Japanese forces that now numbered 13,000. The Japanese had other problems. They were constantly harassed from the air, their supply lines were overextended and they could not handle the steamy jungle climate. But still they kept coming.

On 29 August, the Japanese received orders not to advance past Ioribaiwa, thirty miles from Port Moresby, which they reached on 17 September, while resources were concentrated on Guadalcanal. On 28 September, the Allies, under General Blamey, began a counter-offensive. By now, the Australian troops were experienced in jungle fighting. The Japanese put up no more than token resistance, and by 2 November the Allies had retaken Kokoda. Throughout November, the Japanese continued retreating, but found themselves in difficulties at Wairope, where the bridge had been destroyed. The Japanese commander General Horii was drowned while trying to ford the river and was replaced by General Adachi. The Australians took Gona, which was strongly fortified, after two attempts, then made straight for the Japanese base at Sanananda, while the US troops came under some criticism for their feeble attacks until their commander was replaced by Lieutenant-General Eichelberger. Buna fell on 2 January and Sanananda on 22 January 1943. By this point in the campaign the Japanese had lost 12,000 men; the Australians and the US, 2,800 – though they experienced three times as many casualties from disease as from fighting.

Once Gona, Buna and Sanananda were in Allied hands, 5,400 Japanese fled westwards towards Salamaua, Lae and the Markham Valley. They hacked their way through the jungle and, on 30 January, attacked the airfield at Wau. This was held by the local Kanga force and the Japanese were repulsed with 1,200 casualties. Troops were sent from Rabaul to reinforce them but, on 3 March, 3,000 were drowned when their convoy was sunk in the Battle of the Bismark Sea.

The Japanese retreated towards Mubo and dug in. To break the deadlock, on the night of 20 June, 1,400 US troops made an amphibious landing at Nassau Bay and threatened Salamaua.

Opposite: Up the Jungle Australian troops patrol the jungle, ever watchful for enemy activity.

General Adachi considered Salamaua so important to the defence of his position at Lae that he sent all but 2,000 of his 11,000 troops to defend it. This allowed the Australians to take Mubo on 17 July, then advance around the ridges behind Salamaua. Rather than be encircled, the Japanese withdrew and US troops entered Salamaua on 11 September. During this operation, the Japanese lost 2,722 killed and 7,578 wounded; the Australians, 500 killed and 1,300 wounded; and the US, 81 killed and 396 wounded.

The Allied forces then split in two. The Australian 7th Division pushed down the Markham Valley towards Madang, on the coast, cutting off the Huon Peninsula. They reached Dumpu, some 50 miles from Madang in early October. Meanwhile the Australian 9th Division and the US forces hopped along the coast of the Huon Peninsula in a series of amphibious landings, though they were held up by fierce fighting along the Bumi River and a counterattack outside Sattelberg, which they eventually took on 25 November.

General MacArthur then halted the advance to allow the Allies to build up supplies. This pause further weakened the Japanese who now had no air or naval support in the area. Six understrength Japanese divisions had been left to fight fifteen Allied divisions. On 2 January 1944, the US 32nd Infantry landed at Saidor, 100 miles ahead of the Australians advancing from Sattelberg. This cut off 12,000 Japanese on the Huon Peninsula. The Australian 7th Division forced their way over the mountains west of Saidor and took Bogadjim, Madang and Alexishafen on 24–26 August, forcing General Adachi's Eighteenth Army and his remaining 30,000 men back towards Wewak. The Allies left

Adachi's men, along with 20,000 civilians, there without supplies while they made a further series of amphibious landings up the coast, taking their objectives with no significant opposition. Meanwhile Adachi tried to break out, but the US II Corps was ready for him. Some 8,800 Japanese died, while US troops suffered 450 killed and 2,500 wounded.

MacArthur decided that the tactic of leaving enclaves of Japanese troops in position without any supplies worked well and made a further series of amphibious assaults, isolating enemy troop concentrations. However, someone would eventually have to take the enclaves on. The Australians advanced through the Torricelli Mountains under terrible conditions, and took Wewak on 11 May at the cost of 442 killed and 1,141 wounded. Another 16,203 were hospitalized through a combination of a variety of tropical diseases and sheer exhaustion. The Japanese lost 9,000. Adachi and his remaining 13,500 men only surrendered in 1945, at the end of a war which had long passed them by.

CHAPTER 21

Guadalcanal

'And when he gets to Heaven
To St Peter he will tell:
One more Marine reporting, Sir –
I've served my time in Hell.'

SGT JAMES A DONOHUE, US MARINE CORPS

At the same time as the offensive in New Guinea, the US made an advance in the Solomons, landing on a small, volcanic island that would give its name to one of the most famous engagements in Marine Corps history – Guadalcanal. The largest island of the Solomon Islands – some 2,047 square miles in area – it was named by the Spaniard Álvaro de Mendaña de Neira when he visited it in 1568, but in 1942 it was a British protectorate. Its mountainous spine, the Kavo Range, rises to 8,028 feet at Mount Makarakomburu. Many short, rapid streams, including the Mataniko, Lunga and Tenaru, tumble from the jungle-clad mountains to the coast, which is dotted with mangrove swamps.

On 3 May Admiral Takagi had landed a small force unopposed at Tulagi, immediately to the north of Guadalcanal across the Ironbottom Sound. On 1 July, a radio message from

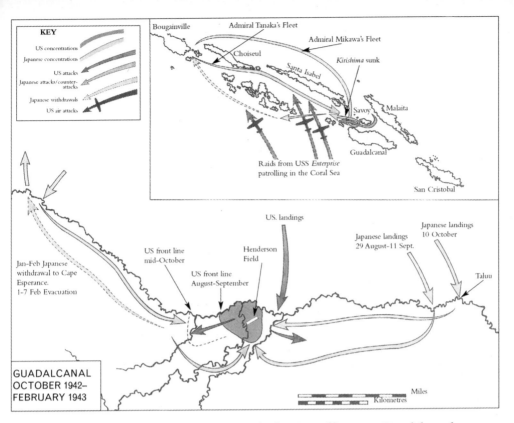

KEY

US concentrations
Japanese concentrations
US attacks
Japanese attacks/counter-attacks
Japanese withdrawals
US air attacks

Bougainville
Admiral Tanaka's Fleet
Admiral Mikawa's Fleet
Choiseul
Kirishima sunk
Santa Isabel
Savoy
Malaita
Guadalcanal
San Cristobal

Raids from USS *Enterprise* patrolling in the Coral Sea

Jan–Feb Japanese withdrawal to Cape Esperance.
1–7 Feb Evacuation

US front line mid-October

US front line August–September

Henderson Field

US landings

Japanese landings 29 August–11 Sept.

Japanese landings 10 October

Taluu

GUADALCANAL
OCTOBER 1942–
FEBRUARY 1943

Miles
Kilometres

Martin Clemens, a young British district officer on Guadalcanal, reported that 1,000 Japanese troops had landed at Lunga, on the north of the island. By 5 July, they were clearing an area just inshore from their beachhead to build an airstrip. This made an attack on Guadalcanal a priority. It was to be under the strategic command of Vice Admiral Robert Ghormley and the tactical commander would be Rear Admiral Fletcher.

OPERATION WATCHTOWER

Operation *Watchtower* – or Operation 'Shoestring' as the invasion of Guadalcanal and Tugali became known among the men – was prepared hastily. Its commanders fell out and the troop morale was low. The under-strength 1st Marine Division commanded by Major-General Archer Vandegrift, a gritty Virginian of thirty-three years service, was assigned the task. With just a few

371

weeks to go before the attack, half of Vandegrift's men were in Samoa or still at sea. They were green – few of them had been in uniform before the beginning of the year. However, time was of the essence. Once the airfield was up and running and the Japanese moved their Zeros and attack-bombers in, any amphibious invasion would be suicidal.

All Vandegrift knew about the island came from a handful of old photographs taken by missionaries, an ancient maritime chart and a short story by Jack London. However, he was getting good reports from Martin Clemens whose local scouts now said that there were between 2,000 and 10,000 Japanese troops on the island, with a smaller force on Tulagi and the twin islands to the north, Tanambugo and Gavutu.

As D-Day for Guadalcanal approached, some Australians were found who had lived on the Solomons. They were flown in to advise Vandegrift and helped him draw up sketch maps of the landing area. These would be out of range of the guns that now dominated the beaches at Lunga, east of the Ilu River. Unfortunately the Australians mis-identified the Tenaru River as the Ilu. Normally this stream was dry in August, but a sudden deluge had turned it into a raging torrent.

Things did not augur well. The unseasonable rains also soaked the men who were loading the transports. These were inadequate, only carrying enough ammunition for ten days' fighting and enough food and fuel for sixty days. The 19,000 men of the 1st Marines were to be put ashore by a huge invasion fleet of eighty-nine ships. Vandegrift had hoped that the Navy would give his Marines artillery and air support throughout the operation. But Admiral Fletcher was convinced that the invasion was going to be a failure. He did not want to risk his three precious aircraft carriers in the restricted waters of the Solomons and planned to pull out after two days.

Fortunately, the enemy were no better prepared. The Japanese army commander Lieutenant-General Haruyoshi Hyakutake in Rabaul had not been told about the Imperial Navy's defeat at Midway. He believed the propaganda claims that numerous American ships had been sunk and their planes annihilated, so he dismissed the possibility of an American counter-attack. The Navy had not even told him about the airstrip they were building on Guadalcanal. So he concentrated all his forces on the invasion of New Guinea, imagining the seas around him were patrolled by the all-powerful Imperial fleet.

At 0613 hours on 7 August, the Japanese were still asleep on Tulagi and Guadalcanal when the bombardment began. Clemens had picked out key targets which were taken out by Dauntless dive-bombers and Avengers. On Tulagi, the Marines, supported by a battalion of Raiders and paratroopers, overran most of the island with hardly a shot being fired. Then they encountered fierce resistance. In the end, it took 6,000 Marines two days to defeat 1,500 Japanese soldiers. On 9 August, Admiral Gunichi Mikawa, commander of the Japanese naval task force 600 miles to the north-west, received a despairing message. It read, 'The enemy force is overwhelming. We will defend our positions to the death, praying for everlasting victory.'

However, Gavutu and nearby Florida Island fell easily. But the Marines who stormed Tanambugo met withering fire. The island had to be bombarded by dive-bombers and destroyers before it fell the next day.

By comparison, Guadalcanal was a walkover – at first. At 0900, the Marines came swarming ashore on the palmfringed beaches practically unopposed. The 2,200 Japanese on the island were largely construction workers who had fled when the first bomb fell. By nightfall, 17,000 Marines were ashore. The 10,000 men of the main force had then moved on to Landing Beach Red in the middle of Guadalcanal's northern coast. Again they stormed 2,000 yards of sandy beach unopposed. The 5th Marine Regiment moved westwards towards the fishing village of Kukum, while the 1st Marine Regiment, which followed them ashore, advanced south-west towards the high ground that overlooked the airstrip. The heat and humidity were overpowering and they made slow progress through the jungle and over the switchback terrain. The rain came down in torrents and they had to wade chest deep through unexpectedly swollen rivers. But four miles inland they reached the grassy knoll above the airstrip. There they dug in for the night, alert for the enemy. But all they heard were the grunting of wild pigs, eerie bird calls, the scuttling of land crabs and the whine of the ubiquitous mosquitoes. It was all too easy.

Admiral Mikawa had also picked up a message from Guadalcanal. It said, 'American landing forces encountered, we are retreating into the jungle.' He passed this on to Admiral Nagumo, who ordered the fleet to make the recapture of Guadalcanal their immediate objective. Mikawa was given permission to launch a night attack on the US fleet in the New Georgia Sound, the narrow body of water that runs the 300 miles north-west from Guadalcanal to Bougainville Island. Soon, twenty-four Mitsubishi G4M 'Betty' torpedo bombers, escorted by twenty-seven Zeros, were on their way. They were spotted by the fleet when they were still an hour's flight away and six Wildcats went up after them. They waited at 20,000 feet, shot several of the Betties down and harassed the rest enough to make their bombing ineffective. A number of Zeros were downed too, and of the fifty-one planes the Japanese sent, thirty were shot down.

After an uncomfortable night on the knoll, 1st Marines seized the airfield with hardly a shot being fired. They found it was much more than an airstrip: some 17,000 Japanese naval pioneers had already built a road to the shore and dug deep bunkers that housed a radio station, warehousing facilities and power and oxygen plants. This was quickly named Henderson Field, after Major Loften Henderson, a Marine flying ace who had been killed at Midway.

The 5th Marine Division took Kukum unopposed and found that the Japanese defenders had fled in panic. They had abandoned their rifles, uniforms, mosquito nets and large amounts of mouldering rice. By 9 August, the Marines had set up a perimeter along the high ground and rivers surrounding Henderson Field and Kukum. With the airfield not yet operational, they were still being supplied across the beaches. Dozens of small craft shuttled back and forth bringing food, fuel, water, arms and ammunition quicker than it could be moved from the dumping grounds on the shore up to the airfield. These small craft were sitting ducks – or so the Japanese thought. Escorted by Zeros, another forty-five Betties attacked. But in the withering fire put up by the US Navy, only one limped away, having caused little damage.

Despite these two easy victories, Fletcher felt that the risk to his three carriers was too great and withdrew them, along with their escort of sixteen destroyers, six cruisers and one battleship. But Admiral Mikawa was not discouraged by the failure of his fliers. He steamed southwards towards the New Georgia Sound, aiming to attack the transport fleet bringing in the Marines' supplies. Luck was on his side. US daylight reconnaissance planes did not spot him, and when he was sighted at last, the report took eight hours to reach Admiral Richmond Turner at his headquarters in Australia. He was furious when he discovered that Fletcher had withdrawn leaving the Marines undefended and ordered Rear Admiral Sir Victor Crutchley, commanding the Australian naval squadron, to block the western approaches of the Sound, while another naval force under Rear Admiral Scott blocked the eastern approaches.

However, the Japanese spotted Crutchley's squadron of six heavy cruisers and four destroyers in the narrow straits between Guadalcanal and Savo Island and attacked. Within half an hour the American cruisers *Astoria* and *Quincy*, along with the Australian cruiser HMAS *Canberra*, were blazing hulks, bound for the bottom of Ironbottom Sound. The USS *Vincennes* hit the Japanese cruiser *Kinugasa*, but followed the others to the bottom. Another cruiser was badly damaged, and 1,270 men were killed, drowned or devoured by sharks. Over 700 wounded were rescued, however. In memory of this action, the next US Navy heavy cruiser to be commissioned was named *Canberra*, the only American warship ever to be named after a foreign city.

Turner had to withdraw the undefended transports and supply vessels to New Caledonia. Next morning, when the Marines from Henderson Field arrived at the beach all they could see was blue sea: the supply ships and warships were gone. They were now on their own.

THE MARINES STAND ALONE

They gathered up what supplies remained on the beach, then set about completing the airstrip in the hope that they might get some fighter support. To hold the airfield, which would become their lifeline, they had to maintain a perimeter that was 3,500 yards deep at its widest and 7,500 yards long. It ran inland from the beach between Kukum and the village of Tenaru to a tortuous ridge of hills along the southern flank. The Matanikau River and Kukum hills formed the western flank, the Tenaru River the eastern. Defences were dug and positions manned, while Vandegrift massed his artillery and tanks in the middle of the enclave so that he could bring down concentrated fire on any point around it. The airfield was defended by 90mm ack-ack guns dug in to the northwest of the airstrip and 75mm guns on half-tracks which were dug in to the north. Positions were also prepared for the half-tracks on the beaches, so they could defend against any seaborne landing. This was where Vandegrift expected the Japanese to attack, so extensive trenchworks were dug along the top of the beaches with other further defensive lines inland.

The first air attack came on 9 August. Anti-personnel bombs that burst into a thousand flying steel slivers were dropped, along with 500-pound bombs. Next came a naval bombardment from Admiral Mikawa's cruisers and destroyers sailing up and down the coast in what the Marines came to call the 'Tokyo Express'. Three days later came the gruesome curtain-raiser to the land battle, when a Japanese force landed at night near Matanikau. On 12 August they ambushed a 26-man patrol, cutting the Marines down with hidden machine-guns. The three survivors who made it back told their fellow Marines that the wounded had been hacked to death with sabres. From then on, the Marines decided that they would be every bit as brutal.

On 13 August General Hyakutake received orders from Imperial General Headquarters in Tokyo to retake Guadalcanal without delay. He sent Colonel Kiyono Ichiki with 2,000 crack troops who had been trained for the invasion of Midway. On 16 August, Colonel Ichiki and the 915 men in his preliminary force set sail on six destroyers. The rest would follow later in slower craft. The main advance force landed at Taivu Point, twenty-two miles east of the Tenaru River, with a diversionary force going ashore to the west. Vandegrift knew about the landings: at night in the South Seas, the wash of boats becomes luminous. This had been spotted by a sharp-eyed sentry. Clemens and ten of his scouts had put themselves at Vandegrift's service and told him of the arrival of the Japanese. US Naval Intelligence confirmed the reports. On top of that, a message bound for the original Japanese force hiding to the west of Kukum fell within the perimeter. It read, 'Help is on the way. Banzai.'

The Imperial High Command believed that the battle for Guadalcanal would force the US to return the remains of its Pacific fleet to the area. Eager for revenge for Midway, Yamamoto mustered three aircraft carriers, three battleships, five cruisers, eight destroyers and a sea-plane carrier and sent them to the Solomons. Admiral Mikawa already had four cruisers and five destroyers there, supported by 100 warplanes flying from Rabaul.

Yamamoto was right in his assessment of the situation. When the Allies saw where his fleet was heading, Ghormley ordered Fletcher to guard the approaches to the Solomons and sent the carrier *Hornet* and its escort of destroyers and cruisers as reinforcements.

Unsure of the enemy's deployment, Vandegrift sent three companies of Marines to attack the Japanese defences along the Matanikau. At the same time he sent a patrol in force to the east. The Matanikau attack was successful and the Marines mounted an amphibious assault further to the west at Kukumba. This came under fire from the Tokyo Express and a Japanese submarine, but the Marines got ashore and managed to drive the Japanese defenders into the jungle.

A patrol from Colonel Ichiki's force to the east was surprised by the Marine patrol and a map was taken from them showing that Ichiki knew the weakest point along the Tenaru defence line. Vandegrift strengthened it immediately. Shortly after 0010 on 21 August, 500 of Ichiki's men rushed the Americans guarding the sand spit at the mouth of the Tenaru River. Mortars rained down on the defenders. The attackers yelled 'Banzai!' and sprayed the Marines' positions with automatic and machinegun fire. But the Marines kept cool and held their fire – then opened up with everything they had. It was a bloodbath. At 0500, Ichiki sent a second wave of 400 men. This time they were cut down before they even reached the American wire. Ichiki's elite force was wiped out without even making so much as a dent in the American line. In shame at his utter failure, Ichiki burnt the regimental colours and shot himself. But some of his men fought on. Wounded Japanese soldiers tried to kill the American medics who were going to help them. Vandegrift sent in light tanks to make sure that there was no further resistance.

But Yamamoto was not to be thwarted. Operation *Ka* to recapture the airfield on Guadalcanal would continue. The remaining 1,500 men of Ichiki's main force were still on their way. Yamamoto reinforced them with another 1,000 men sent on fast transports. Meanwhile, he was determined to get the better of Fletcher. On 22 August, he sent twelve submarines to set up a screen south-east of Guadalcanal, while his main force was concentrated 200 miles north of the southernmost of the Solomons. The light carrier *Ryujo* was then sent out as bait. Yamamoto's plan was to destroy the American carriers while their planes were attacking the *Ryujo*. Then his massive battleships could sail though Ironbottom Sound and annihilate the Marines, while his troops retook the airfield.

Fletcher took the bait and torpedo planes and dive-bombers from the Enterprise and the Saratoga obliterated the *Ryujo*. Yamamoto had counted on Fletcher keeping his three carriers together for the attack, but he had already sent the *Wasp* to refuel. He was also ready for Yamamoto's counterattack. The *Enterprise* had kept back fifty-three Wildcats which were circling in the clouds as the carrier waited for its attack planes to return from the *Ryujo*.

Then thirty Val dive-bombers came screaming from the sky. The battleship North Carolina fired a canopy over the *Enterprise*, but still three dive-bombers found their mark. The *Enterprise* sped on at 27 knots, ablaze. An hour later she was able to swing into the wind to pick up the returning planes, but after that she was out of action for two months. However, in the Battle of the Eastern Solomons, the Japanese lost daytime control of the sea, along with one more carrier and numerous planes, although some of the surviving Japanese pilots claimed that two US aircraft carriers had been sunk. In Rabaul, Admiral Mikawa gave the okay for the invasion convoy to continue to Guadalcanal.

In preparation for the invasion, Admiral Tanaka, commander of the invasion fleet, sent five destroyers into New Georgia Sound to bombard Henderson Field. This left the convoy undefended. On the night of 24 August, with the transport just over 100 miles from Guadalcanal, a formation of Dauntlesses caught up with them. The Japanese were so confident that the US carrier force had been dealt a serious blow in the Battle of the Eastern Solomons that they did not even have their guns loaded. The American dive-bombers hit Tanaka's flagship, the cruiser *Jintsu,* and a large troopship laden with men. They then called up Flying Fortresses which finished off the burning transport and a destroyer that was trying to rescue the men. The other ships turned northwards and fled out of range.

CHANGING TACTICS

Yamamoto then decided to change tactics. Instead of landing a large invasion force, he would build up slowly, landing men on the island by stealth at night. Next ashore was to be the crack Kawaguchi Brigade. But their advance units were so eager to get into the fray that they left Borneo on destroyers at night, guaranteeing that they would be in New Georgia Sound in broad daylight. Marine dive-bomber pilots spotted them and soon two of the four destroyers had been torn apart with explosions and a third was on fire.

Japanese Bunker *US Marines examining a Japanese machine gun emplacement dug into the jungle floor at Guadalcanal, 7 September 1942.*

General Kawaguchi and his main force were on shore in the Shortland Islands south of Bougainville with Yamamoto. A row broke out. Kawaguchi refused to have his men transported by destroyers, insisting that they be landed by barge. A compromise was reached. Eight destroyers would carry the bulk of the force. The rest would follow up in the limited number of barges available. Some 3,500 men were landed from destroyers at Taivu Point on Guadalcanal on the night of 31 August. Several nights later, the remaining 1,000 men turned up in their barges, but a heavy swell prevented them from landing. At first light, they were spotted out to sea by the Marine aircraft now flying from Henderson Field, and decimated.

The Imperial General Headquarters was now getting impatient with the loss of life the recapture of Guadalcanal was costing. They sacked Admiral Tanaka, though he had frequently warned against the use of barges, and made the taking of Henderson Field their top priority. The already over-stretched General Hyakutake was ordered to go on the defensive in New Guinea and concentrate his forces against Guadalcanal. This halted the Japanese forces within thirty miles of Port Moresby and allowed the Allies to regroup for their counteroffensive which eventually pushed the Japanese back across the island. The entire resources of the Southeast Area Air Force would also be put at Hyakutake's disposal and he would be supported by the powerful Eighth Fleet.

Henderson Field was being bombed daily and the Japanese were now deploying fifty-eight more planes against it. However, Henderson now had its Cactus Air Force – as they called themselves – who quickly shattered the myth of the invincibility of the Zero with their new Wildcats. With its superior firepower, the formation flying of the US pilots outweighed the greater speed and manoeuvrability of the Zeros. Spotters along the coast gave Henderson an early warning of the approach of enemy aircraft. This meant that the stubby, radial-engined Wildcats could get airborne and attack the incoming bandits out of the sun. Enemy planes were being shot down at a rate of between six and eight for every Wildcat lost. However, they could do nothing to counter the nightly Tokyo Express and the US Navy still did not dare to enter New Georgia Sound.

The situation at Henderson Field grew dire. The Japanese forces around them were building up. The Tokyo Express meant that the Marines got little sleep at night and were subjected to surprise attacks during the day. They were also suffering from dysentry, jungle rot, malaria and the effects of eating little but stodgy rice. But things picked up when the First World War fighter ace Brigadier-General Roy Geiger flew in to take command of the Cactus Air Force and a battalion of Navy Seabees, expert in airfield construction, arrived to make improvements to Henderson Field.

Vandegrift was short of reinforcements and called in the Raiders and paratroopers from Tulagi. They were ferried across the Ironbottom Sound at night by the light destroyers *Gregory* and *Little*. But after they had delivered their precious cargo, the ships were mistakenly illuminated by an American flare and shot to pieces by the Japanese Navy.

With the airfield now extended, Skytrain air transports brought in machine guns and took out the wounded. This became a regular service and did much to boost the Marines' morale. Then two transports got through with reinforcements, bringing the garrison up to 23,000.

On 12 September, the Japanese began a massive air and sea bombardment to cover the advance of Kawaguchi's 6,200 men in a three-pronged attack. However, he had overestimated how quickly his men could move through the slimy swamps and tangled jungle that characterised the terrain. Soon they were strung out and disorganized.

Forewarned, Vandegrift reinforced the steep ridges the Japanese were aiming for and brought his headquarters up. But the bombardment left Henderson Field with only 11 airworthy Wildcats. Despite protests, Admiral Nimitz ordered Fletcher to sent 24 of his fighters from the Saratoga to reinforce Henderson. This was done reluctantly as Ghormley now considered the position of the Marines on Guadalcanal untenable. As there was no way that the US Navy could risk taking on the Japanese Imperial Navy in the confined waters of the Solomons, he ordered the fleet to stay away.

On the night of 12 September, the American defenders on the ridge above the Tenaru River saw a rocket. Next they heard the crackling of automatic fire and the cry of 'Banzai' as the Japanese came charging up the hill. In some places they forced the Marines back. In others they broke through. But Kawaguchi had misjudged the jungle. He had sent his first wave in while the second were still clawing their way through the undergrowth. Vandegrift then concentrated artillery fire on the places the Japanese had broken through, causing any who had survived the bombardment to flee back into the forest. A counter-attack by the Marines at dawn retook what they were now calling Bloody Ridge. As it seemed certain that the Japanese would attack there again, they rolled out barbed wire and cleared the slopes so that, next time, the Japanese would have to charge across a hundred yards of open ground raked by machine-gun fire.

Back at Henderson Field, three air raids had depleted the complement of Wildcats again, but sixty more planes, including six Avenger torpedo bombers, arrived from the *Wasp* and the *Hornet*. At the same time, 140 new planes arrived at the Japanese bases on Bougainville and at Rabaul.

Henderson was given a day's rest, while General Hyakutake waited for the news that Kawaguchi had taken the ridge. His planes were instead sent to bomb Tasimboko, to Kawaguchi's rear, where there had been an erroneous report of an American landing. Mistaking them for Americans, the Japanese planes made a devastating raid on Kawaguchi's rear echelon troops.

In the jungle below Bloody Ridge, Kawaguchi tried to muster his remaining 2,500 troops into an organized assault. That night, while Henderson Field was under bombardment from seven destroyers, he sent 2,000 men in six waves up the slope against just 400 Raiders under 'Red Mike' Edson. The American artillery decimated the oncoming Japanese. Some made it across the newly-prepared killing grounds and threw themselves into hand-to-hand fighting. Others were knifed to death as they jumped into American foxholes. The Japanese also called in naval gunfire from the Tokyo Express, though soldiers from both sides were in close combat. The American line bent, but held. The surviving Japanese were put to flight by P-400s swooping in low with cannon firing, and were chased away by five Marine tanks. The Raiders had suffered 224 casualties; the paratroopers 212; and the Marines, who had been sent in as reinforcements, 263. The Japanese dead were uncountable and Kawaguchi's men carried away 400 wounded on litters through the jungle towards Matanikau. Meanwhile, six more transports carrying 4,000 more Marines got through. They had been escorted by a substantial force, including the *North Carolina*, the *Hornet* and the *Wasp*. These big ships were quickly withdrawn under cover of darkness on the night of 14 September. The following day, the *Wasp* was fatally hit by torpedoes and a battleship and destroyer were damaged, but Yamamoto could not follow up and finish off the US fleet because his ships had been recalled for refuelling. Instead, he continued his tactic of building up the ground forces on the island, sending in the battle-hardened Nagoya Division and the crack Sendai Division.

On 18 September, in a lightly defended convoy, Admiral Kelly Turner landed more Marines inside the perimeter at Guadalcanal. He also brought 155mm 'Long Toms' and 5-inch naval guns. Also on their way were USAAF Lightnings, diverted from the Anglo-American landings in North Africa, which had the range to attack the Tokyo Express when the ships stayed away from the island during the day.

Although the conditions at Henderson Field were by no means luxurious, the Japanese out in the jungle were in a pitiful state – disease-ridden and starving, with no prospect of evacuation. Vandegrift decided to increase their woes. On 27 September, he sent a three-pronged attack against their strongpoint at Matanikau. The Marines would rush across the sand spit at the mouth of the river, while the Raiders were to cross the river a mile inland, wheel around to the Japanese rear and meet up with another Marine battalion that was to land behind them. But the Marines charging across the spit were driven back, the Raiders were pinned down and the landing force found that they had walked into a trap. Vandegrift cancelled the offensive.

The monsoon was on its way and Admiral Nimitz landed amid heavy rain to reassure the defenders that he would support them with the 'maximum of our resources'. The embattled defenders were in need of reassurance. The ground troops arrayed against them seemed to increase every day. The Marines were, however, winning the war in the air. The next two air raids on Henderson Field cost the Japanese six fighters and twenty-nine bombers, without destroying a single American plane. By the end of September, the Cactus Air Force had lost thirty-two planes; the Japanese more than 200.

INCREASING THE PRESSURE

Determined to make sure that the Japanese forces did not fail again, Hyakutake left Rabaul for Guadalcanal on 9 October to direct operations personally. He estimated Vandegrift's strength at just 10,000 – it was over 19,000 – and believed that his Sendai Division alone could vanquish them. Nevertheless, he took the precaution of bringing the 38th Division in from Borneo and established his Seventeenth Army headquarters on Guadalcanal. The plan was to attack in force from Matanikau on 17 October. The Sendai commander, Lieutenant-General Masoa Maruyama, issued an order of the day setting the tone for the engagement. It said, 'The occupying of Guadalcanal island is under the observation of the whole world. Do not expect to return, not even one man, if the occupation is not successful.'

At the same time, Vandegrift decided to launch another attack, this time in more force, against Matanikau. On 17 October they met head-on in the jungle. Furious fighting ensued. By nightfall both sides were pinned down as the monsoon started. The following day, the Marines caught a battalion of Sendai resting in a ravine and called artillery fire down on them, killing them all. Around 1,000 Japanese died at the cost of sixty-five Americans, and the 'unbeatable' Sendai were then forced to retreat.

As the Marines had held their position on Guadalcanal for

two months now, their prospects were starting to be viewed with more optimism. Even the Army chipped in. The 164th Infantry Regiment sent 3,000 men on two transports from New Caledonia, and the USAAF sent twenty Wildcats. And Ghormley sent all the warships available to challenge the Japanese dominance in New Georgia Sound. The landing on Guadalcanal had started out as a small-scale engagement. Now it was a major battle.

The Japanese were also reinforcing. Hyakutake brought in 1,000 more men from the Sendai Division on six destroyers, and another battalion on sea-plane carriers. The convoy was guarded by a huge force, including three cruisers, two destroyers and numerous aircraft. Artillery, stockpiles of medical supplies and ammunition and sixteen tanks were landed. The ships, under Admiral Aritomo Goto, were then to bombard Henderson Field, putting it out of action. That night, 11 October, they were to run straight into Rear Admiral Norman Scott's convoy coming in from New Caledonia, which had four cruisers and five destroyers protecting the troopships. Goto felt safe, believing that the Americans would not attack after nightfall. But Scott's convoy had radar so he could see where the Japanese ships were, and his crews had been extensively trained in night fighting.

Scott's fleet almost gave their position away when a spotter plane caught fire on take-off, but Japanese look-outs mistook the conflagration for a signal fire on the landing beaches. At 5,000 yards, the American ships opened fire. The first salvoes hit the cruiser *Aoba*, Goto's flagship, setting it on fire and fatally wounding the Admiral. To take stock in the midst of the confusion, Scott ordered a ceasefire. Not all the gun crews heard the order and before the guns fell silent the cruiser *Surutake* was also on fire. Searchlights also revealed that the destroyer *Fuvuki* had been blown to pieces. On the US side, the destroyer *Duncan* had been caught in the crossfire and sank, and the cruiser *Boise* was badly damaged. The Battle of the Cape of Esperance, as the engagement became known, ended Japanese domination of the waters around Guadalcanal for the time being. This point was emphasized when the Japanese destroyers that landed the Sendai reinforcements were attacked by dive-bombers from Henderson Field and annihilated.

Progress was being made by the US forces, but painfully slowly. As soon as the 3,000 American infantrymen Scott had brought set foot on Guadalcanal, there was a massive Japanese air raid. Japanese ground troops had attacked and killed the coastal spotters, so Henderson Field had no warning. The Wildcats could not climb fast enough to intercept the attackers. Planes on the ground were badly damaged and fuel stores set ablaze. The Japanese had now brought in artillery that could out-range the American guns and an artillery barrage hit the runways, putting the airfield out of action for the first time.

Another 10,000 Japanese troops were to be landed on the night of 14 October, ready for an all-out offensive on 20 October. They were supported by Yamamoto's massive fleet which comprised five aircraft carriers, five battleships, fourteen cruisers and forty-four destroyers. The battleships bombarded Henderson Field for an hour and a half, leaving the men there speechless and barely sane. Forty-one were killed, many of them pilots. All thirty-four Dauntlesses were badly damaged, along with nearly all the Avengers and sixteen out of the forty

Wildcats. Both runways were pitted with huge craters.

The Seabees got to work on the runways and, using fuel siphoned from two wrecked Flying Fortresses and a stash captured from the Japanese, the remaining twenty-four Wildcats got airborne to fend off further air raids. Ten Zeros and nine bombers were shot down at the cost of one army pilot and

Death on the Beach *The bodies of Japanese soldiers on the beach at Guadalcanal, after a disastrous attempt to land reinforcements, 26 October 1942.*

two Marines. Then, working around the clock, the mechanics managed to patch up the P-400s, Aerocobras, Dauntlesses and more Wildcats which went out to strafe and bomb the incoming troopships. Fuel was flown in and, towards the end of the day, a formation of Flying Fortresses from the New Hebrides joined in the attack. Four motor torpedo boats began harassing the convoy by night, while the Cactus Air Force threw everything they had at them by day. Two of the transports were wrecked, and another three turned back. In all, Hyakutake only got 4,500 of the reinforcements for his big offensive.

Yamamoto's fleet continued pounding Henderson. On the night of 15 October, hundreds of 8-inch shells finished off the fuel stocks and smashed the planes until there were only twenty-seven left. The converted destroyer *McFarland* arrived with 40,000 gallons of aviation fuel. It was unloading as fourteen Japanese dive-bombers came screaming from the sky. At that moment a squadron of Wildcats sent in from the New Hebrides, at the limit of their range, arrived. With his fuel tanks almost empty, the squadron's leader, Lieutenant-Colonel Harold Bauer, shot down four Vals in one swoop and the *McFarland* finished unloading.

Hyakutake now prepared his attack with 22,000 men. General Maruyama was to take 7,000 men on the same route as Kawaguchi's ill-fated assault. But this time, a road would be hacked through the jungle. He would then break through the perimeter and take the airfield. Meanwhile, the remaining 15,000 men would stage diversionary attacks to prevent the Americans reinforcing Bloody Ridge. And the defenders would be harassed constantly by land-based planes flying from the airfields at Rabaul, on the nearby island of Buka, and from the Buin airfield on Bougainville. They would be joined by planes from Yamamoto's carriers and the fleet would be on hand if any further bombardment were needed. The Japanese strength was so overwhelming, Hyakutake believed that the whole thing would be over in two days.

However, the jungle came to the defenders' rescue again. On 22 October, after a five-day march, General Maruyama's Sendai had only covered twenty-nine of the thirty-five miles to their starting point. Nevertheless, Maruyama reported that he would be ready to start the battle on 23 October. That day, the Japanese sent in a formation of bombers. The Wildcats took off to greet them and take on their escorts. In the attack, twenty Zeros were downed for the loss of not a single Wildcat. None of the bombers got through.

On the ground, things were going even more badly for the Japanese. Maruyama was in position, but Kawaguchi, who was supposed to attack on his right, was not yet in place. Kawaguchi was relieved of his command and the attack was rescheduled for 24 October. However, news of the delay did not get through to Major-General Sumoyoshi. At dusk he attacked across the mouth of the Matanikau River. His men and his tanks were blown to pieces by the American artillery.

Vandegrift was away at the time, seeing the new commander in the South Pacific, Admiral Halsey. Intelligence reported that an all-out attack was expected on the night of 24 October. Halsey sent in the *Enterprise* and the *Hornet* to take on Yamamoto's fleet while the battle raged on land. In Vandegrift's absence, Geiger was in command. Sumoyoshi's premature assault on the Matanikau

River convinced Geiger that the attack would come from the west and he switched a battalion from the southern defence line to reinforce his right flank.

Maruyama's attack was due to begin at 1700. But at that moment the monsoon came. The jungle tracks turned into seas of mud. His units lost touch with each other and communications broke down. He postponed the attack for two hours. At 1900, the rain had stopped, but Kawaguchi's successor, Colonel Shoji, had still not managed to get his men up to the start line to the right. Nevertheless, Maruyama sent his left wing in. The jungle was so dense that it was impossible to advance with any degree of stealth. An American outpost warned their comrades on the ridge that the attack was coming. The Marines held their fire until the Japanese reached the wire. The first wave was cut down to a man. The second wave tried to scramble over the corpses of their fallen comrades, but even the Sendai could not take this kind of slaughter and a few survivors fled back into the forest. At one point, however, the Japanese did make it through. Led by Colonel Furumiya with his sword held high, they rushed the American machine guns, killing a number of Marines. The line simply closed behind them and, when they were all dead, the positions were remanned.

At 2130, the Sendai tried again. This time Shoji had his men in place on the right wing and they were determined to cleanse the dishonour of being late for the battle with their ferocity. At a number of places they managed to penetrate the Marines' line. Thinking that his men had got through, Maruyama radioed that he had taken the airfield and Hyakutake sent a message to Admiral Mikawa asking him to land the remaining men he had on three destroyers at Koli Point to the east of Tenaru to finish off the Americans once and for all.

All this was very premature. The Marines' line had been penetrated, but not broken. The gaps were filled and the Japanese who had got through were hunted down and killed. At 2330, a fourth wave of Sendai warriors were sent in. Instead of finding the line broken, they were met with intense fire. When the slaughter abated, a few survivors slunk away into the dark depths of the jungle. At dawn, the Americans saw the terrible carnage around their positions. At one place, an anti-tank gun had hit a Japanese column at point-blank range, blasting the entire unit to pieces. Shamefacedly, Maruyama radioed Hyakutake, 'Am having trouble capturing the airfield.'

But it was too late to stop the landings. As the destroyers carrying the troops approached Koli Point, they met five-inch shells from the Marines' guns and were forced to turn away. Once the morning sun had dried out the airfield, a wing of Dauntlesses took off to attack the convoy. They set one Japanese cruiser on fire, sent four destroyers fleeing for the open seas and forced another onto shore. Twenty-six Japanese planes were shot down over Henderson Field and Admiral Nagumo, fearing another Midway, turned tail, taking with him the carrier *Junyo* whose planes were to have landed at Henderson, once it was safely in Japanese hands.

That night Maruyama tried to redeem his honour with one more assault. This time he got all his men in place and in communication. They came screaming out of the jungle. Hundreds were slaughtered, but as the battle developed the attack swung towards Hill 67 and the sea. The Sendai charged headlong at the machine-gun nests. Those who got through hacked at the Marines with knives and swords. Such was the ferocity of the attack that some of the machine-gun positions were overrun. But the Marines counter-attacked, forcing the Sendai back, leaving some 2,500 of their dead on the ground. Maruyama ordered a full retreat. The land battle had been won. There now followed a battle at sea.

THE BATTLE AT SEA

While the Sendai were being decimated in the jungle and America was winning its first land battle of the war, the *Enterprise* and the *Hornet* were steaming with their escort ships towards Guadalcanal from the Santa Cruz Islands in the south-east, under the command of Admiral Thomas Kincaid. The huge Japanese fleet, with its four carriers, turned south looking for them. On 26 October, a reconnaissance plane from the *Shokaku* found the US ships 200 miles to the east. Admiral Nagumo sent bombers from all three of his carriers, while the *Junyo*, 100 miles to his rear, launched a separate attack. At about the same time, an American spotter plane found Nagumo's fleet.

Shortly before 0700, a patrol of Dauntlesses came hurtling down through the canopy of Zeros onto Nagumo's carriers. The *Zuiho* quickly made smoke and zigzagged, but two bombs hit her, putting her out of action.

The Japanese pilots could not find the *Enterprise*, which was hidden under cloud, but the *Hornet* was caught out in the open by fifteen dive-bombers and twelve torpedo planes. A Japanese pilot smashed his plane through the flight deck in a kamikaze attack, starting a huge fire. Two torpedoes then struck home, followed by three bombs. Although at one point the whole ship threatened to blow up, the fires were soon brought under control.

Meanwhile, the *Hornet's* dive-bombers had located the *Shokaku*. Diving through heavy flak, they put 1,000-pound bombs through her deck, setting the whole ship on fire. However, the Avenger torpedo bombers did not find her to finish her off. Instead they disabled the cruiser *Chikuma*. The *Shokaku* also headed out of the battle, but in nine months she was at sea again.

While she was turning to avoid torpedoes from a Japanese submarine, the *Enterprise* was hit on the flight deck by two bombs. She evaded more torpedoes dropped by Kates and survived in good enough shape to take on her returning aircraft. The battleship South Dakota downed twenty-six of the Japanese dive-bombers that attacked her, taking scarcely a scratch herself. The *Hornet*, which was being towed by the cruiser *Northampton*, was hit again by Japanese bombers and Admiral Kincaid ordered that she be scuttled. American destroyers tried to torpedo her, but of the eight Mark 15 torpedoes launched by the USS *Mustin*, only three ran straight, and they failed to do the job. So, while American float planes illuminated the target with flares, the destroyer hit her with 430 five-inch shells. Still she would not go down and had to be abandoned. Eventually the Japanese sunk her with four 'Long Lance' torpedoes.

As Kincaid sped away from the advancing Japanese fleet, the Japanese announced that they had won the Battle of the Santa Cruz Islands. But Nagumo was replaced. He had won victory at too high a price. The *Shokaku* and the *Zuiho* had been put out of action and more than 100 planes, along with their highly trained crews, had been lost. On top of that, the *Hiyo* had damaged its engines during the engagement. But at least the defenders on Guadalcanal did not have to worry about being attacked by carrier-borne planes for some time.

Since late October, the conflict on the island had become deadlocked. But soon both sides began to reinforce again. It had come to the attention of President Roosevelt how vital the battle for Guadalcanal was becoming. Cactus Air Force was now down to twenty-nine planes, and he ordered all available aircraft, ships and weapons to be rushed there. Meanwhile, Japanese Imperial Headquarters planned yet another all-out offensive from Matanikau, accompanied, once again, by a massive naval bombardment.

On 1 November, Vandegrift did his best to upset these plans by sending 5,000 Marines to stop the Japanese consolidating their position to the west of Matanikau and to silence their longrange artillery there. Fierce fighting ensued, but the Japanese were eventually pushed back. Then two battalions of 155mm 'Long Tom' guns were delivered to the defenders, giving the US artillery the ascendancy again.

On 3 November, Nagumo's successor, Admiral Tameichi Hari, transported more troops to reinforce the Sendai survivors, who were quietly starving at Koli Point, and renewed the Tokyo Express with three cruisers and eight destroyers. By 10 November, the Japanese had built up their forces on the island to 30,000, against Vandegrift's 20,000 Marines and 3,000 infantrymen. Another 6,000 were on their way. But before they were to attack again, the Japanese wanted overwhelming superiority. On the night of 12 November, they planned to land 28,000 more troops and add two aircraft carriers, four battleships, eleven cruisers and forty-nine destroyers to the Tokyo Express. These were spotted by Australian coastal watchers on occupied Bougainville, and Halsey decided that he would have another crack at the Imperial fleet. In Noumea Harbour on New Caledonia, hundreds of engineers were working day and night on the *Enterprise*. The Imperial Fleet was expected to arrive at Guadalcanal on 12 November. On 11 October, the *Enterprise* sailed from Noumea with repair teams still working on board. She was escorted by the battleship *Washington* and the damaged *South Dakota*, two cruisers and eight destroyers.

Under cover of a rainstorm, the Japanese fleet slipped into New Georgia Sound. American reinforcements were landing when eight Zeros and twenty-four Betties, flying from the fleet, attacked. But the guns of the American naval escort downed three Zeros and twenty-three Betties in minutes.

In the forthcoming battle, the planes on Henderson Field were a vital asset, so Admiral Turner sent two heavy cruisers, the *Portland* and the *San Francisco*; three light cruisers, the *Atlanta*, the *Helena* and the *Junea*; and eight destroyers to attack the Japanese fleet in an attempt to stop it bombarding Henderson Field. Admiral Hari had not anticipated this. When his fleet arrived off Savo Island, its decks were stacked with high-explosive shells to bombard *Henderson*. When the lookouts spotted the American ships, there was consternation. One shell hitting the ammunition would blow the ship out of the war. The high-explosive shells were quickly taken below, the gunners reloading with armour-piercing shells to take on the American ships.

The American ships, under Rear Admiral Callaghan,

advanced in a single line because they had not trained together as a squadron. Even this simple manoeuvre required more co-operation between the ships than they could manage, and the situation was not helped by the fact that Callaghan's flagship *San Francisco* did not have radar. At 0140, in the darkness, the destroyer *Cushing* almost ran into the two Japanese destroyers, *Murasame* and *Yudachi*. Only five minutes later did Callaghan give the order to open fire. Almost immediately, the *Cushing* was blown to bits by the battleship *Hiei*. A point-blank blast from the *Laffey* set the *Hiei* on fire, but the counter-blast blew the *Laffey* out of the water. The *Portland* and the *San Francisco* hit the *Hiei* and damaged two Japanese destroyers, the *Yudachi* and the *Akatsuki*. But when Callaghan found that the *San Francisco's* guns had also crippled the *Atlanta* he gave the order to cease fire. This allowed the 14-inch guns of the battleship *Kirishima* to fire a massive broadside into the *San Francisco*, killing Callaghan and his staff. The crippled *Atlanta* was also caught in the Japanese searchlights and blasted, killing Admiral Scott. In the maelstrom, the Americans lost five destroyers and two light cruisers, and the *San Francisco* was badly damaged. Only one Japanese ship, the *Akatsuki*, sank, though the *Yudachi* had to be abandoned. Nevertheless, the Japanese abandoned their plans to bombard *Henderson* and withdrew, leaving the damaged *Hiei*. The next day, it was bombed and sunk.

But *Henderson* was not to be spared for long. The next night, Admiral Mikawa's flagship, the *Chokai*; three heavy cruisers, the *Kinugasa*, the *Maya* and the *Suzuya*; and six destroyers arrived off Savo Island at midnight. The *Enterprise* was still too far away to be of any help. Kincaid sent the greater part of his escort – the battleships *South Dakota* and *Washington* and four destroyers – but they would not arrive before dawn. Mikawa's ships bombarded *Henderson* at will on the night of 13 November, destroying eighteen planes. But next morning the Cactus Air Force had its revenge. Its planes torpedoed the *Kinugasa* and the destroyer *Izuso*. Then planes from the *Enterprise* turned up to finish off the *Kinugasa*. Soon after noon, eleven Japanese troop transports were spotted by US planes some 150 miles from Guadalcanal. By nightfall, there were only four left.

On the night of 14 November, the Japanese attempted to bombard Henderson Field again. A squadron under Vice Admiral Kondo – the heavy cruisers *Atago*, *Kirishima* and *Takao*; the light cruiser *Nagara* and three destroyers – sailed into Ironbottom Sound. The US submarine *Trout* spotted them as they passed Savo Island and warned Rear Admiral Willis Lee. The *Washington* and the *South Dakota*, supported by four destroyers, went to attack them. But the Japanese had split their force into four groups. The cruiser *Sendai* was sent to shadow the American ships. When Lee realized this, he opened fire. While the *Sendai* returned fire from the rear, the destroyers *Ayanami* and the *Uranami* attacked them for'ard. In the gun battle that followed, the American destroyers *Preston* and *Walke* were sunk.

The destroyer *Gwin* was also out of action and a shot from the *Kirishima* knocked out the *South Dakota's* electrics so it could not move its guns. At this point, only the *Ayanami* was damaged, so Kondo and his squadron closed in. They fired three torpedoes at the *South Dakota*. All three missed. The *Washington* retaliated. Soon the *Kirishima* was crippled and sank. Kondo broke off at 0030, his destroyers also having been badly mauled. However, the Japanese did manage to drive their transports aground at Tassafaronga and the reinforcements disembarked under fire. Only 2,000 got ashore, along with 250 cases of ammunition and 1,500 bags of rice. On 30 November, eight Japanese destroyers attempted to land more troops and were beaten off in the Battle of Tassafaronga, losing one destroyer sunk and one crippled – the cost to the Allies was one cruiser sunk and three damaged.

VICTORY

Even though the Japanese forces on Guadalcanal outnumbered their American counterparts, the Japanese had lost the battle for the sea: the forces on Guadalcanal could not be resupplied. During the naval battle, they had lost two battleships, one cruiser and three destroyers to the Americans' two cruisers and five destroyers. It would become increasingly difficult to resupply their men while the Americans still held Henderson Field. The Japanese mounted a fifth and final offensive on Guadalcanal, but it never really got off the ground, and the Japanese troops on the island were soon reduced to eating grass and roots.

On 4 January 1943, after bitter disputes between the army and the navy, Imperial General Headquarters decided to evacuate all Japanese forces from Guadalcanal. Between 1 and 7 February, the Japanese withdrew the 13,000 survivors so stealthily that the Marines, now 50,000 strong but still fearful of a new attack, did not even know about it. Guadalcanal was the first land victory for the Allies in the South Seas and the beginning of the end for the Japanese Empire. During the six-month campaign on the island, the Japanese lost 50,000 men, 25,000 of those on land and 9,000 to disease. But the greater loss, militarily, was 600 planes and their crews – all for what the Imperial High Command had called, at the time of the first American landing, an 'insignificant island in the South Seas'.

Guadalcanal had cost the Marines 1,592 lives. And for America the island was not so insignificant. It kept open the route to Australia which was fast becoming a forward base in the war against Japan. The battle for Guadalcanal had also been well covered in the press and newsreels, and victory there gave the Allies' morale a much-needed boost.

CHAPTER 22

Island-Hopping

The Japanese empire in the Pacific consisted largely of strings of islands, all of which would have to be captured, one by one, for the US to get close enough to mount an assault on the Japanese home islands.

O n 21 February 1943, the US infantry landed on the Russell Islands to support advances on Rabaul. In the summer of 1942, British forces had begun an invasion of Vichy French-held Madagascar. Hostilities ceased on 5 November and the Free French took over on 8 January 1943. In the North Pacific, the United States had decided to expel the Japanese from the Aleutians. Landing forces on Adak in August 1942, they began air attacks against Kiska and Attu in September while a naval blockade prevented the Japanese from reinforcing their garrisons. Bypassing Kiska, US forces invaded Attu on 11 May 1943 and killed most of the island's 2,300 defenders in the following three weeks, and the Japanese evacuated Kiska. With these strategic bases in the Aleutians now safely back in American possession, the US could bomb the Kuril Islands at the north of the Japanese archipelago.

RABAUL

In mid-1943, the Allies drew up new plans for the invasion of Japan proper. It was decided that the main offensive should come from the south and the south-east, through the Philippines and through Micronesia, rather than from the Aleutians or from the Asian mainland, where the Chinese with Allied backing were still fighting the Japanese.

The key to the invasion plan was the Philippines, which the Japanese had taken in 1941. Retaking them would disrupt Japanese communications with the East Indian islands and Malaya. And the conquest of Micronesia, through the Gilbert Islands, the Marshalls, the Carolines and the Marianas, offered the prospect of drawing the Japanese into a naval showdown and winning land bases for massive air raids on the Japanese mainland in the run-up to any invasion.

To reach the Philippines, it would be necessary to encircle Rabaul – the strategy was to isolate it rather than attack it directly. The encirclement of Rabaul began with the capture of the Treasury Islands in the Solomons by New Zealand troops in October and November 1943. And on 1 November, US troops landed at Empress Augusta Bay on the west of Bougainville. US reinforcements subsequently held off Japanese counter-attacks in December 1943, when they sank two American destroyers, and in March 1944, when they killed some 6,000 men. But by then, what remained of the Japanese garrison on Bougainville no longer had the strength to fight, although it did not surrender until the end of the war.

On 15 December 1943, American troops landed at Arawe on the southwest coast of New Britain. This drew the Japanese

Hill Taken *US Marines storm a peak on the island of Tarawa, November 1943.*

away from Cape Gloucester on the north-west coast, where there was a major landing on 26 December. By 16 January 1944, the airfield at Cape Gloucester had been secured. Talasea, on the road to Rabaul, was captured in March 1944. With western New Britain now in American hands, the Allies controlled the vital straits between New Britain and New Guinea.

On 15 February, New Zealand troops took the Green Islands south-east of New Guinea. American forces invaded Los Negros in the Admiralty Islands on 29 February and captured Manus on 9 March. With the fall of the Emirau Islands on 20 March, the Allies' stranglehold on Rabaul was virtually complete and the 100,000 Japanese troops there could be ignored for all practical purposes. Then, when the Allies subdued the Japanese in western New Guinea and built airbases there, they were all set to push on towards the Philippines.

TARAWA

Although there were no plans for a major offensive westward across the Pacific before mid-1944, the US Joint Chiefs of Staff decided to launch a limited offensive in the central Pacific in 1943, hoping to draw the Japanese away from other areas and to speed the pace of the war. In November 1943, Admiral Nimitz's central Pacific forces invaded the Gilbert Islands. Makin fell easily, but the amphibious landings on the Tarawa atoll became another blood-bath.

Tarawa is an atoll to the north of the centre of the Gilbert Islands, comprising fifteen islets with a total land area of twelve square miles. They are laid out in the shape of a right-angled triangle – the hypotenuse being the north-eastern side. This is made up of a string of islands. The southern side is the same, but the western leg is largely a reef which shelters the central lagoon. The only entrance to the lagoon is through a break in the reef on the western side, just north of Betio Island in the south-western corner. Before the war, Betio had been the British administrative headquarters. On the north side, in the lagoon, there was a pier where a small boat could land at high tide. The island was just two miles long and only a few hundred yards wide. But it was flat, rising no more than ten feet above sea level, and the Japanese had built an airstrip there for medium bombers. It was the main air facility in the region. Consequently, the island was well fortified.

Despite having been British territory before the war, detailed information about the island was scant. The only charts of the area were over a hundred years old and carried no information about currents and tides. However, aerial reconnaissance had located an estimated ninety per cent of the Japanese defensive positions. It was also estimated that the Japanese had 200 artillery pieces on Betio, ranging from 8-inch guns to 20mm cannon. As the island was so small, almost all the beaches were within range of almost all the guns. Although the island had palm trees and a little undergrowth, there were absolutely no natural features to provide cover. Any invasion was going to be bloody.

With little information to go on, the 2nd Marine Division, who were to make the assault, decided to use amphibious tractors – Amtracs – to get its men ashore, although these had only been used to land supplies on beaches before. The Marines acquired seventy-five of them and began fixing machine-guns to them and welding armour plating in position, while Marine drivers were taught how to manoeuvre them over coral. Fifty more Amtracs, of a newer type designed for beach assaults, were shipped out from San Diego the day before the invasion. But even that was not enough. The plan devised by divisional commander Major-General Julian C. Smith called for 100 tractors to carry the first three waves of the assault, with twenty-five tractors to be held in reserve. This meant that the fourth and fifth waves would have to be brought in on landing craft. These would need at least four feet of water over the reef which ran between 800 and 1,200 yards out to sea all around the island. No one knew much about the local tides but, for strategic and logistical reasons, the assault would have be made during a neap tide. If they waited seven days for a spring tide, the high tides came at night, which was no good for a beach assault. Delaying for over a month until spring high tides came during the day would have been too late. So D-Day was set for 20 November 1943 and H-Hour was 0830.

The Japanese were expecting an invasion. At the top of the beach all around the island they had built a wall of palm logs three to five feet high, reinforced with wire. Behind it they had dug machine-gun emplacements and rifle pits. Behind those there were more well-fortified machine-gun posts made of logs, coral and reinforced concrete, and covered with sand. They were hard to see and even more difficult to silence. Further back there were another twenty-five pillboxes and concrete emplacements housing 75mm field guns and 37mm anti-tank guns trained on the shore. At each corner of the island and dotted in between the other emplacements there were fourteen coastal defence guns ranging in calibre from 80mm to 203mm. Their magazines and crews were protected by bombproof shelters. The guns were trained on the sea approaches and the beaches themselves, and concrete beach obstacles had been laid to concentrate any invasion force into their field of fire. The Japanese also had seven Type 95 light tanks, each armed with two machine-guns and a 37mm, acting as a mobile reserve.

The defenders were commanded by Rear Admiral Keiji Shibasaki. Under his command there were 1,497 sailors from the 7th Special Naval Landing Force, and 1,122 sailors from the 3rd Special Base Force. Also ashore were 2,170 Korean construction workers.

Careful study of aerial photographs showed that the south and west of the island were most heavily defended. The Japanese plainly expected the attack to come from the open sea. But the beaches there lay in a series of concave bays where it would be easy for the defenders to concentrate their fire. The northern beaches, however, were convex, so it was decided to attack the island from the lagoon side. A scouting platoon would be sent in to clear the jetty there, which could be used for resupply and the evacuation of the wounded. Three reinforced battalions would then land on the beaches Red 1 and Red 2 to the right of the pier, and Red 3 to the left. A separate landing would take place on Green Beach at the western end of the island. The 2nd Marine Regiment, under Colonel David M. Shoup, was to lead the assault on Betio, reinforced with a battalion of the 8th Marines.

The 2nd Marines had some experience of jungle fighting on Guadalcanal, but their intensive training with the tractors gave them the impression that they were going to be involved in a landing rather than an assault. They thought it was going to be a walkover. On 18 November, the 2nd Marines were joined by the 27th Army Division, under Major-General Ralph C. Smith. Along with the 2nd Marines divisional commander Major-General Julian C. Smith, there was yet another Major-General Smith involved in the operation: the Marine Corps commander Major- General Holland M. Smith — known to his men as H.M. 'Howling Mad' Smith — who had supervised the 27th Division's amphibious training on Hawaii.

On the night of 19 November, the assault force closed on Tarawa. Long before they reached the beaches things began to go wrong. Unbeknownst to the planners, the area where the Marines were supposed to transfer from their ships into the Amtracs and landing craft was subject to strong currents. The ships began to drift and in the darkness what was supposed to be an orderly transfer turned into chaos.

Air raids over the previous few nights were supposed to have knocked out the shore batteries. At first light, it was discovered that they hadn't. However, the Japanese aim was bad – perhaps because the fire control system had been damaged. No ships were hit, but shells landing all around them in the water did little for the men's morale. The Navy then opened up in an attempt to silence the Japanese guns, but the vibration knocked out the communications equipment on board the command ship USS *Maryland*. This meant the invasion force had no communication with the carrier-borne air attack that was to come in and soften up the beach defences. This had been scheduled for 0545, so the Navy stopped their bombardment at that time to avoid hitting their own planes. When no planes appeared, they started it again. When the bombers eventually turned up at 0615, the naval bombardment had kicked up so much dust that they could not see their targets.

At the same time, two minesweepers moved into the lagoon, followed by two destroyers which laid smoke-screens and bombarded the beaches from close range. After an hour the gunfire was supposed to slacken as it was assumed the Marines would be nearing the beaches, but a strong off-shore wind had slowed their progress and they were still nowhere near their start line. This line was supposed to be marked by the minesweepers, but one of them had drifted out of position, adding to the confusion. Rear-Admiral Harry Hill worked out that it would take the Amtracs forty minutes to travel from the start line to the beaches, so he stopped his bombardment at 0855 to avoid hitting his own men as they landed. However, the Amtracs were a lot slower in the water than he had calculated. So, when the bombardment stopped, they were still a long way from the beaches.

The carrier-borne planes were then supposed to strafe the beaches but, due to the breakdown in communication, few turned up and those that did left a full ten minutes before the first Marines arrived. Meanwhile, the carrier pilots were telling their debriefers that the island's defences had been completely destroyed. Along with their bombing and strafing, 3,000 tons of shells had hit Betio, and the Marines, it was said, would walk ashore.

Shortly before 0910, Lieutenant William D. Hawkins and his scout patrol arrived on the pier and cleared it of Japanese snipers. A few minutes later, the three assault battalions reached the beaches and landed with little opposition. They ran up the beaches to the log wall, where they stopped. By this time the Japanese had begun to recover their senses after the bombardment. A few men got over the log wall, but the majority were pinned down behind it.

The men coming in behind them were in even more trouble. There was only three feet of water over the reef, so the landing craft had to drop them at the edge and let them wade ashore, presenting irresistible targets to the Japanese gunners. Amphibious assaults from landing craft were at this time still relatively new. By the time the Allies stormed the Normandy beaches they had learnt to put the officers and NCOs at the back. At Tarawa they were at the front, and they got shot down, leaving those men that did get ashore leaderless. Only one of the battalion commanders from the landing craft reached the beach alive. The men from the landing craft were in danger, not just from enemy fire, but from the reef itself, which had deep holes in it. Fully-laden Marines disappeared into them and drowned.

At noon the next wave arrived with the tanks. These drove in across the reef. On Red 3, one platoon of four medium tanks helped the 2nd Battalion of the 8th Marines under Major Henry P. Crowe consolidate their position, but they made little progress inland. By the end of the day, three of the tanks had been destroyed – two of them hit by American bombs. A battalion from the reserves, under Major Robert H. Ruud, was sent in to help Crowe. Again they took heavy casualties crossing the reef, especially among the officers and NCOs, though Ruud himself made it ashore; by the time they reached the beach, their number was less than that of the battalion they had come to support. There was no prospect of making an attack on the Japanese, and by nightfall, the Americans controlled a stretch of beach only 300 yards long and had penetrated no further than 250 yards inland.

On Red 2, the situation was worse. Intense fire during their landing had dispersed the landing force and their commander had been landed so far to the right that the men effectively had no leader. But a liaison and observing officer from Corps Headquarters, Lieutenant-Colonel Walter I. Jordan, was with them. He took charge but, as he pointed out later, Marines are not inclined to take orders from people they do not know.

Nevertheless, under his command, the Marines moved inland some seventy-five yards before being pinned down by sniper and machine-gun fire.

Seeing that the centre of the beach was in trouble, Colonel Shoup committed his 3rd Battalion. Enough of the Amtracs had made it back through the intensive shelling to the start line to carry two of its three companies back to the beaches. The other company would have to wait until the Amtracs dropped off those men and made the hazardous return journey.

The first two companies approached the beaches at about 1130. On their way they passed the mouth of a small valley bristling with Japanese guns. They took 200 casualties before the tractors even hit shore. Some landed on the wrong beach and those who had arrived on the right one had lost most of their equipment.

Shoup followed them ashore, followed by four 75mm howitzers. He set up a command post and established contact with Crowe to his left. But no communication was possible with Red 1, as the Japanese were dug in between them. He had no communication with his divisional commander J.C. Smith either as most of the radio sets had got wet during the landings and were not working.

Neither Smith nor Shoup had any idea what was happening on Green Beach. The 3rd Battalion under Major Michael P. Ryan landing there found they were facing a considerable Japanese force. But with stragglers who had drifted there from other beaches he managed to consolidate a position on the north-west tip of the island. At 1200, two tanks drove in across the reef to support them. Engineers then blew a hole in the log wall and, following the tanks, Ryan's men advanced 500 yards before the tanks were knocked out. But they were unable to hold this forward position as they had bypassed several Japanese positions, which they lacked the heavy weapons to take out. So at nightfall, Ryan fell back to a defensive perimeter.

That evening, one of Ryan's radios dried out sufficiently to work. He reported to J.C. Smith that without heavy weapons he could not advance. Smith got the impression that the situation was far worse than it was, and although reinforcements could have been landed safely, he sent none. Instead he called up the Corps reserve and prepared to send the 1st Battalion of the 8th Marines to make a fresh landing east of Crowe, fearing that the Japanese had a force there set to counter-attack. Due to a mix up, this landing never took place – which was fortunate as it would surely have resulted in a massacre. Before Smith had issued his orders, a Marine spotter plane saw Shoup's howitzers going ashore on Red 2 and assumed it was the 1st Battalion. Smith was told that the 1st Battalion had already been committed and binned his plan. As it was, the men of the 1st Battalion suffered an uncomfortable night in the landing craft. The following morning they were sent to Red 2. A message from Shoup saying that there was a deep-water channel running all the way up to the jetty did not get through and the 1st Battalion sustained heavy casualties as they waded ashore across the reef. The survivors were sent to defend Shoup's right. He then pushed forward and, by the end of the day, Marines from Red 2 had made it across the island to the opposite shore, cutting the Japanese in two.

Although Ryan had been denied troop reinforcements, he

received two more medium tanks and some flamethrowers during the night. Air strikes were called in on the Japanese artillery and at 1000 hours he moved out against little opposition. Soon he had cleared the western beach and arrived at the southern coast opposite the pier.

That evening, two battalions of the 6th Regimental Combat Team under Colonel Maurice Holmes were to land on Green Beach. In the morning they were to advance on the airstrip while the rest of the Marines were to attempt to break out of their beachheads. The Japanese had been seen moving off Betio onto the next island in the southern chain, Bairiki. As J.C. Smith's orders were to clear the entire atoll, he sent a battalion of 75mm howitzers and a battalion of the 6th Marines to Bairiki to prevent the enemy making a stand there. On Bairiki they met two machine-gun posts manned by fifteen Japanese. But Bairiki was also used as a fuel dump. A preliminary air strike strafed the island and hit the dump with .50 calibre incendiary bullets. The resulting explosion burnt out the machine-gun posts and the Marines landed unopposed. Once the howitzers were in position, they could cut off the retreat of the Japanese, leaving the infantry free to return to the battle on Betio.

Late that afternoon the 1st Battalion of the 6th Marines under Major William K. Jones landed on Green Beach. They were the first unit to reach the island in an organized condition. During the night they moved forward to reinforce Ryan's position. The following morning they pushed along the southern coast until they met up with the Marines who had crossed the island from Red 2 the day before. With the aid of flame-throwers, naval gunfire, the one remaining medium tank and seven light tanks, they pushed forward a mile and a half by midday. The rate of progress slowed that afternoon, partly because the light tanks were found to be ineffective. Their 37mm guns made little impression on even the defensive positions made out of coral and logs and they did not have enough weight to crush them. However, the M4 medium tank worked wonderfully and by the end of the day, they had joined up with Crowe, Ruud and the 8th Marines at the end of the Japanese airbase's runway. With the exception of small pockets, the Japanese forces were now corralled in the eastern end of the island. There they were pounded by naval gunfire and the howitzers on Bairiki.

On the morning of 23 November, Shoup began clearing the remaining Japanese resistance in the valley that ran inland from Red 2. By midday he had driven through to the southern tip. Meanwhile, the 3rd Battalion of the 6th Marines passed through the American lines and advanced on the Japanese positions. At 1312, J.C. Smith announced that Betio was clear. The rest of the atoll was cleared by 28 November. The defenders lost 4,690 killed, and 146 were taken prisoner. Only seventeen of them were Japanese. The rest were the remnants of the benighted Korean construction workers.

Tarawa had cost the Marines over 1,000 killed and 2,100 wounded. The casualty list would have been longer if the Japanese commander had not depended on stopping the invasion on the beaches and prepared a more effective defence inland – admittedly, as Admiral Shibasaki was killed by a shell in the preliminary bombardment, he was in no position to organize this as the battle developed. But as it was, the Battle of Tarawa shocked the American public because of the huge number of casualties sustained in so short a time. However, it had taught the military some important lessons. Programmes were developed to improve the accuracy of naval gunfire and aerial bombing and strafing, and changes were made to the organization of amphibious assaults that would pay dividends on other islands and on the beaches of Normandy.

THE MARIANAS

Having lost the Gilbert Islands, the Japanese defended the Marshalls in an effort to tie up Allied forces and put a strain on their extended lines of supply. Nimitz made his first attack on the Kwajalein Atoll, which he subjected to such a heavy preliminary bombardment that the Allied infantry had no problems landing on 30 January 1944. Eniwetok fell on 17 February.

To support their landings on the rest of the Marshall Islands, the US fleet began day and night attacks on the Japanese base at Truk in the Carolines on 17 February, destroying 200,000 tonnes of merchant shipping and around 300 aircraft. That put the base out of action and the Allies could safely bypass it. The Allies then mustered over 125,000 troops and 500 ships to attack the Mariana Islands, which lay 3,500 miles from Pearl Harbor and 1,000 miles from the westernmost limit of their advance, Eniwetok.

Knowing the attack was coming, the Japanese planned to counter-attack using their remaining 1,055 land-based aircraft in the Marianas, the Carolines, and western New Guinea, along with the 450 aircraft on their nine aircraft carriers. But in the spring of 1944 the Allies were establishing superiority in the skies. The Japanese had also suffered the loss of several high-ranking officers: Admiral Yamamoto had died when his plane had been shot down over Bougainville in April 1943 and his successor, Admiral Koga Mineichi, was killed along with his staff in a plane crash.

On 15 June, two divisions of US Marines went ashore on Saipan Island in the Marianas. But the 32,000 Japanese defending it put up a fierce fight. The Japanese fortified themselves in underground caves and bunkers that protected them from American artillery and naval bombardment. The same defensive tactics were used on other small islands. The only way to deal with the defenders was to clear out the bunkers and caves one at a time. This was time consuming and caused such a high rate of casualties that an entire Army division had to be brought in as reinforcements. Gradually, the Japanese defenders were pushed into smaller and smaller pockets. The Japanese position was hopeless. To encourage their men to fight to the last, Admiral Nagumo, now Commander-in-Chief on Saipan, and Lieutenant Gaito, head of the garrison, committed suicide. Organized resistance ended on 7 July with a suicidal counter-attack, the biggest of its kind in the war. Some 8,000 civilians also committed suicide en masse by jumping off the cliffs at Marpi Point. Only 1,000 out of the garrison of 32,000 survived. In all, 22,000 civilians also perished. American casualties were also high – 3,426 were killed and 10,595 wounded.

The loss of Saipan was such a setback for the Japanese that prime minister Hideki Tojo and his entire Cabinet resigned. Even some in the Imperial High Command realized that the loss of the Marianas meant the war was lost, but dared not say so. However, Tojo was succeeded by General Koiso Kuniaki, who pledged to carry on the nation's historic fight with a renewed vigour. The loss of Saipan meant that the US could build bases there for its new B-29 Superfortresses, which had been developed for the sole purpose of bombing Japan. Now the Japanese would have to suffer air raids like their German allies. The first flight of 100 B-29s took off from Saipan on 12 November 1944. It bombed Tokyo, the first air raid on the city since 1942.

While the Japanese were still resisting on Saipan, Admiral Jisaburo Ozawa put Admiral Mineichi's plan into action. The Japanese Combined Fleet was steaming from its anchorages in the East Indies and the Philippines to take on the American Fifth Fleet, under Admiral Raymond Spruance. Ozawa had nine aircraft carriers against Spruance's fifteen, but he could count on help from land-based planes from Guam, Rota and Yap. They met west of the Marianas in the greatest carrier battle of the war known as the Battle of the Philippine Sea. It is also known as the 'Great Marianas Turkey Shoot'. Battle was joined on 19 June, but Ozawa had already lost. He did not know that raids on the Japanese airfields had put his land-based aircraft out of action. At 0830 Ozawa sent 430 planes in four waves against Spruance's ships. As the second wave left, the carrier *Taiho*, Ozawa's flagship, was hit by a torpedo from a submarine. US planes intercepted the Japanese aircraft and only twenty planes from the second wave got through to inflict minor damage on the *Wasp* and Bunker Hill. At 1220, the *Shokaku* was recovering the thirty of its planes that had made it back when it was hit by a torpedo from the US submarine *Cavalla*.

Advance *Storming the Orote Peninsula on Guam, July 1944.*

The *Shokaku* blazed for three hours before it sank. Shortly after, at 1532, the *Taiho* exploded. Even then Ozawa did not realize what a disaster the battle had been, believing that his missing planes had landed on Guam. In fact, over 300 planes had been shot down. Hoping that they might return, Ozawa held on until late in the afternoon of 20 June. US aircraft counter-attacked, sinking the *Hiyo*, damaging the *Zuikaku*, putting a hole in the flight deck of the *Chiyoda* and destroying nearly 100 more planes. As the Japanese fleet retreated northward towards Okinawa, the American pilots tried to make it back to their ships in the growing dark. That night, only 43 of the 216 aircraft launched in the air strike found their carriers. Many ditched in the sea and most of the crews were picked up. The US lost only 16 pilots and 33 aircrew.

Despite the American aircraft losses the Battle of the Philippine Sea was ultimately of more strategic importance than the fall of Saipan. After it, Nimitz's forces could occupy other major islands in the Marianas. Of particular satisfaction was the retaking of Guam, which had been an American possession since the Spanish-American war in 1901. Garrisoned by 365 Marines, it was the first US possession to fall into Japanese hands, on 9 December 1941.

GUAM

The island of Guam is about ten miles long and thirty miles wide. There are mountains to the south and the centre is a flat limestone plateau. It had a fine anchorage in Apta Harbour and the Japanese had built an airbase on Orote peninsula, next to the old Marine Corps barracks. The invasion was delayed because the Marines were held up by the prolonged fighting on Saipan, so the Army's 77th Infantry Division was brought in from Hawaii to reinforce the assault force. After eleven days of bombing and shelling, the 3rd Marine Division was put ashore at 0829 on 21 July at Asan. By mid-afternoon they held a beachhead just 2,000 yards wide and 1,200 yards deep, with the Japanese pouring fire down on them from the surrounding hills. Mortars were fired from the caves on the front of the hills and artillery from the reverse slopes, causing huge casualties among the Marines. But accurate naval gunfire helped them fight their way up the slope and on 24 July they held the ridge. The following night seven battalions of Japanese soldiers with bayonets fixed charged, shouting, 'Banzai' and 'Wake up Yankee and die'. In heavy fighting some of the enemy got so far through the American line that the wounded in the field hospital had to pick up rifles and defend themselves from their beds. But the ferocious Japanese counter-attack failed to push the Marines back into the sea. It petered out, leaving massive Japanese casualties.

A second landing on 21 July by the 1st Provisional Marine Brigade (Shepherd) to the south on Agat beach came under heavy Japanese artillery fire the moment they hit the beaches. Some 350 Marines died and twenty-four Amtracs were destroyed. But once ashore the Marines made rapid progress, soon penetrating to a depth of 2,000 yards. On the first day, they also managed to land 3,000 tonnes of supplies and a platoon of Sherman tanks which helped them hold off Japanese counter-attacks on the following few nights. When reinforcements arrived from the 77th Infantry, the Marines fought their way out of the beachhead and joined up with the Marines at Asan to the north. Together they fought north until they had cut off the Orote peninsula. This was defended by an infantry battalion, whose commander told his men to drink whatever alcohol they could lay their hands on. Intoxicated on beer, saki and synthetic whiskey, the Japanese staged a night attack. They charged, giggling hysterically, reeling about and firing their weapons indiscriminately. But just because they were drunk did not mean they were not dangerous. They were shelled and machine-gunned. In the morning, the Marines counted more than 400 Japanese corpses.

The 1st Provisional Marine Brigade then fought its way

yard by yard up the Orote peninsula against fierce resistance. But fire support from naval artillery helped force the enemy back. Resistance cracked on 27 July. By 29 July the peninsula had been cleared and the airfield was in action again on 31 July – this time for American planes. But there were still Japanese units on the island who put up a tremendous fight. Gradually, the 1st Marines and 77th Infantry drove them up into the northern tip of Guam.

Resistance ceased on 10 August. Of the 54,891 US troops who landed, 1,440 were killed, 145 were missing and 5,648 were wounded. Of the Japanese garrison 10,693 were killed and ninety-eight taken prisoner. The rest disappeared into the jungle to fight on. A Lieutenant-Colonel and his 113 men surrendered on 4 September 1945, but the last known survivor, Colonel Yokoi Shoichi, only emerged in January 1972.

The last important island in the Marianas, Tinian, fell on 24 July, when two Marine divisions from Saipan landed on the beach taking the Japanese commander, Admiral Kakuda, and his 9,000-man garrison by surprise. By the evening, the Marines had established a large beachhead and 1,200 Japanese died when they tried to force them back into the sea. The 4th Marines cleared the southern part of the island, while the 2nd took the north.

Within a week the island was in American hands. The Marines had lost 327 killed and 1,771 wounded. The Japanese had lost their garrison almost to a man. In all, the Marianas cost the Japanese 46,000 killed or captured; the Americans, 4,750 killed.

THE PHILIPPINES AND BORNEO

On 28 July 1944, President Roosevelt had approved General MacArthur's plan to take the Philippine archipelago. This was of special interest to MacArthur as he had been commander of the US forces on the Philippines when the Japanese attacked in 1941. With 180,000 men under arms he thought he could hold the islands, but by 27 December he was forced to abandon the capital Manila and withdraw to the peninsula of Bataan. They fought a delaying action there, but found themselves short of supplies. MacArthur left on 11 March 1942 with the words, 'I will return'. The men in Bataan fought on until 8 April. Six days later they were subjected to a march into captivity, the infamous Bataan Death March. Some 16,000 died. A small US force fought on, on the island of Corregidor, until 6 May.

In preparation for the invasion, MacArthur's forces from New Guinea seized Morotai, the most north-easterly island of the Moluccas, in mid-September 1944. This was on the direct route to Mindanao, the southernmost landmass of the Philippines. Meanwhile, Nimitz's fleet from the east landed troops in the Palau Islands.

US intelligence had discovered that the Japanese forces were unexpectedly small both on Mindanao and on Leyte, a smaller island north of the Surigao Strait. It was decided that they should bypass Mindanao and begin the invasion of the Philippines on Leyte. On 17 and 18 October 1944, US forces seized offshore isles in Leyte Gulf. And on 20 October, they landed four divisions on the east coast of Leyte itself. The threat to Leyte was the cue for the Japanese to put into action their latest plan *Sho-Go* – 'Operation Victory'.

Under *Sho-Go*, the next Allied invasion would be met with concerted air attacks. The problem was that the Japanese army and navy air forces only had 212 planes in the immediate area. However, Admiral Ozawa would send four carriers with 106 planes south from Japanese waters. It was also hoped that this carrier force would lure the US aircraft carriers into a new engagement. By this point in the war, the Japanese were training 'kamikaze' pilots who would fly planes loaded with fuel and explosives into the Allied shipping. They hoped to knock out the US carrier fleet in a desperate effort to protect their homeland.

At the same time, a Japanese naval force from Singapore would split itself into two groups and converge on Leyte Gulf from the north and from the southwest. The weaker of the two groups – two battleships, one heavy cruiser and four destroyers under Vice-Admiral Nishimura Teiji – would pass through the Surigao Strait. The stronger group, consisting of five battleships, twelve cruisers and fifteen destroyers under Vice Admiral Kurita Takeo, would enter the Pacific through the San Bernardino Strait between the Philippine islands of Samar and Luzon. On the way, two of Takeo's heavy cruisers were torpedoed by submarines on 23 October, and one of the mightiest of Japan's battleships, the *Musashi,* was sunk in an air attack the next day. However, three groups of American escort carriers Takeo met on the way also suffered heavy damage.

As the commander of the US Third Fleet, Admiral Halsey, had diverted his main strength towards Ozawa's fleet further to the north, Takeo made his way unopposed through the San Bernardino Strait on 25 October. But Teiji's fleet had been spotted going through the Surigao Strait and, when it arrived in Leyte Gulf in the early hours of 25 October, it was practically annihilated by the US Seventh Fleet under Admiral Kincaid. Finding himself all alone in Leyte Gulf, Takeo turned back. Meanwhile Halsey had destroyed all four of Ozawa's carriers, together with a light cruiser and two destroyers. 'Operation Victory' had been a terrible defeat. Japanese losses amounted to one large aircraft carrier, three light carriers, three battleships, six heavy cruisers, four light cruisers and eleven destroyers. The US had lost only one light carrier, two escort carriers and three destroyers. However, this was the first time the American fleet faced the kamikaze in force and their deliberately suicidal attacks meant it was clear that the war was going to be hard won.

After the Battle of Leyte Gulf, the Japanese navy was no longer a threat and the way was clear for the invasion of the Philippines. But that did not mean the Japanese were going to give them up easily. Even after their naval defeat in the Leyte Gulf, they landed reinforcements on the west coast of Leyte. Japanese resistance was so stubborn that the Americans had to be reinforced before the main city of Ormoc fell on 10 December 1944. Only on Christmas day could the US claim control of the whole of Leyte – even then, there was still some mopping up to be done. The defence of Leyte cost the Japanese some 75,000 killed or taken prisoner.

From Leyte the Americans took Mindoro, the largest of the islands immediately south of Luzon, on 15 December. Again the kamikaze pilots made the victory costly. Suicidal attacks continued after the US forces surprised the Japanese by landing at Lingayen Gulf on the west coast of Luzon itself, the most important island of the Philippines, on 9 January 1945. There was no hope of reinforcement and, in the long run, there was no prospect of victory, so the Japanese commander, Lieutenant-General Yamashita Tomoyuki, tried to tie down the American forces for as long as possible in the mountains. Manila itself was strongly defended. One American corps approached it from Lingayen over the Central Plains. Another was landed at Subic Bay, at the northern end of the Bataan Peninsula, on 29 January. The two corps met up at Dinalupihan a week later. More troops landed at Nasugbu, south of Manila Bay, on 31 January, surrounding Manila. It fell on 3 March, but Japanese resistance continued in the mountains until mid-June 1945. Meanwhile, an American division landed on Mindanao at Zamboanga, on the south-west peninsula, on 10 March, and a corps began the occupation of the core of the island on 17 April.

While US forces consolidated their positions in the Philippines, the Australians started the reconquest of Borneo by bombarding Tarakan Island, off the north-east coast, on 12 April. On 30 April, they landed on nearby Sadau Island in the Baragan Straits, from where they could shell the beach fortifications. They landed on Tarakan on 1 May. After four days of fighting the town of Tarakan fell at a cost of 225 Australians killed and 669 wounded; 1,540 Japanese were dead. On 10 June, 2,900 Australians went ashore at Brunei on the north-west coast, where they met little opposition. Balikpapan, on the east coast far to the south of Tarakan, was attacked on 1 July and the Japanese defences collapsed, depriving Japan of oil supplies for southern Borneo. The British then began preparing an advance base for the retaking of Singapore there. But by the time the air base in Borneo had been built, Japan had surrendered.

CHAPTER 23

Endgame

While the campaigns on the Philippines and on Borneo were still under way, plans were being laid for the invasion of Japan. This would begin, the planners decided, with landings on Kyushu, the most southerly of the major Japanese islands.

In preparation for the planned landings on the Japanese home islands, B–29 Superfortresses under General Curtis E. LeMay, stationed on the Mariana Islands, began a campaign of bombing Japanese cities nad industrial centres in the closing months of 1944. But it was a round trip of 3,000 miles from Saipan to mainland Japan, a long flight even for the Superfortresses, with their increased fuel capacity. If US forces could take the little volcanic island of Iwo Jima in the Bonin Islands, which lay some 760 miles south-east of Japan, they would halve the distance to Tokyo and, with fighters stationed there, the USAAF would be able to defend its bombers over their targets. Iwo Jima was a doubly important target because Japan considered the island its 'unsinkable aircraft carrier'. It was a radar and fighter base whose aircraft intercepted the Superfortresses on their bombing missions over Japan.

IWO JIMA

Irregularly shaped, Iwo Jima is about five miles long and anything from 800 yards to two and a half miles wide. The Japanese were determined to hold on to it. They garrisoned the island with 21,000 troops under Lieutenant-General Kuribayashi Tadamichi and it had the strongest defences of all the Japanese possessions in the Pacific. It had been under constant bombardment since the fall of the Marianas, but the prolonged fighting in the Philippines had delayed the attack, giving the Japanese a few months to build up the island's already formidable fortifications. As on other Pacific islands, they had created underground defences, making the best possible use of natural caves and the rocky terrain.

For days before the landings, Iwo Jima was subjected to massive bombardment by naval guns, rockets and air strikes using bombs carrying the recently developed napalm. But the Japanese were so well dug in that no amount of shelling or bombing could knock them out.

On 19 February, 4th and 5th Marine Divisions under General Harry Schmidt went ashore on the south of the island, confidently expecting to take the island in four days. Of the 30,000 men landing on the beaches on the first day, 2,400 were hit by the Japanese. The Marines soon had a 4,000-yard long beachhead, but they were slowed down inland by the island's ashy volcanic soil. 5th Marines then divided their forces. Half struck inland and took the first of the two Japanese airfields – a third was under construction. The other half turned south to take Mount Suribachi, an extinct volcano soon nicknamed Meatgrinder Hill for the casualties taken there. The Marines eventually took

Mount Suribachi on 23 February. The raising of the American flag on its summit was photographed by Joe Rosenthal of the Associated Press. It became one of the best-known images of the Pacific war, and statues, paintings and American postage stamp designs have been based on it. However, the photograph actually depicts a second flag being raised over Mount Suribachi. The first flag had been raised some hours earlier, but it was too small to be seen by the other troops on the island.

While 5th Marine Division moved up the west coast, 4th Marines fought their way up the east, but the fighting was so fierce that 3rd Marines, a floating reserve, had to be landed. They moved up the centre and by 9 March they had reached the north-east coast. On 26 March the Japanese staged their last suicidal attack with 350 men near Kitano Point on the northern tip of the island. After that, resistance collapsed. Some 20,000 Japanese were killed, the remaining 1,000 captured. The Marine and army losses were 6,812 killed and 19,189 wounded. The Battle of Iwo Jima was a costly, but decisive victory. Now the allout assault on the Japanese mainland could begin and, in the next five months, over 2,000 Superfortresses flew bombing missions from the airfields of Iwo Jima.

While the fighting on Iwo Jima had been going on, the war in the air took a new turn. The USAAF abandoned high-altitude strikes during daylight as they seemed to be making little impact on Japan's industrial output. Instead they began low-level strikes at night, using napalm. These were a startling success. As Japan was in an earthquake zone, buildings were

Opposite: Stars and Stripes The US flag is raised on Iwo Jima, 23 February 1945.

traditionally made out of lightweight wood and paper. They burnt easily. In the first fire-bomb raid on the night of 9 March 1945, about twentyfive per cent of Tokyo's buildings were destroyed, killing over 80,000 people and leaving one million homeless. Strategic planners then came to believe that Japan could be defeated without an invasion by ground troops and the massive casualties that would entail. Similar fire-bombing raids were launched against other major cities – Nagoya, Osaka, Kobe, Yokohama and Toyama. However, the invasion plans were not discarded immediately and there would be one more island hop before the end of the war. It would be the largest amphibious operation of the Pacific war. Its objective was Okinawa, an island some seventy miles long and seven miles wide just 350 miles south of Kyushu. Okinawa was considered the last stepping stone before the invasion of Japan itself.

OKINAWA

American reconnaissance planes put the strength of Okinawa's garrison at 65,000. In fact, the Thirty-Second Army under General Mitsuru Ushijima was almost 120,000 strong. Some 10,000 aircraft defended the island and the Imperial Navy sent a task force headed by the *Yamato*, the biggest battleship ever built.

For the invasion of Okinawa, codenamed Operation *Iceberg*, the commander of the US ground forces, Lieutenant-General Simon Bolivar Buckner, assembled the largest array of battle-hardened troops yet deployed in the Pacific. There were three Marine divisions and four army divisions – over 155,000 men in all. But by the time the fighting was finished, over 300,000 Americans had been committed to battle. Admiral Spruance assembled over 1,300 vessels of all sizes for the landing, including a large British carrier force under Vice Admiral Sir Bernard Rawlings.

Air raids on Okinawa began as early as October 1944 and culminated in March 1945 in an attack that destroyed hundreds of Japanese planes. The invasion was scheduled for 1 April and the preliminary naval bombardment began on 18 March. US forces then began taking some of the outlying islands, including the Kerama Islands which would be used as a forward base. On the Keramas, 77th Infantry captured 200 suicide boats, packed with explosives which would have posed a major threat to the Fifth Fleet, which was already being harassed by kamikazes. In all, twenty-seven suicide pilots penetrated the wall of fire the escorts put up to reach their targets. Four carriers were damaged in the run up to the landings. The USS *Franklin* and the *Wasp* were knocked out and kamikazes also hit a battleship, a cruiser, four destroyers and six other ships.

On 1 April, the island was bombarded with 44,825 rounds of five-inch and larger shells, 32,000 rockets and 22,500 mortar rounds. The troops clambered into their landing craft at 0400 for the four-and-a-half hour run into Hagushi beach on the west coast of the island, which had just been cleared of mines. They hit the beaches at 0830 and found, to their surprise, no opposition. By nightfall, 60,000 men were ashore, holding a beachhead eight miles wide and three miles deep.

The next day US troops drove across the island to the east coast, occupied the entire central zone of the island and captured two airfields. Buckner then sent three Marine divisions south, while 6th Marines went north where they met some resistance on the Motubu Peninsula. By 21 April, they had cleared the north of the island, killing 2,500 Japanese defenders at a cost of 218 Americans killed and 902 wounded.

On 4 April, the XXIV Corps under Major-General John Hodge reached the Japanese southern defences at Shuri, where Ushijima was determined to fight a war of attrition that he could not win. Meanwhile, on 6 April, the 77th Infantry Division took the small island of Ise Shima off the north coast of Okinawa. It was held by 2,000 Japanese who put up a fierce fight for five days.

That same day the kamikaze resumed with new vigour. Some 700 suicide planes attacked the Fifth Fleet damaging or sinking thirteen destroyers. The *Yamato* along with its escort of the cruiser *Yahagi* and eight destroyers were also sent on a suicide mission. With their tanks filled with nearly all Japan's remaining stocks of oil, they did not have enough fuel to sail back to port. So the flotilla had been ordered to beach itself on Okinawa and use their guns to defend the troops there. But the mighty *Yamato* was spotted by a submarine just off the southernmost tip of Kyushu. She had no air cover and was a sitting duck when carrier planes caught up with her the next day. In two hours, she was hit by seven bombs and twelve torpedoes, blew up and sank. Then, in what proved to be the last naval action of the war, the *Yahagi* and four destroyers were also sunk.

Meanwhile, despite reinforcements, XXIV Corps could not make much of a dent in Ushijima's defences and were suffering high casualties. Even though his men were suffering ten times the casualty rate of the US forces, on 12 April, Ushijima went on the offensive. For two days he sent wave after wave of men in suicidal attacks on the American positions. All of them were repulsed. Thirty-Second Army then went back on the defensive.

That same day a new Japanese suicide weapon – christened the 'baka' by the Allies from the Japanese word for fool – claimed its first victim, the US destroyer *Abele*. The baka was a rocket-powered glider that was towed into range by a bomber. When released, its solitary pilot flew at the target. There was no parachute and no way to get out. Dropped usually from an altitude of more than 25,000 feet and over fifty miles out, the baka would glide to about three miles from the target before the pilot ignited its three rocket engines, accelerating the craft to more than 600 miles an hour in its final dive. The explosive charge in the nose weighed more than a ton. Plane, pilot and – in thirty-four cases – ship were destroyed in one massive explosion.

Frustrated with the slow progress on land, Buckner ordered a more intensive bombardment. But the Japanese fortifications were well prepared and costly to overrun and the Marines could make no breakthrough. On 2 May Ushijima went on the offensive again, but was driven back, losing 5,000 men. On 11 May, Buckner ordered a new offensive to push back the Japanese flanks. Fearing that he was about to be encircled, Ushijima pulled back on 21 May to make a final stand on the southern tip of the island. A rearguard continued a ferocious fight against XXIV Corps, while the rest of Ushijima's men made an orderly retreat to a new line. On 31 May, the city of Shuri finally fell, after its defences had been reduced to rubble by bombardment.

The US Tenth Army made a last push, aided by 6th Marines who made an amphibious landing on Oroku Peninsula on the south-west corner of the island to take out a strongpoint and an airfield there. Buckner's main force moved forward painfully slowly using flamethrowers and high explosives to clear enemy positions. The Japanese fought on fanatically, but the front gradually began to crumble.

On 18 June, General Buckner was wounded, and later died. He was replaced by General Geiger for the final stages of the battle. Three days later Ushijima was also dead, by his own hand. Scorning an American offer of surrender to prevent any further unnecessary loss of life, on 21 June he and his Chief of Staff knelt outside their headquarters and committed hara-kiri. His final order was that his men should revert to guerrilla warfare. They continued fighting until the end of the month when some 7,400 gave themselves up – the first time the Japanese had surrendered in large numbers. At least 110,000 Japanese soldiers were dead and there had been a large number of civilian casualties. For the Allies it was the costliest operation in the Pacific, with some half a million men involved in the fighting. US ground forces had lost 7,203 killed and 31,807 wounded. The navy had lost some 5,000 killed and a similar number wounded.

Japan had lost its entire navy and, during the Battle of Okinawa, 7,800 Japanese aircraft had been destroyed for the loss of 763 Allied planes. The Japanese mainland now lay wide open. It had no defence against the continual bombing raids the USAAF flew against it, and the British and American fleets that surrounded the islands could shell it at will.

General Joseph 'Vinegar Joe' Stilwell was brought in to command the Tenth Army and plans were laid to bring over the First Army, which had recently been victorious in Europe. They were to form a new army group under General Douglas

MacArthur, ready for the invasion of Kyushu, scheduled to begin on 1 November. But they were upstaged by history.

President Roosevelt had died on 12 April and President Harry S. Truman was now in the White House. Military assessments of the situation given to Truman estimated that it would take well into 1946 to defeat Japan, at a cost of perhaps a million casualties, a figure many in the military found unacceptably high. President Truman agreed. There had to be another way to decisively defeat the Japanese at a lesser cost in American lives.

SECTION SEVEN
THE ATOMIC BOMB

By August 1945, it was clear the war was over, and
it was also clear who had won it. When a Japanese
surrender was not forthcoming, the US began to
plan the invasion of the Japanese home islands.
When the projected casualty figure for this invasion
reached the million mark, however, it was regarded
as unacceptably high. Another way would have to be
found to bring the Japanese to the negotiating table.

CHAPTER 24

A Blinding Light

'I am become Death, the destroyer of worlds.'

ROBERT OPPENHEIMER, 'FATHER OF THE A-BOMB',
AFTER THE FIRST SUCCESSFUL ATOMIC TEST.

By May 1945, it was clear to the Japanese that they had lost the war. Their European allies had been crushed. They were in retreat in the face of overwhelming force on all fronts. Allied submarines had brought the economy to a standstill. The home islands could not produced enough food to support the population and Japan itself was being pounded by bombs and incendiaries in an unremitting air campaign. However, the Japanese government still hoped for a negotiated peace.

Despite the Tripartite Pact between Berlin, Rome and Tokyo, Japan had not declared war on the Soviet Union when the Germans attacked in 1941. Neither had Stalin declared war on Japan after Pearl Harbor. However, the Russians refused to help when the Japanese put out peace feelers. Forty years before, Japan had soundly beaten Russia in the Russo-Japanese War, sinking two Russian fleets and putting an end to Russian expansion in the east. Now, with the defeat of the Japanese, Stalin hoped to make territorial gains.

But the Japanese still had an army of two million men and nine thousand kamikaze aircraft. They believed that they could inflict sufficient casualties on the Americans to force them to the negotiating table.

US Army Chief of Staff General George C. Marshall had already drawn up plans for the invasion of the island of Kyushu with 190,000 men on 1 November and the invasion of Honshu five months later. The landings on Kyushu alone, it was estimated, would cost 69,000 American casualties. This was a terrible price to pay. Another alternative was discussed in the White House on 18 June 1945. At that meeting an engineer from the top-secret US Army Manhattan Project said that it could have two atomic bombs ready for operational use by late July.

DEVELOPING THE ATOM BOMB

Before the Second World War, Germany had been the world's leading scientific nation and German scientists had developed the physics that made it possible to build an atomic bomb. However, Hitler's anti-Semitic policies had forced a number of key scientists into exile.

One of them was Albert Einstein. He had left Germany after Hitler came to power in 1933 and moved to Princeton, in New Jersey. In the summer of 1939, he wrote to President Roosevelt, alerting him to the possibility of using uncontrolled atomic fission to produce a bomb of unimaginable power. When World War II began, exiled scientists in Britain began work on the bomb. In the autumn of 1941, a delegation from the US visited England in an attempt to set up a joint effort. However it was not until 1943 that a combined policy committee was set up between the US, Britain and Canada. Physicists from the three countries moved to the US, where work got underway at Los Alamos, New Mexico, and other laboratories around the country.

By 1945 they had developed two bombs. One, 'Little Boy', had a core of fissionable Uranium-235, laboriously extracted from other more stable isotopes at a giant plant at Oak Ridge, Tennessee. It was triggered by a simple gun mechanism that fired a plug of U-235 into the U-235 core to create a critical mass and trigger a nuclear chain reaction.

The other weapon was 'Fat Man'. It used plutonium which had to be manufactured in the nuclear reactors at Hanford, Washington, using a method developed by Enrico Fermi at the University of Chicago. This was fired by imploding a sphere of the metal using TNT. Scientists were not sure that this would work, so 'Fat Man' was tested at 0530 on 16 July 1945 at the Alamogordo air base, 120 miles south of Albuquerque, New Mexico. It did work.

The USAAF had already set up the 509th Composite Group under Colonel Paul W. Tibbets. Its 393rd Bombardment Squadron had the most advanced longrange B-29s, the only bombers big enough for the task. After training in Utah, the group was shipped out between April and May 1945 to Tinian Island in the Marianas, from where they flew bombing raids over Japan to familiarize themselves with the area. They dropped 'Pumpkin Bombs' – 10,000-pound bombs painted orange and filled with TNT – which had the same ballistic characteristics as 'Fat Boy'.

A list of targets was drawn up. These included Hiroshima,

Kokura, Niigata and Kyoto. However, Secretary of War Henry L. Stimson objected to Kyoto's inclusion because of the city's priceless art treasures, and the port of Nagasaki was substituted.

TAKING THE DECISION

For the Japanese, one of the key requirements of any peace settlement was the retention of their Emperor. However, when the Potsdam conference on 26 July called for Japan to unconditionally surrender, or face 'prompt and utter destruction', there was no mention of the Emperor. The result was silence. That same day, the US cruiser *Indianapolis* delivered 'Little Boy' to Tinian. Four days later the *Indianapolis* was sunk by a Japanese submarine.

President Harry S. Truman had known nothing of the Manhattan Project when he took office after the death of President Roosevelt on 12 April 1945. He now had an agonizing decision to make. Would he use this terrible new weapon. or would he risk losing tens of thousands – possibly hundreds of thousands – of men invading Japan? Based on the invasions of Iwo Jima and Okinawa, the US military had estimated that the casualty figure for an invasion of the Japanese home islands could be as high as one million, casualties who would be, in effect, civilians in uniform. For the sake of both his own men and the civilian population of Japan he decided that he must put a speedy end to the war.

General Carl A. Spaatz was in Washington, D.C. on his way to take command of the US Army Strategic Air Forces in the Pacific when he was told of the atomic bombs and Truman's decision. He refused to drop such weapons on a purely verbal order and was given written orders that the 509th Group would deliver the first bomb as soon after 3 August as weather permitted.

ENOLA GAY

The weather forecast held off the attack until 6 August. At 0245 that day, a B-29, named Enola Gay by Tibbets after his mother, clawed its way into the sky. The nine-thousand-pound 'Little Boy' had put the plane eight tons over its normal bombing weight. As there was a danger that the plane would crash on take-off, US Navy ordnance expert Captain William S. 'Deac' Parsons was on board. He would arm the bomb once they were airborne. The target was Hiroshima, chosen as it was home to the Japanese Second Army, responsible for the defence of the south-west sector of the homeland. It was this army that any invading force would be up against.

At 0715 Major Claude Eatherly in a B-29 over Hiroshima acting as a weather- scout signalled that the skies over the city were clear. When he left, the all-clear was sounded in the city below. By 6 August Hiroshima had almost completely escaped bombing and few people took any notice when, at 0806, two B-29s appeared, flying at 31,600 feet. They were so high that no air-raid alarm was sounded as it seemed they would simply overfly the city.

The Enola Gay dropped 'Little Boy', then turned sharply away. The second plane dropped a parachute carrying a package of scientific instruments. At seventeen seconds after 0815, the bomb exploded just below two thousand feet over the most built-up part of the city. There was a blinding flash of bluish-white light, followed by a searing heat. There was a roar a thousand

Enola Gay *The crew of the B-29 Enola Gay plane, including pilot Paul Tibbets (centre), which dropped the first atomic bomb in history on the Japanese city of Hiroshima.*

times louder than thunder and the ground shook. The blast was equivalent to seventeen thousand tons of TNT. Some 4.7 square miles of the city were completely flattened in the ensuing firestorm, and sixty thousand of the ninety thousand buildings within 9.5 square miles were destroyed or badly damaged.

It is not known how many people perished. The names of 61,443 people are inscribed on the cenotaph that sits at ground zero, directly under the point where the bomb exploded. However, the US Strategic Bombing Survey estimated that there were 139,402 casualties, including 71,379 known dead, and missing presumed dead. Over 20,000 of the dead were schoolchildren. There were also 68,023 injured, 19,691 of them seriously. Ironically, the city's munitions factories, which were on the outskirts, survived.

News of the destruction of Hiroshima was not carried in the newspapers. It was said that it had come under attack by incendiaries. No surrender was forthcoming. However on 8 August, the Soviet Union declared war on Japan, invading Manchuria, seizing the northern part of Korea and taking over two million Japanese prisoners before the end of the war.

NAGASAKI NIGHTMARE

At 0349 on 9 August the B-29 Bock's Car, piloted by Major Charles W. Sweeney, took off from Tinian, carrying 'Fat Man'. This was an altogether more hazardous procedure as the plutonium bomb had to be armed before take-off. Kokura, with its enormous army arsenal, was the primary target; the harbour at Nagasaki, with its four large Mitsubishi factories involved in war production, was the secondary target.

A storm brewing over the Pacific delayed the aircraft carrying the British observers. While Bock's Car waited at the rendezvous point, the clouds closed in over Kokura, so Sweeney headed for Nagasaki. It too was obscured by cloud, but Bock's Car was running low on fuel. A radar drop was authorized, but at the last moment a hole opened in the clouds. At 1101 hours, 'Fat Man' was dropped three miles from the designated dropping point, but directly over the city's industrial heart. Sweeney then headed back to Okinawa where he made an emergency landing with just a few gallons of fuel left.

As the dropping of an atomic bomb on Hiroshima had not been carried in the Japanese papers, no one was prepared. There had been an air-raid alert at 0748, but only around four hundred people were in the shelters, which were in any case only big enough for around a third of Nagasaki's 195,290 residents.

Hills surrounding the area where the bomb was dropped concentrated the blast, but protected the rest of the city. Only 1.45 square miles were completely destroyed. The official Japanese casualty figures recorded 23,753 killed, 1,927 missing and 23,345 injured. Again the US Strategic Bombing Survey put the figures higher, with over 35,000 dead and more injured. There was no fire storm and little panic, but sixty-eight per cent of the industrial capacity of the city was destroyed.

At both Hiroshima and Nagasaki, many victims died later of burns, radiation sickness, thyroid cancer and leukaemia. Survivors suffered from cataracts. Men suffered from a catastrophically low sperm count. Women miscarried and there was a twenty-seven per cent rate of premature births, compared to the normal rate of six per cent.

The question remained whether the dropping of the two atomic bombs was really necessary. The US Strategic Bombing Survey concluded that it was not. It said: 'Certainly prior to 31 December 1945 and in all probability prior to 1 November 1945, Japan would have surrendered even if the atomic bombs had not entered the war, even if Russia had not entered the war, and even if no invasion [of Japan] had been contemplated.'

However, it should also be remembered that on the days

Mushroom Cloud The atomic bomb explodes over Hiroshima, 6 August, 1945.

the atomic bombs were dropped, more Japanese died from conventional bombing, and the naval bombardment inflicted on Japanese cities by the British and American ships that now surrounded the islands.

Even after the atomic bomb had been dropped on Hiroshima, Japanese militarists were arguing that the US could not possibly have amassed enough radioactive material to continue such attacks. But after the bombing of Nagasaki, Emperor Hirohito – still a god in the eyes of the Japanese – told his government that 'to continue the war means nothing but the destruction of the whole nation' and that 'the time has come when we must bear the unbearable'.

SURRENDER

In the early hours of 10 August, a cable was sent to Japan's representatives in Stockholm and Berne accepting the Potsdam ultimatum, with the one proviso that the Japanese could keep their Emperor. This was accepted.

Emperor Hirohito recorded a message to be broadcast at noon on 15 August, calling for all Japanese to accept the surrender. The people of Japan had never heard his voice before. He warned them to 'beware of any outburst of emotion', as there were some who still wanted to fight to the finish.

Indeed there was a small group of officers in the palace itself who wanted to continue the war. On the night of 14 August, they approached General Nuzo Mori and asked him to join them. When he said that he would go and pray in a Meiji Shrine to help him make up his mind, they shot him, then used Mori's seal in an attempt to locate the recording of the Emperor's broadcast. When their coup failed, the officer who shot Mori committed hara-kiri on the Imperial Plaza. Other hard-liners also committed suicide.

On 30 August the first American occupation forces, accompanied by a small British contingent, arrived at Yokosuka. Then at nine o'clock in the morning of 2 September the new Japanese foreign minister Mamoru Shigemitsu went on board the USS *Missouri* in Tokyo Bay. He signed the surrender document on behalf of the Emperor and the Japanese government. This was accepted on behalf of the Allies by General Douglas MacArthur. Then a scratchy record of 'The Star-Spangled Banner' was played over the ship's PA system and the Second World War was officially over.

The war had cost between thirty-five and sixty million dead. There are no reliable estimates of the number of people wounded or permanently disabled in the conflict. The governments of the belligerent nations expended more than one trillion US dollars prosecuting the war. As a result, millions were left homeless and undernourished. Many of the centres of economic activity in Europe and the Far East were destroyed, along with countless lives. In Europe alone, the war created some twenty-one million refugees and displaced persons.

SECTION EIGHT

WAR CRIMES TRIALS

'War Crimes: namely, violations of the laws or customs of war. Such violations shall include…murder, ill-treatment or deportation of civilian population of or in occupied territory, murder or ill-treatment of prisoners of war or persons on the seas, killing of hostages, plunder of public or private property, wanton destruction of cities, towns, or villages, or devastation not justified by military necessity.'

From Article 6 of the Charter of the International Military Tribunal at Nuremberg

CHAPTER 25

In the Dock

*Some voices on the Allied side, notably
Winston Churchill, called for Nazi and Japanese
leaders to be shot on sight. Cooler heads
prevailed, and military tribunals were set up
in both Germany, at Nuremberg,
and Japan, at Tokyo.*

Winston Churchill was not in favour of war crimes trials after the Second World War. He thought top Nazis should simply be executed. However, at the Yalta conference in February 1945, Britain, America and the Soviet Union agreed to prosecute the Nazi leaders and other war criminals.

An International Military Tribunal was set up by the London conference in August 1945. It was given the authority to indict offenders on three counts: crimes against peace – that is, planning and initiating wars of aggression; crimes against humanity – genocide, extermination and deportation; and war crimes – that is, violations of the laws of war. Each of the four victorious powers – Britain, America, the Soviet Union and France – would provide one judge and one prosecutor.

THE NUREMBERG TRIALS

The International Military Tribunal first sat on 18 October 1945, in the Supreme Court Building in Berlin. The first session was presided over by the Soviet member, General Iola T. Nikitschenko. The prosecution entered indictments against twenty-four Nazi leaders and six 'criminal organisations' – Hitler's cabinet, the leadership corps of the Nazi party, the SS (party police) and SD (security police), the Gestapo, the SA and the General Staff and High Command of the army.

On 20 November 1945 the tribunal moved to the Nuremberg Palace of Justice. This was chosen because it was spacious, with about eighty courtrooms and some 530 offices. War damage was minimal and it had a large, undamaged prison attached. The sessions there were held under the presidency of Lord Justice Geoffrey Lawrence (later Baron Trevethin and Oaksey) and procedures followed Anglo-American practice. During the 218 days of the trials, testimony from 360 witnesses was introduced, with 236 witnesses appearing in the court itself.

On 1 October 1946, the verdict was handed down on twenty-two of the original defendants. Slave-labour organizer, Robert Ley had committed suicide in jail, and armaments-manufacturer Gustav Krupp von Bohlen und Halbach was too ill to appear in court and the charges against him were dropped.

Hans Frank, the governor-general of Poland; Wilhelm Frick, minister of internal affairs; Alfred Jodl, Hitler's strategic adviser; Ernst Kaltenbrunner, head of the SD; Field Marshal Wilhelm Keitel; Joachim von Ribbentrop, Hitler's foreign minister; Alfred Rosenberg, minister for the occupied territories; Fritz Sauckel, another organizer of forced labour; Julius Streicher, anti-Semitic propagandist and gauleiter in Franconia; and Arthur Seysslnquart, commissioner for the occupied Netherlands, were all sentenced to death and hanged in the early morning of 16 October 1946 in the old gymnasium of the Nuremberg prison. The bodies were cremated in Munich and the ashes were strewn in an estuary of the Isar River.

The head of the Luftwaffe Herman Göring was also sentenced to death, but committed suicide before he could be executed. Nazi party organizer Martin Borman was sentenced to death in absentia, though he was officially declared dead in 1973 after a body identified as his had been unearthed in Berlin.

Walter Funk, Minister for Economic Affairs and president of the Reichsbank from 1939, was sentenced to life imprisonment, but was released in 1957 due to illness. He died in 1960. Erich Raeder, commander-in-chief of the navy, was sentenced to life imprisonment, but was released in 1955 due to illness, and died in 1960. Rudolf Hess, Hitler's deputy, who had made the dramatic flight to Scotland in 1941, was also sentenced to life imprisonment. He committed suicide in 1987 in Spandau Prison in Berlin, where the other Nuremberg detainees were held.

Karl Dönitz, admiral of the fleet and Hitler's successor, was sentenced to ten years imprisonment. He was released in 1956 and died in 1980. Albert Speer, minister for weapons and munitions, was sentenced to twenty years. Released in 1966, he died in 1981. Baldur von Schirach, head of the ministry for youth and gauleiter of Vienna, was also sentenced to twenty years. He was released in 1966 and died in 1974. Konstantin von Neurath, protector of Bohemia and Moravia, was sentenced to fifteen years imprisonment. Released in 1954 due to illness, he died in 1956.

Hans Fritzsche, head of the news service section in the Ministry of Propaganda and essentially a stand-in for Goebbels, who had committed suicide, was acquitted, but in the subsequent denazification procedures he was sentenced to nine years imprisonment. He was released in 1950 and died in 1953. Franz von Papen, vice-chancellor in Hitler's first cabinet was acquitted. In the denazification procedures, he was sentenced to eight years imprisonment. Released in 1949, he died in 1969. Also acquitted was Hjalmar Schacht, president of the Reichsbank up until 1939 and Minister of Economics until 1937, who had been imprisoned in the concentration camp at Flossenbürg since 1944. The German authorities imprisoned him until 1948. He died in 1970.

Guilty verdicts were also handed down on the leadership corps of the NSDAP, the SS, the SD and the Gestapo.

THE 'DOCTORS TRIAL'

Although it was originally intended for the International Military Tribunal to sit again, the Cold War had started and there was no further co-operation among the participants. However, more military tribunals sat in the separate French, British, American and Soviet zones of occupation. The US tribunals sat at Nuremberg, and on 9 December 1946 proceedings began against twenty-three German doctors accused of participating in the Nazi 'euthanasia' programme to murder the mentally deficient, and conducting medical experiments on concentration camp inmates. The trial lasted 140 days. Eighty-five witnesses appeared and 1,500 documents were introduced in evidence. Sixteen of the doctors were found guilty. Seven were sentenced to death and executed on 2 June 1948.

In the twelve subsequent proceedings at Nuremberg, 175 Germans were convicted. In all, 10,000 Germans were convicted and 250 sentenced to death.

TRIALS IN JAPAN

The Potsdam declaration of July 1945 also called for the trial of those who had 'deceived and misled' the Japanese people into war. As commander of the occupation, General Douglas MacArthur arrested thirty-nine suspects, most of them members of General Tojo's war cabinet. Tojo himself tried to commit suicide, but was resuscitated by American doctors.

In Manila, MacArthur had already held war crimes trials that had resulted in the executions of Generals Yamashita and Homma and there were doubts about the legitimacy of such proceedings. Nevertheless, on 6 October MacArthur was given the authority to try suspects under three broad categories. Class A charges alleging 'crimes against peace' were to be brought against Japan's top leaders who had planned and directed the war. Class B and C charges, which could be levelled at Japanese of any rank, covered 'conventional war crimes' and 'crimes against humanity' respectively. In early November, MacArthur was also given authority to purge other wartime leaders from public life.

On 19 January 1946, the International Military Tribunal for the Far East was established with eleven judges. Sir William Webb, an Australian, was the tribunal's president and US Assistant Attorney General Joseph Keenan was named chief prosecutor.

The Tokyo trials began on 3 May 1946 and lasted two and a half years. On 4 November 1948, all of the remaining defendants were found guilty. Seven were sentenced to death, sixteen to life terms and two to lesser terms. Two had died during the trials and one had been found insane. After reviewing their decisions, MacArthur praised the work of the tribunal and upheld the verdicts.

On 23 December 1948, General Tojo and six others were hanged at Sugamo Prison. Afraid of antagonizing the Japanese, MacArthur defied the wishes of President Truman and banned photography. Instead, four members of the Allied Council were present as official witnesses.

The Tokyo trials were not the only forum for the punishment of Japanese war criminals. The Asian countries that had suffered under the Japanese war machine tried an estimated five thousand suspected war criminals, executing as many as nine hundred and sentencing more than half to life in prison.

BIBLIOGRAPHY

Bauer, Lt-Col E., *The History of World War II*, Orbis, London, 1966

Beevor, Anthony, *Berlin: the Downfall 1945*, Viking, London, 2002.

Beevor, Anthony, *Stalingrad*, Viking, London, 1998.

Carver, Michael, *Dilemmas of the Desert War – A New Look at the Libyan Campaign 1940–42*, Batsford/Imperial War Museum, 1986.

Cawthorne, Nigel, *Fighting Them on the Beaches*, Arcturus, London, 2002.

Churchill, Winston S., *The Second World War*, Penguin, London, 1985.

Clark, Alan, *Barbarossa*, Hutchinson, London, 1965.

Clark, Gen. Mark, *Calculated Risk*, Harper & Row, New York, 1968.

Cunningham, Admiral Viscount, *A Sailor's Odyssey*, Hutchinson, London, 1951.

Dean, Gen. John R., *Strange Alliance*, Viking Press, New York, 1947.

Deighton, Len and Hastings, Max, *Battle of Britain*, Wordsworth, Ware, 1999.

Erickson, John, *The Road to Stalingrad: Stalin's War with Germany*, Harper & Rowe, New York, 1975.

Evans, Martin Marix, *The Fall of France*, Osprey, Oxford, 2000.

Forty, George, *Road to Berlin – The Allied Drive from Normandy*, Cassell, London, 1999.

Gawne, Jonathan, *The War in the Pacific – From Pearl Harbor to Okinawa*, Greenhill Books, London, 1996.

Hamilton, Nigel, *Montgomery of Alamein, 1887–1942*, Allen Lane, London, 2001.

Hastings, Max, *Overlord*, Michael Joseph, London, 1984.

Healy, Mark, *The Battle of Midway*, Osprey, Oxford, 2000.

Johnson, Air Vice-Marshal J.E., *Full Circle*, Ballantine Books, New York, 1968.

Kershaw, Robert J., *The Battle of Kursk*, Ian Allen, Shepperton, 1999.

Kershaw, Robert J., *War Without Garlands – Operation Barbarossa 1941–42*, Ian Allen, Shepperton, 2000.

Kiriakopoulous, G.C., *Ten Days to Destiny – The Battle for Crete 1941*, Franklin Watts, New York, 1985.

Latimer, John, *Tobruk 1941*, Osprey, Oxford, 2001.

Macintyre, Capt. Donald, *The Battle of the Mediterranean*, B.T. Batsford, London, 1964.

Majdalany, Fred, *The Battle of Cassino*, Transworld, London, 1959.

Montgomery of Alamein, *Field Marshal Viscount, Memoirs*, Collins, London, 1958.

Mueller, Joseph N., *Guadalcanal 1942 – The Marines Strike Back*, Osprey, London, 1992.

Perrett, Bryan, *Allied Tanks in North Africa, Arms and Armour*, London, 1986.

Prange, Gordon W., *At Dawn We Slept – The Untold Story of Pearl Harbor*, Penguin, London, 2001.

Ryan, Cornelius, *A Bridge Too Far*, Wordsworth, Ware, 1999.

Trevor-Roper (ed.), *Hitler's War Directives 1939-1945*, Sidgwick & Jackson, London, 1964.

Werth, Alexander, *Russia at War 1941-1945*, E.P. Dutton & Company Inc, New York, 1970.

Whiting, Charles, *The Battle of the Bulge*, Sutton, Stroud, 1999.

Wright, Derrick, *The Battle for Iwo Jima 1945*, Sutton, Stroud, 1999.

INDEX